IN
DESIGN

THEORY
AND PROCESS

New interior of the Judge Institute, Cambridge. Courtesy of John Outram Architects.

INTERIOR DESIGN

THEORY AND PROCESS

ANTHONY SULLY

A & C BLACK • LONDON

I would like to dedicate this book to my wife Penny and my children, Nell, Kim, Jessica, Daniel, George and Jodie.

First published in Great Britain 2012
A&C Black Publishers
an imprint of Bloomsbury Publishing Plc
50 Bedford Square
London WC1B 3DP

ISBN: 978-1-4081-5202-7

Copyright © Anthony Sully 2012
sultony@gotadsl.co.uk

A CIP catalogue record for this book is available from the British Library

Anthony Sully has asserted his rights under the Copyright, Design and Patents Act, 1988, to be identified as the author of this work.

Unless otherwise credited, all drawings are the author's.

Publisher: Susan James
Project editor: Davida Saunders
Assistant editor: Agnes Upshall
Copy editor: Fiona Corbridge
Cover design: Sutchinda Thompson
Page design: Susan McIntyre

Typeset in 10.25 on 12.5pt Minion Pro

This book is produced using paper that is made from wood grown in managed, sustainable forests. It is natural, renewable and recyclable. The logging and manufacturing processes conform to the environmental regulations of the country of origin.

Printed and bound in China

CONTENTS

PREFACE

Interior design concerns itself with more than just the visual or ambient enhancement of an interior space; it seeks to optimise and harmonise the uses to which the built environment will be put.

Frances Mazarella, American Society of Interior Designers

WHY I HAVE WRITTEN THIS BOOK

I have been responsible for managing five interior design degree courses in the UK at different stages of my career, as well as practising as an interior designer. This book is the culmination of my teaching and practice, which has involved constant research and debate, ultimately leading to frustration with the state of interior design in both education and practice.

I decided to teach interior design because I could see the potential for improving design education from the standpoint of a designer. There are many books written on the subject by non-designers, but although these are excellent in many ways, they sometimes fall short on certain aspects of the design process which can only be explained by someone who has been through that creative process. I hope to redress that balance in this book, and with the help of experience, hindsight and assistance from colleagues, provide guidance as to the real potential of a much maligned area of design. I aim to present ways, processes and methods of approaching interior design in a refreshing and illuminating light that will help students, teachers and practitioners alike. I have distilled information to suit my purposes from a variety of scholarly sources rather than regurgitating what has already been written. I would like the book to be a constant companion, almost like a toolkit necessary to be able to do the job. I make no apology if I generalise on certain social issues for the sake of clarity, as I am well aware that the world contains many varied cultures and rituals that demand different design solutions. As Norberg-Schulz states:

It is a paradoxical but common experience that different persons at the same time have a similar and different experience of the same environment. That we do manage to participate in the activities of daily life proves that we have a common world.[1]

Also Claude Lévi-Strauss, the social anthropologist, said in 1958 that myths from different parts of the world, which were very different in their surface details (necessarily since the cultures they came from were so different) might reflect the same basic structure underneath.

AIMS

Many books have been written about interior design and related disciplines, concerning history, styles, professional practice, and the practical issues of designing and making interiors including regulations, green issues and design for specialist groups. This book does not intend to repeat these subjects (except where relevant), but instead sets out to present a personal exploration of interior design which students of the subject can draw upon to influence their own practice and development. My purpose in writing this book is threefold:

1. To expand the theoretical basis of interior design so that designers can feel that they really are specialists in a field that has substance and credibility.
2. To promote and emphasise the art of interior design, which is about being able to interpret people's needs and produce visionary solutions that work as well as lift up the soul.

3. To break the conventional mould of building and indicate new conceptual approaches to the shaping of interior space.

There are recent examples of high artistic achievement in the works of Anish Kapoor for fine art, Zaha Hadid and Enric Miralles for architecture, Santiago Calatrava for structural engineering, Tom Dixon for product design, Tord Boontje for glass works, Jasper Morrison for furniture and product, and Sjoerd Seuters for architecture and interior design; Philippe Starck also deserves inclusion simply for being Philippe Starck. Many lay people will be aware of the work of these designers and it is partly because the subject of interior design is readily accessible via the media (and promoted in DIY stores) that it has become devalued as a serious and demanding discipline.

The common products that are specified for and installed in interiors need to be challenged and comprehensively reviewed in order for radical change to take place. Manufacturers are guilty of following trends and sales charts, and many designers are guilty of paying lip service to their clients. I wish to clarify, at this stage, that an interior decorator is usually responsible for the detailed furnishing of interiors; an interior designer performs the more architectural functions required for dealing with buildings.

DESIGN COURSES

Some readers will have noticed that in certain higher and further educational institutions there are courses described as 'interior architecture' or 'spatial design' rather than the more common 'interior design'. This has come about due to a change in thinking by some educationalists rather than a change in the professional discipline. When a building is viewed from the outside, glimpses of the interior can be seen as was the intention of the architect, but when a person is inside the building, the external appearance of the building is not seen (there are exceptions, I know) as a whole entity. Therefore it is right to assume that the term 'interior architect' is a weaker definition than the term 'interior designer'. There is no such person as an interior architect in the UK. The name may have changed, but the game is the same.

MY VIEWS

Finally, I would like to add that whilst I am trying to reveal design opportunities untrammelled by historical and stylistic rules, conventions or dogma, there will no doubt be evidence of my own personal views and preferences, which I hope will positively contribute to the debate of the subject. I do not intend to discuss wider questions of 'What is art?' and 'What is design?', nor to delve deep into philosophical discourse, as there are many excellent literary sources for the reader elsewhere.

ACKNOWLEDGEMENTS

I wish to give thanks to the following people who have inspired and helped me in the course of my life:

Mr Rudolph, primary school teacher at St Barnabas Church of England School, Pimlico, London, who was so supportive as a general teacher as well as helping me with my art.

Peter Enticknap, art teacher at my school, Lord Wandsworth College, Hampshire. A fine artist himself, he taught me patience and all the skills of the art room.

Tom Simmons, foundation lecturer at Hammersmith College of Art and Building, London. His Lancastrian humour would have the class in stitches, but it was always served up to make an important point. He showed concern for the individual, and was distressed that I chose interior design and not art for my career.

Geoffrey Bocking, interior design course tutor at Hammersmith College of Art and Building, and the most exciting and deep-thinking person I had ever met. He taught me how to think, how to analyse and how to enjoy the fruits of problem-solving. Through him I met Buckminster Fuller, Keith Critchlow, George Mitchell, B. F. Skinner and Anthony Hunt.

Keith Critchlow, tutor at Hammersmith College. I was amazed by the amount of hand-drawn, beautifully executed A1 teaching sheets he would pin up to support his studio teaching. Listening to him deliver theories and philosophies with great articulacy was like having a massage!

Norman Potter, my first year tutor at the Royal College of Art, London. An inspirational and totally underrated person. He was a wonderful teacher and friend of Geoffrey Bocking. A left-wing rationalist, humorist and behaviourist, he would sometimes answer a question by twisting his finger around his cigarette whilst it stayed in his mouth, and look through you with his penetrating stare; whatever he said was mesmerising.

Graham Hopewell, interior designer and mentor, with whom I had a good working partnership and learned how a small practice was run.

Richard Padovan, architect and writer, fellow tutor at Buckinghamshire College of Higher Education. He believed in my teaching approach, and was supportive of many initiatives. I had the greatest respect for his clarity of vision and intellectual grasp of design issues.

Chris Patrick, Osaka Gas Europe. She effectively monitored my design research, guiding it into a manageable form which culminated in very comprehensive reports. A good listener who chaired briefing sessions admirably.

Graham Frecknall, architect. I owe a huge debt to Graham for his partnership with me throughout the Glendower Chapel conversion in Monmouth. I respected his professionalism, integrity and skill in managing the contract and grant funding.

I would also like to thank all the students whom I have had the privilege to teach over the years. To see many of them become successful designers gives me the greatest of pleasure. I thank them for their responsiveness, their commitment and their company.

Thank you to the following people for their advice and help in the preparation of this book: Bill Haley, Giles Alldice, Eleanor Bird, Susan Redgrave and Tomris Tangaz. I also owe a huge debt of gratitude to my wife Penny, who helped with the preparation of all the images for publication.

I would also like to thank the following practices for providing me with the professional experience in this field: Duffy Eley Giffone Worthington, Llewelyn Davies Weeks, Frederick Gibberd, Austin Smith Lord, and John Bonnington.

I would like to thank the publisher, A&C Black, for taking on this book, and in particular the following for their help and support throughout the whole process: Susan James, Davida Saunders, Agnes Upshall, Susan McIntyre, and Fiona Corbridge.

FOREWORD

Finally, here it is – the complete guide to navigating the often confused waters of the interior design discipline. I am so pleased that Anthony Sully decided to title this book 'Interior Design, Theory and Process' and not 'Interior Architecture, Theory and Process' or 'Spatial Design, Theory and Process' or any of the myriad of other vaguely fashionable titles this subject has recently been given. Interior design is what it is; it has its own integrity, its own theory and its own particular processes.

Anthony Sully's passion for the subject leaps off the pages of this important book. The book plots a clear road map through the pitfalls, obstacles and traps of this complex discipline, and charts the many points of reference required to gain a full understanding of the process. It is an essential resource for anyone interested in the changing landscape of interior design.

In my opinion you cannot have a great building without a great interior; however, you can have a great interior without a great exterior. The importance of interior design as a discipline matches that of architecture. In spite of this, though, it is an often maligned subject. This is in part due to the plethora of TV make-over shows and publications confusing interior design with interior decoration. The book makes a clear definition between interior design and these related activities under the broader headings of architecture, design, decoration and art. It does, however, suggest that interior design is in fact an art in its own right. This book surveys the subject in its broadest sense, and to its furthest boundaries. It is rich in quotes, all of which give context to an understanding of the discipline itself and where the subject belongs within our ever changing society.

Anthony Sully's aim is to provide "a toolkit" but also "an enabling book that promotes a fresh look at the discipline". He describes fully "the complex and misunderstood discipline of interior design". All of this assists in providing a complete and comprehensive understanding of the subject from both an outsider's and a practitioner's perspective. This is a book of many riches, and should be made compulsory reading for every student and practitioner of interior design. Furthermore, and perhaps more importantly, it might be a good idea for clients and the many agencies involved in the procurement process of interior design projects to be encouraged to use this book as a "toolkit" or "enabling book".

My own mission as an interior design practitioner has been to produce spaces that hopefully enrich our lives and occasionally make the hairs on the back of our necks stand on end. There are endless examples of great interiors throughout history. They range from bathrooms to palaces, libraries to nightclubs. We inhabit interior spaces all of our lives; it is the remit of the interior designer to produce spaces that improve our lives and inspire us in every human activity.

Ben Kelly
January 2012

INTRODUCTION

WHAT IS INTERIOR DESIGN?

Interior design comes under the umbrella activity of design, which brings together many disciplines, often for commercial reasons. These disciplines are outlined at the beginning of Chapter 1 and serve to reinforce the notion that there are certain generic processes common to all design disciplines. (interior architecture, as the name suggests, is no longer a design subject and becomes part of architecture and hence subordinate to it. This is why I persist in retaining the name 'interior design').

In this book, having examined issues under design (a creative field of activity), we will then move on to look at the specifics of interior design. Historically, in the media the subject of design is dominated by the discipline of product design. The reason for this is that technological innovation naturally begins with a material, which is manipulated under the guise of 'product development'. The item is explored under laboratory, factory or workshop conditions. When innovations such as the telephone, the motor car and plastics appeared, they led the way. During the twentieth century, many more new products continued to act as signposts in representing technological innovation as well as the culture of the times rather more easily than interiors could. An interior may contain an assemblage of new products and materials, but the whole interior is not defined or recorded iconically in the same way that products have been. This of course highlights the very hybrid nature of interior design because 'an interior', unlike any other art, architectural or design artefact, cannot be parcelled up into an identifiable piece of form and sold as a product. It is acknowledged that within the field of interior design, 'prototype interiors' are not made in the same way as in product design, but rather the whole process relies on tried evidence of use of materials and products elsewhere, plus some degree of workshop testing, should the project so desire it. In a sense, *all* interior projects are unique prototypes in that they are witness to the first combination of products and services of their kind (unless part of a reproductive commercial chain).

The interior environment is a 'wraparound' inter-active experience, second only to the clothes we wear, of objects, structures, surfaces, space and light, felt by people *moving* through a building. There is nothing static about experiencing interior spaces. People walk through this environment in a processional sequence of experiences covering a variety of space–use functions. The understanding of this combinational experience describes the very essence of the skill of designing an interior. The designer, by responding to the needs of the user, and to the exigencies of the building and location, is a form-maker, an artist and a problem-solver. Interiors ultimately give life to a building and the designer sets the stage for the 'actors' (the users) to perform. The building, as architecture, can be perceived as an object of form relative to the viewer because of its profile against the land and sky.

Roberto Rengel put it well when he said:

Design requires the resolution of a multitude of problems at many different levels and scales. The solutions to these design problems (adjacencies, privacy, connections, enclosure, views, details, furnishings, lighting, and so on) are layered next to and over one another in intricate ways that create specific effects. On any given job, the designer needs to manipulate control, and, ultimately, resolve these combinations, pushing, pulling and twisting to achieve engaging and evocative designs.[1]

WORKING ON AN INTERIOR DESIGN BRIEF

Here is an example of the way that an interior design project might progress (see also the diagram on p.18).

Once a contract has been awarded to a designer, the client issues a more detailed brief outlining requirements, activities and needs, and a budget. This is analysed and amended after questions have been asked, in order to arrive at an interpretation (this can be reviewed and amended as the job proceeds). The designer then draws up a team of professionals, which may include architects, engineers and other design professionals, to assist him with the contract. He needs to carry out research into the client's organisation and the topic of the contract, such as commercial offices, for example.

The next stage is to familiarise himself with the building and location before producing sketch ideas. A few sketch design options are presented to the client and one is selected to proceed with. A full design scheme is presented; if approved, further detailed drawings of construction and building services, together with a specification of works, will be produced as tender documents to send to several building contractors for costing. At the same time, approvals are obtained from the local authority for doing the work and to ensure that the proposed designs satisfy building regulations.[2] The successful contractor will be appointed and a programme of works on site will be produced, which contains a target completion date. The designer attends site meetings with all the parties involved, usually once a week, to monitor the building process.

The designer needs to be in possession of a great deal of skills and specialist knowledge in order to carry out the above. This book concentrates on those theoretical aspects which fortify the designer's intellectual and philosophical stance and which give credence to the design solution being presented.

ABOUT THIS BOOK

WHO WE ARE
The interior design industry – to be informed about the professional context.

WE SHAPE AND MANIPULATE
The basic elements that make up an interior environment – definition of the major components that we handle throughout a project, from which design concepts develop.

WHO WE DESIGN FOR
The human form – it is essential that we know as much about the way the body works and functions, so that the right prescriptive measures can be delivered.

OFFERING CONTROLLED ARRANGEMENT
Geometry and proportion – the theoretical reasoning of shape and form.

HOW WE SEE THINGS
Perception – to understand visual judgement and effect.

JUSTIFICATION AND REASONING
Expression and meaning – powerful motivating factors to ensure uplifting solutions.

HOW WE DESIGN
The tools for the job.

WHERE ARE WE NOW?
New directions.

We begin by analysing the essence of interior design in terms of the elements, such as space, environment, ground plane, support and so on that are the forming blocks which designers manipulate in order to achieve their solutions. This is followed by an examination of the geometric and proportional controls that designers use, and the theoretical basis for the design process to work. We will investigate the powers of expression and meaning through an abbreviated look at the main historical design movements in order to establish current directions. We then concentrate upon the relationship of the human form and its activities and needs in relation to defined space uses, in order to explore suggested ways forward that may serve to inspire the reader. Chapter 8, 'Searching for Codes', is the final chapter, and singles out those individuals from the past who developed an influential style; this is followed by an exploration of new conceptual approaches in the shaping of interior space.

This book's approach, through analysis, is to try and break down subjects into categories and groups wherever possible, for the purposes of classification and ordering. It is not meant to be an exhaustive coverage, but serves as a selection which is easy to use, manipulate or extend as the reader thinks fit. It is not a definitive, all-encapsulating bible, but rather an enabling book that promotes a fresh look at the discipline. It is for designers to dip into as and when motivated to do so. In the research stages of the design process, familiar terms will be used as a starting point, but the aim is to re-establish a neutral base whereby solutions are offered that require new terminology. Existing terms carry with them preconceptions and prejudices that need removing. We will be challenging existing norms and asking questions to prompt some original responses. At the end of each chapter, a review section will sum up the content.

SIMPLIFIED SEQUENCE THAT PRODUCES THE FINAL BUILT SOLUTION

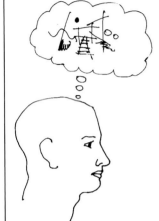

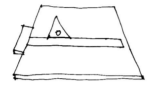

1) Ideas formulated

2) Drawings and model to convey ideas

3) Completed interior (Courtesy of the Natural History Museum, London)

We will not investigate the human psyche, behavioural psychology, gender and sexual studies, ethnic studies, nor any of the applied sciences in any great depth, as there is much material available in the marketplace. Of course, the feelings and attitudes of people and the way that they respond to certain spaces, materials and visual effects is important to designers, and if a project demands more specialised research, then that is the time to explore further. My own basis of working has been entirely through my own observations of people using a variety of buildings. It is rather like comedians saying that their material is sourced from their own observations of people. We, as designers, have to have the sensitivity, curiosity and general desire to become informed about the way that people use interior spaces, and possess the necessary recording equipment to store that information. Designing from one's own experiences of life is better than designing from hearsay or second-hand sources. From my experience, the enemies of design in our era are:

■ **Compactness** – Implies tight spaces and minimum facility.

■ **Miniaturisation** – Small is not necessarily the answer.

■ **Efficiency** – The modern disease of being clever, driven by economic forces.

■ **Fashion** – The pursuit of trends and gimmicks blinds original thinking.

■ **Compromise** – The final solution, but not to be aimed for.

■ **Sedentary life** – A reflection of the 'couch potato' syndrome.

■ **Public complacency** – There is nothing worse than apathy and indifference.

■ **Health and safety regulations** – Being too cautious: it is part of human nature to take risks.

Clearly this list can only be believed or understood through experience of working in the business, and therefore readers may well come to different conclusions. There is one more enemy to design and this is perhaps the most difficult to handle, especially within a design practice with very young designers: long design experience. With the best will in the world, an experienced designer will already be formatted to use previous experience to solve a variety of design and construction problems, no matter how hard that designer tries to be innovative. This can also affect relationships with clients. With age, it becomes increasingly comfortable to use tried and tested methods. This is entirely natural and I am not making accusations here. Experience is necessary to steady the ship when a storm is circling. But when quieter waters are found, opportunities should be given to younger designers in the office (if their training has been good) to produce challenging ideas. Another problem that may surface is that the experienced designer's idea will be cheaper to implement, in an office cost-planning scenario. The younger designer's idea, however, could prove to be more expensive because it will demand more research and preparation time, as well as creating a new format for office procedures. The biggest danger to a young designer's growth is if he or she produces a design that conforms to the existing office format and is subsequently congratulated for it – there is no growth in that young designer's development. I see many examples of current interior designs that clearly reproduce past techniques and ideas with visual tweaking that is only on the surface.

Here are some further comments that help our general understanding of this complex subject:

The space within becomes the reality of the building.

Frank Lloyd Wright, *c.*1900[3]

All architecture functions as a potential stimulus for movement, real or imagined. A building is an incitement to action, a stage for movement and interaction. It is one partner in a dialogue with the body.[4]

Bloomer and Moore

Since the days of Imperial Rome, the formation of interior space has been the major problem of the art of building.[5]

Sigfried Giedion

ADVICE TO STUDENTS

To fully understand and appreciate the physical reality of interiors, apart from any programme of study, you need to visit as many buildings as possible. You should try and seek permission to visit the interior during construction so that you can merge this experience with the theory of your teaching programme. Ensure that you have permission to take photographs, make sketches and take notes. As a designer, you should always carry around equipment for such tasks, including a measuring tape. Also visit completed interiors with the intention of carrying out similar tasks. Always ask the building's owner who designed it and when was it built. You should build up a dossier of the many interiors you have been to, recording as much information as you can, including your own comments and opinions. This activity should be ongoing throughout your career. Talk to as many users of buildings as possible to ascertain their views and obtain feedback from their experiences.

PART ONE
CLARIFICATION

1: THE PRESENT SITUATION
IN THE DESIGN INDUSTRY

ABOUT THIS CHAPTER

Interior design is placed in the context of those disciplines that require creative design thinking, even though these disciplines may not have any direct commercial link. For example, designing a building is very different from making a film, yet the actions and aims of the people involved can be related. Each discipline can learn from, and be inspired by, the other. In this chapter, we examine contractual relationships in interior design and answer a series of questions on why we choose interior design as a profession, who makes interiors, what skills are necessary, who does what in the industry, which sectors interior design covers, and the sequence of work in a job, with the purpose of setting the stage before exploring the discipline further.

In order to understand the complex and misunderstood discipline of interior design, it is necessary to describe how it exists professionally, educationally and theoretically within the design industry. The following categories are used initially for the purposes of simplicity and clarity, acknowledging that commercial practice can be multidisciplinary, and cross-fertilisation will occur. Also, current design activity suggests that recognised boundaries are changing and newer disciplines are emerging, hence overlaps can occur.

ASSOCIATED PROFESSIONAL DESIGN DISCIPLINES

The profession of interior design coexists with seven other major three-dimensional (3D) design disciplines (architecture, product design, art/craft, theatre, event design, film and fashion/textiles) and one two-dimensional (2D) design discipline (graphic design), with varying degrees of interaction and involvement. (Graphic design is usually described as a 2D discipline, but may have applications within a 3D context.) Architecture is the major 'holding' discipline, simply because it provides the buildings within which interior design is carried out. The film industry is perhaps the main outsider to all of the other disciplines in terms of its final product, which is a screened moving/still image. Yet its designers can come from all other disciplines by way of producing a real environment composed of all the daily objects that we are familiar with. It is the only discipline whereby the consumer does not touch or experience the reality of its being.

Design can sometimes be seen to be an ephemeral subject dictated by the fashion of the day, so I think it is worth pondering upon the relative life of design work in order to ascribe our attachment to it. The lifespan charts below show the expected life of the product, rather than the actual or possible lifespan. The design disciplines are summarised below:

■ **Architecture** – The design and landscaping of buildings by architects (building designers). Embraces interior design. Lifespan of hundreds of years; refurbishment gives new life.

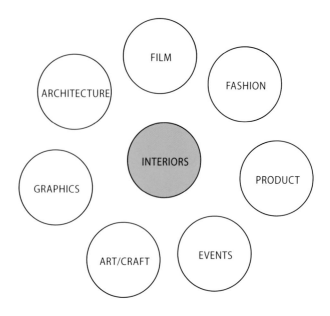

■ **Product design** – The design of objects, from hand-held items to motorbikes, cars and furniture. Lifespan of a few months to a few decades; open to wear and tear.

■ **Art/craft** – The work of craftspeople making artefacts reliant upon their skill in handling certain materials. Lifespan of hundreds of years, depending on how well an item is looked after.

■ **Theatre** – The design of sets for the stage, covering all forms of entertainment. Lifespan of days to years, depending on how successful the production is.

■ **Event design** – A specialisation that has grown out of exhibition design in the last 30 years and encompasses pop concerts, corporate events, sound and light shows, circuses etc. Lifespan of days to weeks.

LIFESPAN CHARTS

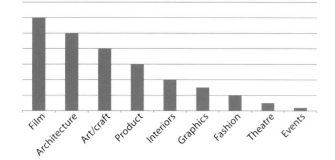

Chart 1 illustrates the average length of a product's life, acknowledging that there are many variables at work.

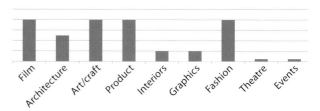

Chart 2 shows degrees of ownership, from total ownership of an item to temporary ownership, such as paying to see a show.

■ **Graphics** – Also known as visual communication/spatial communication. Deals with signage, posters, corporate identity, packaging etc. Lifespan of weeks to a few years.

■ **Film** – Producing moving/still images for mass viewing. Lifespan: forever, depending upon technology.

■ **Fashion/textiles** – The production of clothing for the public, sold through mass retailing and haute couture, as well as all types of soft furnishings. Lifespan of years, depending on usage and maintenance.

■ **Interior design** – The adaptation of interiors in old buildings or the design of interiors for new buildings. Lifespan varies; generally years.

INTERIOR DESIGN EDUCATION IN THE UK

Over the past thirty years many changes have taken place, which have affected entry requirements, educational provision and the type of institution offering courses of study. Whereas UK universities were once answerable to the Council of National Academic Awards (CNAA)[1] or professional organisations, they are mostly now independent and can exercise their own strategy and regulations. With countless mergers and empire-building campaigns, they have become lumbering, impersonal places of conflict and agitation. I and many designers of my generation were financially supported by a grant when we were students – which in my case resulted in seven years of uninterrupted full-time study (a five-day week that consisted of eight-hour days) – and we had no debts at the end of it all. Contrast that with the horrendous costs and debts that students have to face now, and with only a few hours' tuition a week! Where is the progress here, and how can we hope to produce designers of the same quality that we used to?

The main qualifications that can be obtained in the UK are either a BTEC[2] two-year National Diploma in design (when entering a further education college at 16), followed by a two-year Higher National Diploma (HND) in interior design; or a three-year degree course at a higher education institution. Students passing the HND can be accepted directly on to the second year of a degree course. Applicants who are straight out of school with A-levels (age 18) have the option of studying on a one-year art foundation course before applying for a degree course, or they may apply direct for a degree course. The recommended route has always been via the foundation course, but unfortunately, due to universities' urgent need to fill student places, they have discouraged this and invited students to go straight for a degree course directly after completing their A-levels. From my own experience, this has been a disastrous policy as it has reduced the capability and maturity level of the applicants and placed an intolerable burden upon the teaching staff. Foundation courses have subsequently become an expendable option and many have disappeared. We now need a revival of independent art schools that can thrive without the stifling bureaucracy and anonymity of the larger institutions.

It is fundamental for the future status of the discipline of interior design that the theoretical scope of the subject is defined by making an informed, detailed study, and this is what I aim to do in this book.

CONTRACTUAL RELATIONSHIPS

First let us look, in simplistic terms, at the working scenario of the interior designer, describing the main players in the field.

OFFICIAL BODIES

When running an interior contract, permissions usually have to be obtained from the following Local Authority departments and members of the public (if applicable). See p.25 for the sequence of operations during a contract.

■ **Planning department** – Permission for an extension to a building or a change of use in a building.

■ **Public health department** – Permission regarding changes to water supply and drainage.

■ **Building regulations department** – Permission for proposed materials and construction method, to ensure relevant codes are followed.

■ **Listed building[3] consent** – Permission for alterations if the building has important historical elements.

■ **Local community** – People need to be consulted if the project affects them in any way.

CLIENT

The client is the person or organisation commissioning the project.

CONTRACTOR

The contractor, who could be a builder or a shopfitter, will provide a foreman to manage the project on site, and organise suppliers and sub-contractors.

DESIGNER

The designer is responsible for producing the design to submit to the client and a specification and working drawings for the contractor.

DESIGN MANAGER

The design manager (who may not be a designer) is a specialist in organisational issues covering all the people and organisations who participate in the whole programme of the project.

THE USER

The user may be the resident or occupier of the building, who operates and manages the services and spaces; or a visitor, a short-term user who has come to make use of the interior for the purpose for which it was designed.

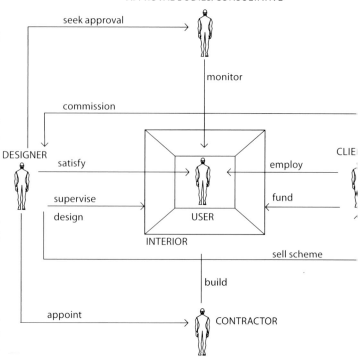

CONTRACTUAL RELATIONSHIPS

Figure 1. The London office of HOK (formerly Hellmuth, Obata and Kassabaum). Project manager Eve Chung, 2009. Photo: Hufton + Crow.

WHY CHOOSE INTERIOR DESIGN AS A PROFESSION?

Your reasons for choosing interior design as a profession may be any of the following – or perhaps all of them.

- You want to improve the quality of people's lives.
- You want to enrich buildings and bring new life to them.
- You want to apply your artistic skills to this field.
- You want to seek an outlet for your creative and visionary skills.
- You enjoy using different materials.
- You enjoy building and making things.
- You want to explore technology to the fullest.
- You enjoy the architectural process and its history.
- You want to make money.

Many young people choose their professional route based on how well they did at school, backed up by careers advice which can sometimes be inadequate. They have no idea what the profession is really like. The last reason above for choosing to be an interior designer – to make money – is in my view a poor one on its own, but it is one that has been given to me by many young people. It perhaps reflects on those designers who look upon the whole affair as being primarily a business, and work so produced is usually devoid of the higher qualities that design offers. We would do well to bear the following reflections in mind:

> *The concept of function has been abused by justifying social and cultural mediocrity.*
>
> Cedric Price, 1982

> *The designer is a servant who uses his talents and skills to satisfy the needs of society. Don't forget that bad taste is popular.*[4]
>
> John Blake, 1979

> *Today's buildings, shaped by function and profit and styled in the self-referential dead end of technique, taciturnly avoid these roles using flexibility and ephemerality as excuses.*
>
> Peter Buchanan, 'Architecture as Art', *Architectural Review*, February 1981

Figure 2. Example of a research visit. This is the Backhausen Museum of Interior Textiles in Vienna. There are original works of Josef Hoffmann[5] on display. Photo by author.

> *The Western world is in danger of being submerged in constructions in which function, beauty and cost may have been the starting point, but where cost is the client's only real preoccupation.*
>
> Peter Hoffer, 'The New Commercialism', *Architectural Review*, March 1980

WHAT DOES AN INTERIOR DESIGNER DO?

This brief outline shows what an interior designer must do, having secured a contract and obtained local authority approvals.

■ **Interpret** the client's requirements from a brief, **research** the topic of the contract, looking at comparable examples, and research products, materials and services.

■ **Survey** the property concerned (or commission a surveyor) to study the condition, character and access of the building, and produce architectural drawings of the property to work on.

■ **Design and plan** things to be made or assembled, working with a team of fellow professionals. Develop a theoretical approach to the job by developing the following eight minor design concepts: planning, three-dimensional form, construction, lighting, colour, material, circulation, building services (see end of Chapter 2, p.55). Submit a major design concept that stems from the eight minor design concepts. Within the enclosing building, plan the elements that define and shape the space and allow circulation. Design purpose-made interior components, fittings and lighting; purpose-made furnishings; and purpose-applied decoration or graphics.

■ **Specify** products, furniture and furnishings from the marketplace; environmental controls and outlets within building services; materials and finishes; light fittings and controls; and IT and audiovisual equipment, as necessary.

■ **Oversee** building work on site together with the project manager and foreman.

Figure 3. Glendower House, chapel conversion, 2002, showing the work of joiners and plasterers. Designer: Anthony Sully. Architect: Graham Frecknall. Photo by author.

WHO MAKES AND CONTRIBUTES TO THE MAKING OF INTERIORS?

The specialists involved in the making of an interior can be divided into six categories:

1. *Component and product manufacturers defined by item:* doors, windows, stairs, ceiling systems, ironmongery, furniture, and other lightweight structures.
2. *Material manufacturers and producers of items supportive of function and defined by effect:* plaster, concrete, glass, wood, metal, brick, stone, plastics, fabrics, decorative finishes etc.
3. *Craftspeople:* specialists in certain materials, who make one-off products, usually to commission, ranging from fine art to furniture, fabrics, lighting and many other products.
4. *Building services:* mechanical and electrical engineers, and manufacturers and suppliers of components for power supplies, communications, heating, ventilation, water, drainage and security systems.
5. *Assembly/construction – installation and fitting out:* building contractors, structural engineers, shopfitters and ancillary trades.
6. *Project manager – site control:* usually the building contractor or appointed specialist.

The associated professionals, who reflect the nature of teamwork, are as follows:

■ **Architects** – Responsible for building design.

■ **Structural engineers** – Responsible for the design of the structure.

■ **Service engineers** – Responsible for the design of building services and IT.

■ **Surveyors** – Responsible for the survey of the site, including building condition and services.

■ **Furnishing consultants and audiovisual specialists**.

■ **Property consultants** – Have expert knowledge of the site and expertise in managing it.

■ **Access consultants**.

■ **Estate managers** – Usually work with property consultants.

■ **Facilities managers** – Responsible for office management.

■ **Landscape consultants** – Responsible for both hard and soft external design.

■ **Conservation officers/groups** – Concerned with the preservation and maintenance of the valuable historic parts of a site.

■ **Local authority** – Monitors standards and approves building applications.

■ **Other specialist designers** – Such as graphic, furniture, textile and product designers.

■ **Space planners** – Interior designers specialising in office interiors.

Anyone who conceives of a corridor with parallel walls, that is as a static prism, does not know the first thing about architecture. Even the arrival spaces – living room, study or bedroom – should not be totally static. They must foster human communication, intellectual tension, or waking after sleep. Life is always full of happenings.[6]

Bruno Zevi

WHAT ARE THE MAIN SKILLS AND QUALITIES OF AN INTERIOR DESIGNER?

It is accepted that, as with many design professions, the discipline of interior design is made up of people specialising in certain aspects of the design process within a business format. This section concentrates on the creative role of the designer ('Who in the design industry shares responsibility for interior design?' on p.23 will expand on all other specialisms that assist with this process). As children, we are taught how to do things as we grow up. We are extremely grateful at the time, and show our satisfaction when we successfully accomplish the task. Gradually, we reach an age when we begin to question what we have been taught for the following reasons:

- We think that there is possibly a *better* way of doing it.

- We think that there is a *different* way of doing it – and this requires experimentation.

- Because of sheer bloody-minded *rebelliousness* – we are opposing authority by not conforming.

- We have *discovered* something from our own enquiry, unprompted by others.

These traits are the beginnings of a creative spirit, and in our case, through promotion of self-interest directed towards the arts, and encouragement from others, we emerge as creative beings. We then secure an educational route to our chosen profession.

To be a successful interior designer requires a range of personal qualities and skills, as shown below.

INTERIOR DESIGNER: PERSONAL SPECIFICATION

Motivation and commitment
- To have the desire to change, restore and improve the environment.
- To be a visionary in pursuing dreams of self-fulfilment as well as satisfying the client.
- To have good management skills.
- To realise powers of expression and meaning in one's work.

Holistic approach
- To be sensitive and perceptive about people's needs and to ask the right questions.
- To maintain a driving force creatively.
- To make strong value judgements concerning quality and costs, meeting the budget.
- To have good verbal and written communication skills and a clarity of intent.

Organisational abilities
- To be able to handle a vast range of materials, products and services, as well as being resourceful in finding them.
- To be able to organise and store information for reference, and for applied use when necessary.
- To be a team player – with other colleagues as well as with consultants.
- To be able to work to a programme and meet deadlines.

Hands-on skills
- To be competent in handling three-dimensional form, space, colour and texture.
- To have a feeling for materials and be able to put things together – construction.
- To be proficient in drafting by hand and using computer-aided design (CAD).
- To be able to sketch and draw for two reasons: to facilitate one's own design process from conception to completion; to aid communication and the presentation of ideas.
- To be competent with latest technological/graphic aids that assist with the design process and presentation (e.g. CAD).
- To have good analytical and problem-solving skills.

As part of his task is to create healthy buildings for humans, he must know something of biology. As he usually hopes that humans will be happy in his buildings, he must be something of a psychologist.[7]

Sven Hesselgren

WHAT THEORETICAL BASIS DOES THE DESIGNER WORK FROM?

Here is one design company's ideology:

Nemaworkshops is a team of architects, designers, and thinkers who create spaces that are conceptually innovative and highly sensitive to cultural and social contexts. The studio approaches projects through research and collaborative brainstorming wherein ideas are discussed and reworked until the team emerges with a single cohesive concept. The process is a non-linear approach, adhering to the conviction that good ideas can come from unlikely places. Ultimately, the designs challenge architectural typologies, demonstrate acute cultural awareness and propose original spatial concepts.

Nemaworkshops, New York, USA

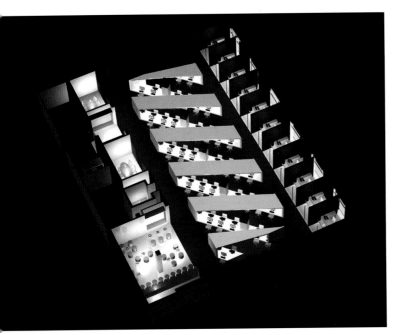

Figure 4. The offices of Groupsoft, designed by Nemaworkshops, 2010. Note the diagonal linked forms.

All of the following checklist items are suggested ways of preparing for the task of design, providing thought processes that support hands-on skills, and finally ensure that the designer has the intellectual and philosophical stance necessary to be able to perform the duties of an interior designer.

CHECKLIST: THE TASK OF DESIGN

Problem-solving
- Make an interpretive analysis of the client's requirements.
- Make an analysis of the site and building (context) – the inherent properties of space, light and form.
- Synthesise data and observational records.
- Evaluate all information in readiness for joint theoretical reasoning with other categories.

Three-dimensional form
- Consider the handling and manipulation of form and space.
- Consider geometric laws and principles.
- Consider proportional systems.

The human form
- Consider anatomy, physiological and psychological characteristics.
- Look at anthropometrics and ergonomics.
- Refer to human behaviour in interiors – movement, posture and responsiveness.

Expression
- Prepare conceptual approaches to the project (see Chapter 2, p.55).
- Form a basis for expressing the client's identity.
- Form a basis for expressing materials and structure.
- Form a basis for using lighting expressively.
- Draw from your own cultural, social and political climate.
- Refer to your own personal theoretical and philosophical ideology.

Perception
- Use your knowledge of psychology of vision on behalf of the user.
- Apply perception theory to your own design work.

Philosophy
- Confirm your own conviction and belief in what you are doing and why you are doing it.

WHO IN THE DESIGN INDUSTRY SHARES RESPONSIBILITY FOR INTERIOR DESIGN?

The following classifications clarify who participates in the whole design process.[8] People may possess skills in more than one of the areas below and the division of manpower may have a degree of fluidity as a project proceeds. If these classifications were acknowledged by educational and professional bodies, and people were trained for the industry according to these classifications, participants would have a better common dialogue of communication than exists at present. It is my contention that new degree courses could be planned embracing these relationships.

Whilst we need people who are skilled designers, we also need a greater number of people who understand design – how to commission and use it. Poor design understanding leads to poor decision making in many areas – not least in the administration of the built environment, which affects us all.

UK Design Commission[9] Inaugural Report 2011: *Restarting Britain – Design Education and Growth.*

DESIGNERS

Design is about making important contributions to the organisations of government, business, commerce and the community, and designers provide professional expertise that helps to shape and determine the quality of the environment. Designers aim to serve the community by being socially responsible, and aware of the resultant effect and influence that their work has on the well-being of society. Designers are essentially problem-solvers, analysts and communicators.

Examples of designers are: Terence Conran, Eva Jiřičná, Philippe Starck, Ben Kelly and John Outram. Professional bodies include the Chartered Society of Designers, and the British Interior Design Association.

PROCESSORS

These are people involved in administration, management, marketing, research and buying activities concerned with the production of an interior.

Figure 5. Visits to exhibitions provide a constant source of research and a means of making contacts.

■ **Specialist researchers** – Identify and collate information covering historical data, current market conditions, other competitors, future trends, availability of materials, legal issues and products, and technical information.

■ **Managers** – Responsible for quality control by ensuring that communications are both effective within the company and with the client and other relevant organisations. They also monitor the project programme and budget.

■ **Procurers** – The buyers (in retail, for example) who ensure that materials and products are available at the right price and delivered according to the programme of the contract. They are skilled in quality selection, appropriateness and assessment.

■ **Marketing managers** – Concerned with promoting design services that meet national and global opportunities and selling design services.

Examples of processing companies are: Headlight Vision, Fitch, BDG McColl, G2, and Ogilvy and Mather. Professional bodies include the Chartered Institute of Marketing, the Institute of Management, and the Advertising Association.

PRODUCERS

The 'makers' in manufacturing, building, crafts and assembly. See 'Who makes and contributes to the making of interiors?', p.20. Examples of companies involved in this area are: Costain, GS Contracts and Thornton Project Solutions. Professional bodies include various institutes covering building, engineering, trades and crafts.

OBSERVERS

These people provide much needed commentary, criticism, appraisal and vision within the industry from the point of view of evolution, current trends and forecasting. They may be designers, journalists, lecturers, writers or historians. They can be highly influential, informative and highly inspirational for designers, as well as enlightening the general public and sparking controversy.

Examples of observers are: Stephen Bayley, Deyan Sudjic, Penny Sparke, James Woudhuysen, Guy Julier, Jeremy Myerson, Jonathan Glancey and Peter Buchanan. Professional bodies include the Association of Art Historians, the Design History Society, the Professional Contractors' Group (PCG), and the International Federation of Journalists.

WHAT SECTORS DOES INTERIOR DESIGN COVER?

All buildings have interiors. Most public buildings have the interior professionally designed, but some buildings have a preordained format that does not require the deft skills of an interior designer. Some interiors are designed as being 'narrative', in the sense that they unfold a story: this usually applies to the museum/exhibition field. The following list contains some of the most popular areas of work:

■ **Residential** – Housing and apartments.

■ **Hospitality and hotels** – From large hotels to boarding houses.

■ **Commercial** – Offices, showrooms and workshops.

■ **Educational** – Schools, colleges and universities.

■ **Industrial** – Factories, workshops, agricultural buildings and power stations.

Figure 6. The Blu Apple Frozen Yoghurt Café in Jakarta, Budi Pradono Architects, 2009. Note the floating, cloud-like ceiling panels. A very yogurty atmosphere!

■ **Retail** – High street shops, department stores, shopping centres and markets.

■ **Sport and leisure** – Swimming pools, sports and recreational halls, fun palaces, stadiums, pavilions and ice rinks.

■ **Entertainment** – Casinos, dance halls, nightclubs, theatres, cinemas and concert halls.

■ **Liturgical** – Churches, chapels and mission halls.

■ **Community** – Community centres, youth clubs and playgroup buildings.

■ **Refreshment** – Bars, pubs, cafés and restaurants.

■ **Civic** – Town halls, law courts, civic centres and libraries.

■ **Heritage** – Museums, tourist-related buildings, ancient and historic buildings.

■ **Health** – Hospitals, clinics and medical practices.

■ **Events** – Exhibitions and promotional events, both temporary and permanent.

■ **Transport** – Bus and train stations, airports, docks and ports for shipping.

■ **Corrective institutions** – Prisons, remand centres and young offenders' institutions.

■ **Protective forces** – Police, army, navy, air force and fire service buildings.

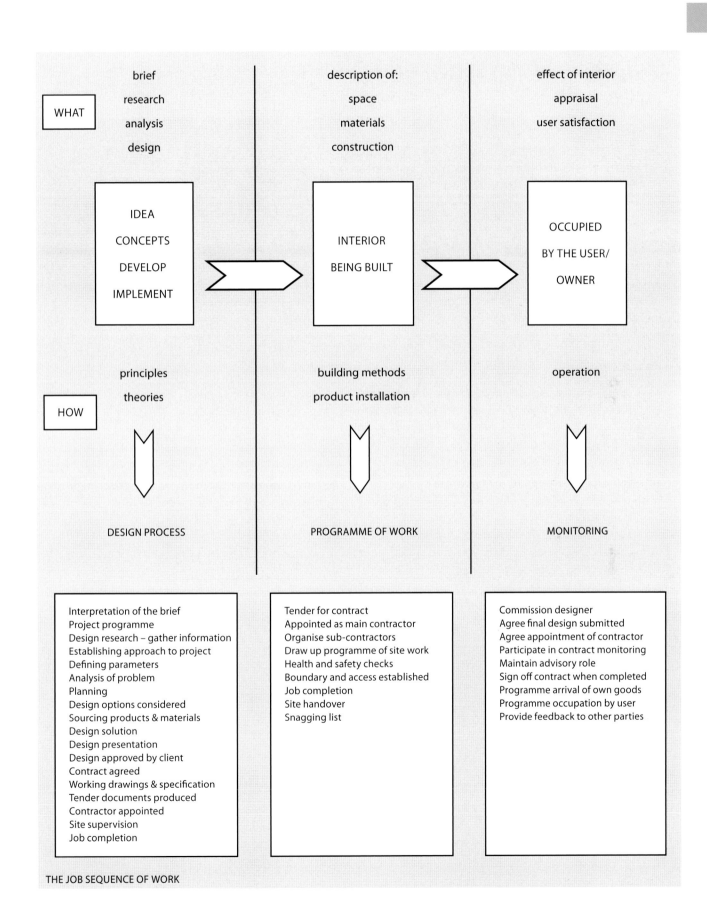

WHAT

brief
research
analysis
design

description of:
space
materials
construction

effect of interior
appraisal
user satisfaction

IDEA
CONCEPTS
DEVELOP
IMPLEMENT

INTERIOR
BEING BUILT

OCCUPIED
BY THE USER/
OWNER

HOW

principles
theories

building methods
product installation

operation

DESIGN PROCESS

PROGRAMME OF WORK

MONITORING

Interpretation of the brief
Project programme
Design research – gather information
Establishing approach to project
Defining parameters
Analysis of problem
Planning
Design options considered
Sourcing products & materials
Design solution
Design presentation
Design approved by client
Contract agreed
Working drawings & specification
Tender documents produced
Contractor appointed
Site supervision
Job completion

Tender for contract
Appointed as main contractor
Organise sub-contractors
Draw up programme of site work
Health and safety checks
Boundary and access established
Job completion
Site handover
Snagging list

Commission designer
Agree final design submitted
Agree appointment of contractor
Participate in contract monitoring
Maintain advisory role
Sign off contract when completed
Programme arrival of own goods
Programme occupation by user
Provide feedback to other parties

THE JOB SEQUENCE OF WORK

WHAT IS THE JOB SEQUENCE OF WORK?

The diagram on the previous page, which presents a vertical sequence downwards as well as across horizontally, is designed to summarise the process from the point when the designer receives the brief from the client through to the occupation of the completed interior. There are three overlapping stages:

- **Design process** – The stages that the designer goes through, from inception to completion. The initial stage includes the formation of a project team, which may include external consultants such as mechanical and electrical engineers (M&E).

- **Programme of work** – The programme of work is a critical time chart, which the site foreman manages in order to ensure that the contract goes smoothly. After a tour of the finished job by the designer and contractor, a snagging list is made of any possible defects in workmanship and uncompleted work. These are then put right within an agreed time frame.

- **Monitoring** – The client is kept informed in order to assist with the programme and makes decisions on items that need his/her approval. The client gives important feedback to the designers during the first few months of occupation so they can ensure that everything is in working order.

To design is to plan, and to organise, to order, to relate and control. In short it embraces all means opposing disorder and accident. Therefore it signifies a human need and qualifies man's thinking and doing.[10]

Josef Albers

REVIEW

The information in this chapter is useful to you as a designer in several ways.

With regard to the design team, it clarifies individual roles, aids communication and bonding within the practice, and assists with strategic reports and marketing.

It helps you to boost a client's confidence in your position within the industry, enables collaborative partnerships to develop, and strengthens your understanding of peripheral issues.

With regard to the users of the building, it promotes more efficient methods of solving problems, provides a deeper understanding of how to satisfy a client's needs, and clarifies your sense of purpose.

In terms of the builder/installer, it helps you to realise the importance of good communication of information and to become a better team player. Your demands and instructions will be applauded for their clarity and appropriateness, and your project monitoring and supervisory skills will be enhanced.

2: DEFINITION OF TERMS

ABOUT THIS CHAPTER

This chapter begins by outlining directions in employment before analysing the nine basic elements of interior design in simplistic terms. It is important to understand the broad terminology of the subject before examining the detail. These elements are analysed and defined in relation to their function in interiors. Various subgroups are presented to ensure a full understanding of the scope of each element. There are also eight concepts that designers must explore before they can develop an overarching concept for a scheme and finally present it to a client.

DIRECTIONS IN EMPLOYMENT

It is vital that students know what work opportunities exist in the industry. There are many strands, which do not necessarily require the same qualifications. These can range from working on an architectural scale in the design or adaptation of buildings, to working for interior decoration and furnishing contract firms. For students who show skill and interest in the making of artefacts, or who deal with the varied skills of applied decoration, the latter may be the route to choose.

To choose who to work for, students need to be discerning when looking at designers' work. Students need to be able to recognise a design that has integrity, soundness of concept, and depth of meaning, allied to the highest ideals of architecture and art. Unfortunately, the profession of interior design has been plagued by many factions who claim to produce interiors of quality, which appear to be enjoyed by the people who use them (henceforth called the user), when in fact these interiors often represent the worst kind of design. The problem is that the field is easily accessed by lay people and members of the public through the DIY industry. It has also been popularised by television programmes in the UK such as *Changing Rooms*, which convince people that they can transform their home or workplace using products and services that are readily available.

Apart from this field of amateur activity, it is important to be aware of the distinction between an interior decorator and an interior designer. An interior decorator does not deal with the architectural and structural alterations to a building as much as an interior designer does. Interior decorators offer excellent contractual services with regard to the final detailed furnishing of an interior. However, problems may arise when the decorator controls the full design of an interior – the end result can sometimes be overdone with decorative elements, whilst lacking in design substance: the choice of furniture, finishes and furnishing may result in a lack of coordination.

SCOPE OF WORK

As we have seen in Chapter 1, the scope of the subject is enormous and, as with architects, many interior designers find themselves specialising in certain sectors. This is because they have either built up a reputation for producing successful projects in the past, or they have built up a research and knowledge base in that sector which means that they are better prepared to take on more jobs in the same sector.

The nature of work has become increasingly multidisciplinary over the years, out of the realisation that interior designers, graphic designers, furniture designers, engineers and architects can work more efficiently if united together as one business. They can subsequently appear to offer a speedier service to the client, but not necessarily one that guarantees quality. A designer may work for the following types of employer:

■ **Specialist design group** – Consists of designers and support staff.

■ **Architect** – Could be multidisciplinary.

■ **Large company** – Working as an in-house architect or member of the design department (for companies such as the British Shoe Corporation or John Lewis Retail).

■ **Local authority** – Such as a county or town council. Working in the architects' department.

■ **Building contractor** – Such as Costain or Taylor Woodrow.

■ **Yourself** – Working as a freelance.

Whatever direction the design business takes, there will always be a need for people with great skill and human understanding to look after, maintain, convert or upgrade the insides of our buildings. In order to carry out these responsibilities in a proper professional manner, interior designers need to be equipped, theoretically and philosophically, to carry out the necessary design work and confidently present a strong rationale to the client for the final design solution. This book examines these duties in detail and begins by analysing the basic interior design elements that shape interiors.

THE ELEMENTS OF INTERIOR DESIGN

The elements of interior design are not to be confused with the visual elements of art such as form, line, colour and texture. The setting up of a body of theory has been essential for my own teaching purposes and professional career, and whilst I have drawn inspiration from many sources, I have developed my own terminology to describe and analyse the various groups of study areas, simply because I have found a lack of such terms when teaching students. A useful terminology, which can be understood, is vital to ensure clarity of communication.

The nine elements of interior design listed opposite (environment; space; light; ground plane; enclosure; support; display, storage and worksurface; decoration; and information) are those that I consider to be the key parts of the physical interior and which designers manipulate in three dimensions in order to arrive at a completed design. These basic elements, in general descriptive terms, are in four groups:

1. *Environmental*
2. *Spatial*
3. *Three-dimensional (3D)*
4. *Two-dimensional (2D).*

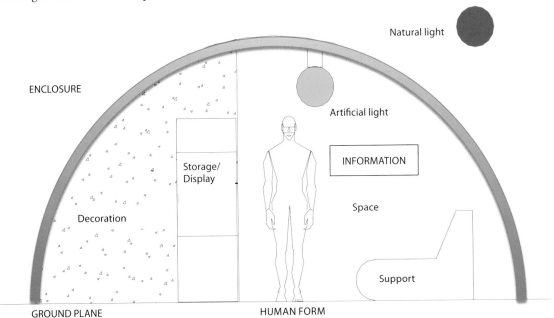

ELEMENTS	WHAT ARE THEY?	EFFECT/USE
1. THE ENVIRONMENT	Natural and adapted environment. It is important to understand what we are doing in relation to the natural environment.	Fusion of both, harmony.
2. SPACE	Air, gas, smoke, mist, fog. Space is the most difficult element to handle because it is the result of the making of the solid.	See distance, views, major impact of interior.
LIGHT	Artificial or natural, task or decorative. Illumination is complex and exists under controlled variations.	To see, emphasise, focus.
3. GROUND PLANE	Gravity, incline, undulate, step. Various levels to contend with.	Hard, soft, polished. Walking, transporting.
ENCLOSURE	Structure, form, openings, entrance, exit, divisions. Main building form and subdivisions of space.	Shelter, protection, connections.
SUPPORT	For: seating, holding, hanging, lying, leaning. Normally described as furniture, but for supporting the human form.	Rest, work, play.
DISPLAY/STORAGE AND WORKSURFACE	Objects – 2D and 3D, visual or applied needs. Usually under the heading of furniture.	Identify, remind, relate, work, reference.
4. DECORATION	Applied or integral with structure. Not an add-on or last minute decision.	Completion of scheme, mood.
INFORMATION	Graphic, signage, time. Communication.	Content, message, directional.

THE ELEMENTS OF INTERIOR DESIGN

Building services (which cover heating, ventilation, telecommunications, IT, security, water and drainage) are excluded from the elements because they are usually the *result* of the design and coordination of the above. If, on the other hand, a chosen building services system begins to influence the design of any of the elements, then it should be put into the equation.

The sectional abstract diagram (left) symbolically illustrates all the basic elements (including the human form) apart from that of the environment, and is not for a specific interior. All interiors can be analysed and broken down into these main headings. When a designer is working out a design, all of the elements have to be fully researched to plan a strategic way forward. The elements are used to help shape the spaces where various activities will take place, and determine the human needs of those spaces. The aim is to produce eight concepts (described in detail at the end of this chapter) that will eventually mature into a conclusive design concept, which will then be honed into a final design solution to present to the client.

ELEMENT 1: ENVIRONMENT

COMMENT ON OUR ADAPTATION PROGRESS

From the beginning of time, humankind has adapted the natural environment to suit the generational demands of changes in the way we live, work and play. Buckminster Fuller[1] demonstrated that due to the way our society is evolving, we are in danger of losing our contact with nature, and that this is undesirable for future survival. Through his own work, he has tried to reunify essential common elements that acknowledge our natural connections on this planet. The Dymaxion House, built in 1929, was an attempt to design a mass-produced home using industrial methods, steel and aluminium. Through his geocentric structures, Fuller attempted to harmonise with nature by using the geometry inherent in nature.

The quotations that follow support creating and maintaining connections with our natural evolutionary roots.

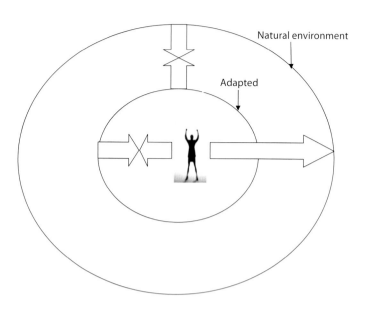

Diagram showing the interaction between living beings, the adapted environment and the natural environment – fusion.

Figure 7. *The Climatron*, Buckminster Fuller's patented design of the world's first geodesic domed greenhouse, 1960. Architects: Murphy and Mackey. Wikimedia Commons licence. Photo: Jet Lowe.

... was the essence of ancient religious science, and its architecture sought literally (as well as symbolically) to unite man with the forces which maintain the biosphere of which he is a part.[2]

Lawrence Blair

Psychoanalysis and anthropology teach and warn us that man has lost some essential values in his rise to civilisation; the sense of the unity of space and time, the freedom of nomadic life, the joy of aimless wandering through unlimited horizons. We can and must recover these values.[3]

Bruno Zevi

Man alone lives in a time-world that transcends the limitations of his local environment: the world of the past, the present and the possible; or, if you will, the real, the realising, and the realisable. Once he loses hold on any of these dimensions of his experience, he cuts himself off from a part of reality.[4]

Lewis Mumford

Martin Pawley's[5] book *The Private Future*, published in 1973, states how he foresaw a society with ever greater technical means of communication becoming paradoxically more insular and dysfunctional. Because we operate in a space–time continuum, we must be sensitive to the evolution of design through the ages. The design of our cities, towns, villages and the means of transport devised represent part of this process of adaptation from the natural environment. The work of interior designers continues with the adaptation process.

The relationship of man to the landscape is highlighted by Amos Rapoport[6], where he lists three classifications of attitude that have been developed historically:

1. *Religious and cosmological* – The environment is regarded as dominant, and man is inferior to nature.
2. *Symbiotic* – Here man and nature are in a state of balance, and man regards himself as responsible to God for nature and the Earth, and as a steward and custodian of nature.
3. *Exploitative* – Man is the completer and modifier of nature, then creator, and finally the destroyer of the environment.

INSIDE TO OUTSIDE

The total urban built environment consists of buildings, streets and open spaces. Robert Venturi[7] talks about contradiction between the inside and the outside of a building. He goes on to explain different theories such as 'the inside should be expressed on the outside', or the way that the inside can be divorced from the outside by an 'unattached lining'. This separation of the inside from the outside can vary in degrees, as further analysed by Brooker and Stone[8] in the following breakdown:

Responsive interiors: design inspired by the character of the existing building

■ **Intervened** – New additions that respond to the existing character.

■ **Inserted** – Separate and distinct from the original building.

■ **Installed** – Allows the existing building and new additions to exist independently.

Autonomous interiors: the new design strongly asserts itself over the existing building

■ **Disguised** – Treats the enclosure as a shell that is to be hidden or camouflaged.

■ **Assembled** – Anonymous space containing a series of interconnected objects.

■ **Combined** – Brings together the Disguised and Assembled approaches.

Some of the most common terms for describing what we do to buildings:

■ **Convert** – Implies a change of use from previous occupation.

■ **Refit** – A total renewal of existing functions.

■ **Renovate** – To renew and update parts of the building to continued usage.

■ **Remodel** – To make a total alteration resulting in an intervention into the building's life.

■ **Retrofit** – To use the latest technology to strengthen future performance.

Because of our connections with nature, it is naturally desirable to emphasise these connections in the design of interiors by using organic materials, living plants and any other source that completes the connection.

ELEMENT 2: SPACE

Forms are not restricted to their corporeal limits. Forms emanate and model space. Today we are again becoming aware that shapes, surfaces and planes serve not only to model interior space. They operate just as strongly, far beyond the confines of their actual measured dimensions, as constituent elements of volumes standing freely in the open.[9]

Sigfried Giedion

It could be said that all the nine elements listed previously compete for attention in one way or another.

The most difficult one to handle is space, in that it is not tangible in the same way as the other elements. It is not something physical that can be planned, moulded or made in a factory. In the conceptual planning of an interior, the eight minor design concepts listed later in this chapter (planning, circulation, lighting, building services, three-dimensional form, construction, material and colour; see p.55) should be coordinated continuously throughout the design process. So how can one define space? Space can be conceived of and described in terms of the *effect* produced when experienced by the user. The following is a selection of examples in terms of dualities.

TYPES OF SPACE IN TERMS OF DUALITIES/OPPOSITES

Compressive
Figure 8. Child's bed and play area. H2O architects, Paris, 2009. Photo: Stéphane Chalmeau.

Expansive
Figure 9. British Airways corporate event at a Gatwick aircraft hangar, 1988. Photo courtesy of Imagination, London.

Liberated
Figure 10. *Merry-Go-Round Coat Rack*, entrance of Museum Boijmans Van Beuningen, Rotterdam. Designed by Studio Wieke Somers, 2009.

Confined
Figure 11. Apartment in Moscow. Peter Kostelov, 2009.

High

Figure 12. The Great Court, British Museum. Foster + Partners, 2000. Atrium-type space. Photo courtesy of British Museum.

Low

Figure 13. ICI offices, London. Tilney Shane, 2001.

Light

Figure 14. Shop for the Italian knitwear brand, Stefanel. Sybarite, Hamburg, 2009. An overall effect rather than a localised source.

Dark

Figure 15. Zimzum restaurant, London. Tilney Shane, 2003.

Organic

Figure 16. Lyon-Satolas Station. Santiago Calatrava, 1994. Inspired by a natural form. Photo courtesy of Tom Godber.

Linear

Figure 17. DIY store. Photo by author.

Public
Figure 18. Circus Zandvoort, youth entertainment centre, the Netherlands. Sjoerd Soeters, 1991. Photo: Viewfinders/ Koos Baaij.

Private
Figure 19. Main ensuite bathroom, Glendower House, Monmouth. Anthony Sully, 2002. Photo: Media Services LCSF, University of Glamorgan.

The types of space listed above – compressive/expansive, liberated/confined, high/low, light/dark, organic/linear, public/private – are determined by the enclosure and by the type of objects within them. We may use the following terms to describe space:

■ **Degree of containment** – Total separation, or partial separation by leakage into other spaces through the planning of the enclosure of wall, floor and ceiling.

■ **Edges** – Visually determined by all enclosing parts of the interior.

■ **Boundaries** – Defined area of activity.

■ **Domain** – Defined by the name of the activity performed within the space.

■ **Context** – The overall type of building and site.

■ **Circulation pattern** – Routes of the people who move through and use the space.

■ **Centre** – The heart of the space.

The main duality is physical mass and space. A major failing of any design is if the solid massing is planned without any feeling for the space, as if it were of secondary importance.

> *Our sense of the interior depends, not simply on empty space, but on its interaction with the material that encloses it; it is that material that grants space a specific character, a particular shape, and dimensional spatial unity.*[10]

Malnar and Vodvarka

DISTINGUISHING FEATURES OF SPACE
The features that distinguish a space are as follows:

■ **Character** – Made by distinctive features, personality.

■ **Purpose** – Defined by the activities carried out there.

■ **Effect** – Impression made upon the user.

■ **Atmosphere** – Overall feeling confirming the relationship of the user to the space.

■ **Style** – A judgement of its place in time by a comparative method.

■ **Mood** – Quality affecting the spirit and attitude of use.

■ **Quality** – Measurement of the standard of finish.

■ **Aesthetic** – Judgement of the visual arrangement of form, colour and materials.

■ **Scale** – Size and impact of the space.

■ **Stature** – Place in the hierarchical use of space.

Malnar and Vodvarka discuss space differentiation in terms of human behaviour as being:

■ **Absolute space** – An uncluttered, clear view.

■ **Object space** – Defined by the presence of objects.

■ **Body-centred space** – Haptic experiences, feelings and memory.

The same authors explain Hall's[11] theories of spatial organisation, which are:

- **Infracultural** – Rooted in our biological past; underlying culture.

- **Precultural** – The physiological basis for perception with regard to structure and meaning.

- **Microcultural** – Organisation of individual and group activities.

In terms of the social level of occasion, spaces can be grouped as either **informal** (with a casual function, no dress code, and not making any demands upon people) or **formal** (would usually involve a dress code and the attendance could be a more programmed function).

Norberg-Schulz sees the description of an interior volume more in the sense of 'place' rather than 'space'. Whilst this view has become popular with the academic community, I feel that both words still have their distinct and different meanings. To me, a place is part of an urban or rural environment, with loose boundaries, and will have a strong associative meaning according to a particular event or one's memory; whereas a space usually refers to the inside of a building and has distinct boundaries. Hence the adjective 'spatial', a derivative qualitative term that is an important part of the interior designer's terminology. The word 'place' does not have an equivalent – there is no such thing as 'platial' – so, the term has limitations.

ELEMENT 3: LIGHT

NATURAL LIGHT
The primary source of natural light is the sun, which also provides us with warmth, vitamin D and psychological pleasure. Interior designers usually work on buildings with pre-designated daylight openings. These could be changed or added to depending on the needs of the user.

Measurement
When daylight enters a building, it is measured in terms of the daylight factor which, without any artificial light present, is a ratio of the interior level of light (lux level) to the outdoor level of light under an overcast sky.

Orientation
It is important to note the orientation of the building in terms of the movement of the sun and the angles of the

sun's rays into the interior throughout the course of a day. Depending upon the project in hand, an assessment will be made as to how much daylight enters the interior and the effects of full sun or an overcast sky. A common rule applied to the position of computers in offices is that the screen should never face a window because the reflections will impair clear visibility of the screen. This will affect the layout of the office.

Control
There are now means of controlling the amount of daylight entering a building through the use of automatic electronic external blinds or shutters, which respond via sensors. Traditionally, the amount of daylight has been adjusted or closed off by curtain drapes, blinds or internal shutters.

The example below shows what an ingenious solution the internal Georgian[12] window shutter was. It consisted of two wings on either side of a window, which folded together and were hinged in order to return to a recess each side of the window. Here they appeared to merge into the rest of the interior as wall panelling, thus concealing their secret. When they were folded across the window, a steel pivot bar dropped on to brackets and locked the window tight – a wonderful security device that goes back to medieval times.

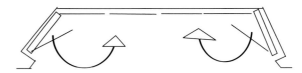

Above. Plan of Georgian window with folding shutters.

Figure 20. Georgian window. Courtesy of Watchet Conservation Society.

ARTIFICIAL LIGHT

Buildings have to be illuminated in order to aid vision under daylight conditions, and to provide light at night. Lighting is required for a variety of working conditions; if it is to fall on a desktop, this is called a 'working plane'. The source of light is emitted from a variety of lamps and fittings, the quality of which ranges in terms of intensity, contrast, glare, visual effect and colour; filters, diffusers and shades are used to facilitate these factors.

Lighting has six basic functions: general or ambient illumination, task lighting, decorative or special-effect lighting, directional or accent lighting, informational lighting, and lighting as a decorative focus.

General or ambient illumination
Figure 21. The offices of Willis, Faber, Dumas, Ipswich. Foster + Partners, 1975. Photo: Tim Street Porter.

Task lighting for specific activity
Figure 22. Desk lamps by Artemide Tolomeo.

Decorative or special-effect lighting
Figure 23. Switch Restaurant, Dubai, UAE. Karim Rashid, 2009. The lighting can be changed to a variety of colours.

Directional or accent lighting
Figure 24. Kimbell Art Museum, Fort Worth, Texas, USA. Designed by Louis Kahn, 1972. Photo: Andreas Praefcke, Wikimedia Commons.

Informational lighting
Figure 25. Illuminated sign by White Villa, London.

Lighting as a decorative focus

Figure 26. *Daedalus Lamp* by Tord Boontje for Artecnica, 2007.

In addition to the functions above, the following three aspects need to be understood.

Measurement

The measurement of the light output from a lamp is by its lumen rating (or luminous flux). Light sources are labelled with an output rating in lumens, and it is quantified by lumens per square metre.

Control

Lamps can be incandescent, fluorescent, HID (high-intensity discharge, such as mercury vapour, metal halide or high-pressure sodium) or LED, though only incandescent reflector or HID lamps are available in a spotlight configuration. The fitting that houses a lamp is designed for a particular method of installation and for a particular location in an interior. Lamps are suitable for many different design schemes because of their varied styles and effects. Other available types of light source are neon, cold cathode, fibre optic and laser. Lighting can be programmed to change in intensity, colour and frequency through computer-controlled settings.

Design concept

The consideration of lighting is a constant factor throughout the design process. The effect of a light is dependent upon the kind of space and the surfaces that the light bounces off. Lighting is not an 'add-on' feature that gives life to a space; it should be thought of in an integrated way along with the development of the three-dimensional element of the space. Consider what needs to be illuminated and plan accordingly. The stages of development in the design of lighting could be as follows:

1. Establish requirements from the client.
2. Define the purpose of the lighting and the effects required (see previous examples).
3. Quantify the amount of light required in response to the given space and surfaces.
4. Decide on the type of light installation – fixed, adjustable, mobile or concealed.
5. Research light fittings that can give the desired effect.
6. Consider possible locations – walls, floor, ceiling or furniture.
7. Match fitting method to fixture in relation to location on wall, floor or ceiling.
8. Plan the location of lighting controls.

ELEMENT 4: GROUND PLANE

The culturally constructed elements of a landscape are thus transformed into material and permanent markers and authentications of history, experience and values.[13]

Michael Parker Pearson

HISTORICAL DEVELOPMENT

The ground plane is the surface we walk on. In buildings it is the floor, steps or ramp. If we examine the natural terrain it is undulating and varied according to whereabouts on the planet we are. Early man would have been a climber, a runner and very athletic, in order to survive. The evolution of our built environment through man's adaptation of the planet has resulted in such observations as succinctly expressed by Mumford:

The path of human development has been from sensation to significance, from the externally conditioned to the internally conditioned, from herdlike cohesion to rational cooperation, from automatism to freedom. Thus the poor be-plagued creature of circumstances who greets us at the beginning of history becomes progressively the shaper of his own character, the creator of his own destiny. But only up to a point … For this increase of self-control is subject to numerous hazards and setbacks: man is the sport of natural forces both outside and within himself, forces he sometimes circumvents, but never entirely sets at naught. Pride trips him; reason unnerves him. Even man's cunningest [sic] efforts to escape nature's dominion may recoil against him: has he not, at this moment of apparent triumph over nature, seen himself slip helplessly back from freedom to automatism, from civilisation to barbarism?[14]

As with Buckminster Fuller's work, Mumford emphasises the risks we run if we do not respect the forces of nature. Our so-called domination of, and detachment from, the natural landscape could ultimately lead to disaster. The earliest forms of structure made by man in the prehistoric world were burial mounds – the re-forming of the natural landscape – such as the West Kennet Long Barrow in Wiltshire, UK.

During the Babylonian period, various peoples built massive raised structures in the form of steps or terraces, called ziggurats (holy mountains). A ziggurat was a temple chamber as well as an observatory, and a mark against the endless 'flatness' of the landscape. (Subsequently, most religious buildings have reached to the heavens in the form of spires, towers and domes.)

As early civilisations developed, they began to build dwellings that were more substantial, with *flat* floors, so if these were on sloping land, they would form a group of stepped structures. I think we can conclude that throughout history, human beings have associated 'flatness' in their environment with efficiency and convenience. However, in many situations, 'flatness' may be described as being rather boring, whilst anything that reaches high up and emphasises the vertical has greater significance due to status (as in places of worship and palaces) and a greater sensation of views and distance.

When we look at ancient settlements, the dwellings hug and follow the landscape. The Babylonians accepted the flat landscape of their country because of the resources offered by the River Tigris and the River Euphrates and, as with many other early examples of habitation, they also built on the edges of rivers for agricultural reasons.

In our urban developments, 'flatness' became popular because of the practicalities of working, as technology developed; the ease of communication it afforded; and the ease of transportation it allowed – especially when wheeled vehicles were established. Yet people also love to visit and work in modern buildings that contain interior atrium spaces, stairways that cut through the space in dramatic fashion, and glass elevators. Why is this? Is it because our desires stem from our ancestral roots, and such devices are designed to help with this assimilation with our natural environment? Hence the sight of the natural external environment from the interior can produce a feeling of comfort in people, and a design that allows for this experience to occur is a gesture of this reunification of humans with nature.

Figure 27. West Kennet Long Barrow, UK, c.3650 BC. Wikimedia Commons. Photo: Troxx.

Figure 28. Yungang Grottoes, near Datong, Shanxi province, China, c.460 AD. Photo: Felix Andrews, Wikimedia Commons.

Figure 29. Atrium of HSBC Bank in Hong Kong. Foster + Partners, 1985. Photo: Ian Lambot.

TYPES OF FLOOR PLANES

Floor planes come in an inexhaustible variety of materials, which are classified in terms of being hard, soft, smooth, rough, polished, matt or transparent. They may have a level surface for perambulation as well as vehicular usage; a sloping surface, facilitating a smooth walk or disabled access; or be stepped for a quick climb from one level to another. Floors, or levels, are usually stacked one above the other. They enable human circulation and can assist with the direction of travel; this interior surface receives the most wear and tear (see Chapter 7, p.143).

Flooring can be summed up as follows: the surface given to a floor depends upon its function; its structural depth is in accordance with the building's form; it can contain building services; and it is designed to allow for the fixing of secondary structures as required.

ELEMENT 5: ENCLOSURE

HISTORICAL DEVELOPMENT

Many early dwellings existed in the form of caves. Other materials such as mud, leaves, reeds, stone and wood were also used to devise a simple structure, or enclosure, to live in. The cave would have been excavated, with a flat floor and a concave surround that echoed the arm movements of the human figure. There would have been certain zones of use.

This series of drawings shows the development of primitive huts and the gradual rise of the vertical wall as part of an enclosure.

TYPES AND PROPERTIES OF FORM

The enclosure developed over centuries, with structural solutions that set the means of future architectural style, as shown in the diagrams opposite.

Primary structures are load-bearing and hold a building up; secondary structures are not load-bearing, and can be removed and altered easily. Structural variations were developed using combinations of walls and columns. The subdivision of interior spaces produces internal walls – described in the plural; curiously, the floor and ceiling are described in the singular simply because they both flow (on the same level) through the building, connecting one space to another, whereas walls turn corners and multiply. Accepting that there

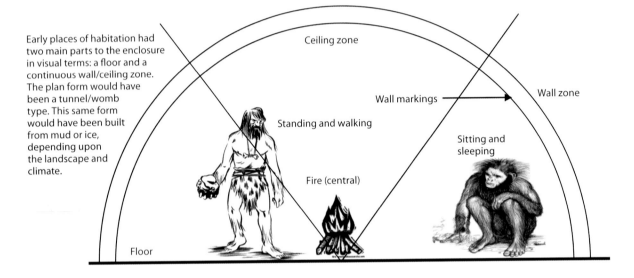

Early places of habitation had two main parts to the enclosure in visual terms: a floor and a continuous wall/ceiling zone. The plan form would have been a tunnel/womb type. This same form would have been built from mud or ice, depending upon the landscape and climate.

Ceiling zone

Standing and walking

Wall markings

Wall zone

Sitting and sleeping

Fire (central)

Floor

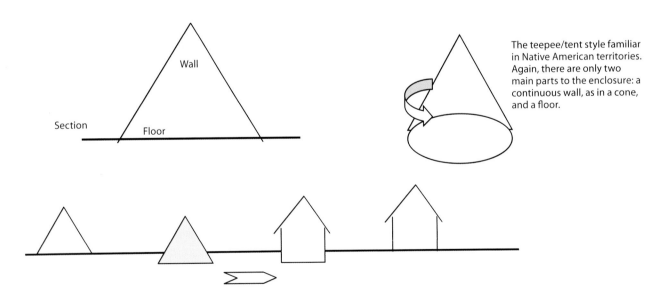

Section

Wall

Floor

The teepee/tent style familiar in Native American territories. Again, there are only two main parts to the enclosure: a continuous wall, as in a cone, and a floor.

can be different levels of floor and ceiling, they are still rarely referred to in the plural. In interior design, we are usually given an existing building, as explained under the section on environment. The brief from the client will be to carry out one of the five tasks listed in that section (see p.31): conversion, refit, renovation, remodelling or retrofit.

FEATURES

The enclosure will be surveyed and its quality, condition and character described. This will set out any remedial work that needs to be done in order for the building to work satisfactorily. This assessment will establish constraints and the basic provision of:

■ Means of access and exit.

■ A primary structure – the system by which the building stands up.

■ Secondary structures – not essential for the building to stand up and can therefore be removed if necessary.

■ Services – power supply, water, drainage and security.

■ Fenestration.

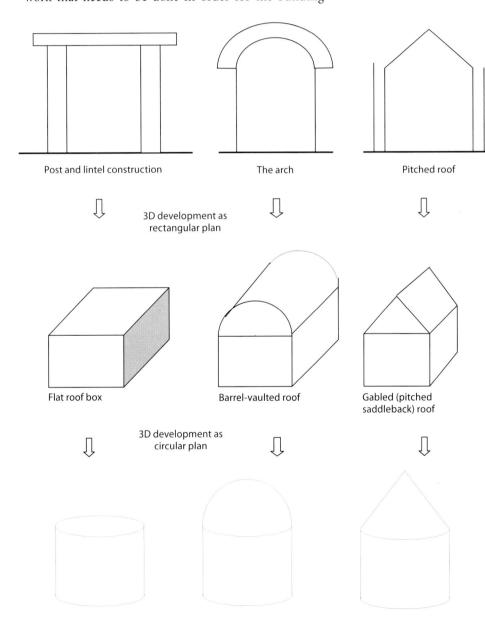

Post and lintel construction

The arch

Pitched roof

3D development as rectangular plan

Flat roof box

Barrel-vaulted roof

Gabled (pitched saddleback) roof

3D development as circular plan

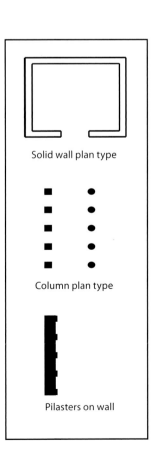

Solid wall plan type

Column plan type

Pilasters on wall

Figure 30. *Top left*. Old Addenbrooke's Hospital ward block, Cambridge (now the Judge Institute: see Figure 31), founded 1766. Courtesy of Cambridge University Hospitals NHS Foundation Trust.

Figure 31. *Top right*. Remodelled exterior of the Judge Institute, Cambridge. John Outram Architects, 1995. Photo: Cambridge 2000.

Figure 32. *Left*. New interior of the Judge Institute. Courtesy of John Outram Architects.

These photos of the transformation of an old ward block at Addenbrooke's Hospital into the Judge Institute reveal a beautifully orchestrated series of forms with a clear delineation of components, demonstrating how an enclosure can be remodelled as well as providing a wonderful modern intervention.

ELEMENT 6: SUPPORT

This element covers all the forms that provide support for human beings, whether they are sitting, resting, lying, sleeping or leaning – in fact in any posture whilst at work, at home or in some form of leisure pursuit, covering such areas as refreshment, the arts and sport. The following table provides a guide to how these support items can be analysed collectively and on a comparable basis. This analysis is intended to help the designer categorise and group items with more thought as to their functions, instead of just specifying the product from catalogues based on cost, size and style. The headings under 'Product' usually fall into separate groups such as furniture, shelving, bathroom appliances and ironmongery/accessories, but these headings are generic and do not show all variants. 'Host image' in the 'Identity' column implies that the product is conforming to a style of space used by the public rather than being tailored to the identity of the owner/user. In other words it has more general usage than specific. Dark grey boxes indicate that there could be more than one person using the piece. This chart is not meant to be exhaustive and readers will be able extend it with further examples.

Product	Application	Posture	Duration of use	Quantity	Status	Identity	Example/ location
chair: – dining	private/public	sitting	1-2 hrs	group	formal	personal/host image	home/ restaurant
– office	commercial	sitting	working hrs	scattered/ single	formal	corporate	office
– lounge	private	sitting	few hours	1 or 2	informal	personal	home
– reception	commercial	sitting	short	group	formal	corporate	office
– folding	various/ portable	sitting	various	single/ scattered	informal	practical	various
high stool	commercial/ leisure	sitting	working hrs/1hr +	group	formal/ informal	host image	office/bar
low stool	leisure/private	sitting	1hr +/ occasional	scattered/ 1 or 2	informal	host image/ personal	bar/café
bench	general	sitting	short	single/ scattered	low	personal/ public	garden/park
shelf	general	standing	short	single/ scattered	supportive	public/ personal	library/home
couch	domestic	sitting/lying	a few hours	single	personal	personal	home
handrail	public/private	standing	short	short/long	communal/ personal	public/ personal	retail centre/ staircase
grip rail	private	various	short	single/ scattered	personal	personal	bathroom
bed	private	lying	a few hours	single	informal	personal	home/hotel
bath	private	lying	short	single	informal	personal	home/hotel
basin	private/public	standing	short single/ group	informal/ communal	personal/ public	home/hotel/ public	home/public
wc	private/public	sitting	short	single/group	personal/ communal	personal/ public	home/public
bidet	private	squatting	short	single	personal	personal	home

SOME INNOVATIVE PRODUCTS

The illustrations below show imaginative and problem-solving responses to various needs. They serve as examples of originality and improvement of public spaces, and are also visually stunning solutions.

Figure 39. *Left.* Folding chair in laminated wood, Ken Okuyama, 2005. It has a second life as a vertical screen.

Figure 40. *Above.* Flip Chair, Boris Novachi Bojic, 2007. This may be used vertically, as an upright chair, as well as horizontally, as a recliner.

FACING PAGE: *Left, top to bottom*
Figure 33. *Stretch Fence*, New York. Jennifer Carpenter, Truck Product Architecture, 2005. A structure for sitting or leaning on, designed for taxi drivers in New York.

Figure 34. Bench made of sea grey granite with LED underlighting, Manchester. Bailey Streetscene, 2009. The rails define five bays, making a ten-seater bench (when seated back to back) and also give it some structural integrity and discipline.

Figure 35. Modern polished tubular steel handrails separately supported by matt flat steel uprights. Photo by author. Courtesy of the Natural History Museum, London.

FACING PAGE: *Right, top to bottom*
Figure 36. Seating that has been sculpted and divided into two separate parts: a wall-mounted back support and floor-standing seating. Zaha Hadid, 1980s. Courtesy of Zaha Hadid Architects.

Figure 37. Victorian brass handrails with finials supported by screw-twisted steel uprights. Photo by author. Courtesy of the Natural History Museum, London.

Figures 35 and 37 show handrails from two different periods, of contrasting designs, in the same museum.

Figure 38. Aluminium bench exhibited at the Max Protetch Gallery. Designer: Zaha Hadid, 2003. Photo © Eli-Ping Weinberg.

FEATURES

Support products have various possible relationships to an interior space. They may be fixed to a structure, moveable (by lifting), or mobile (on casters or wheels). They could be:

- *Freestanding* (on a ground plane, by gravity)
- *Cantilevered* (from a wall)
- *Suspended* (from a ceiling).

They may be made from various materials, such as wood, metal, plastic, stone, marble, rope, cables or fabric upholstery.

When it comes to sourcing products or having something specially made, it has become more common in the UK these days to discover that designers have to look abroad because of the decline in British manufacturing. This perhaps reflects upon the more global nature of working that has developed, and the way that international communications in trade and professional services have become much easier over the past 30 years. The computer has of course helped in this process, with the speed of communication it affords aiding the management of projects and people.

ELEMENT 7: DISPLAY, STORAGE AND WORKSURFACES

Every interior has objects (two- or three-dimensional) that are either meant to be used or seen, or that are stored away for future use. Hence the objects will require structures upon which or in which they will be supported. Two-dimensional items include artwork or mirrors, in which case the surfaces of the enclosure could be used for fixing. Also included here are worksurfaces for various activities, which may need to facilitate access to objects that are displayed or stored.

DISPLAY FORMS

Shelves fixed to walls are common in every interior. The dresser, as found in kitchens for storing crockery was usually in two parts: the upper half as open shelves and the lower half consisting of drawers and compartments.

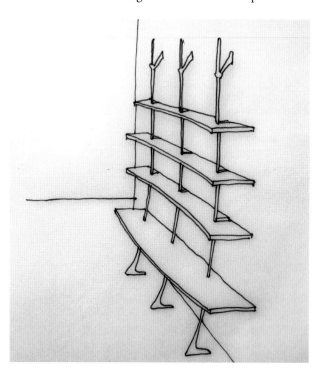

Figure 41. Ladder shelving, 1980s. This just stands and leans – there are no fixings. Designed by Jaime Tresserra. Drawing by author.

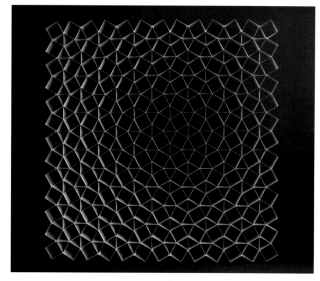

Figure 42. *Cell Screen*, Korban/Flaubert, 2003. This screen has the function of dividing up space yet allowing you to see through it. Made in anodised aluminium, with the geometry inspired by Islamic architecture, mathematical sequences and natural growth patterns.

The hat stand could also hold umbrellas. Many types of screen were used to divide a space and were usually portable. There are various kinds of cabinets, such as those used in dining rooms with drawers and compartments. The whatnot, or étagère, was a cabinet of open shelves usually pyramidal in shape and used for the display of curios and accessories. Bookcases are freestanding shelving units specifically for the storage of books. A cocktail cabinet had the specific function of storing drinks and glasses and a surface for preparing such drinks. The trolley (canteen) had the general purpose of enabling food and drink to be wheeled from one space to another. The desk is a place to work and usually comprises a worktop and drawers. The bureau is the antique version of a desk as a place to write and read, and consisted of a folding down work surface, open compartments for the storage of stationery items, and a cupboard below. A secretaire, or secretary desk, is similar to a bureau but is usually a lighter piece of furniture with slender legs. A clock case, such as a grandfather clock, is usually a substantial piece of furniture with a pendulum as part of the mechanism, which has a distinctive tick. These stand on the floor but smaller versions could be wall mounted or placed on a mantelpiece.

Figure 43. *Carlton Butterfly Desk*, Jaime Tresserra, 1988.

Figure 44. Museum shop's display cabinets. Photo by author. Courtesy of Natural History Museum, London.

PRIMARY STORAGE FORMS

See diagrams on p.48. The cupboard, built-in or freestanding, is an enclosed unit of varying size with hinged or sliding doors for access. The sideboard is a long, horizontal freestanding storage unit that appears in either the sitting or dining room, and contains many household goods used for relaxation purposes. A commode is usually an ornate freestanding storage chest or it can be a taller unit in a bedroom containing a washbowl and jug. A washstand is similar to a commode but can have a washbasin built in, with a marble surround. A chest can vary a great deal but it is simply a low freestanding cupboard. A tallboy is a two-tiered freestanding chest of drawers. A wardrobe is either built-in or freestanding and is specifically for storing and hanging clothes on shelves or hangers with hinged or sliding doors for access. A chest of drawers is usually for storing clothes and is a chest with pullout drawers rather than hinged doors. A credenza is the forerunner of the sideboard, but in the 19th century it was a highly decorative and heavy storage unit with a marble top. A chiffonier is a smaller and more decorative version of a sideboard, with small compartments for storing odds and ends. The dressing table usually has a mirror and storage drawers and has an accompanying stool on which to sit when preparing cosmetic applications. A box settle is basically a bench seat and back, where the seat surface lifts up on hinges to reveal a chest type storage space inside.

Figure 45. *Marie Galante Portable Make-Up Trunk*, Starbay, France, late 19th C. This unique dressing table/make-up trunk is a working piece of furniture with added portable facility.

SECONDARY STORAGE

Secondary storage is achieved by the allocation of space, rather than the use of a designed artefact. It is usually in the form of a loft or a lock-away store.

CHOOSING A DISPLAY OR STORAGE FORM

This is calculated around a specified activity, according to whether the displayed or stored items are used regularly, intermittently or rarely. First, the designer must quantify the amount of storage/display required in terms of surface area and volume. Secondly, shape

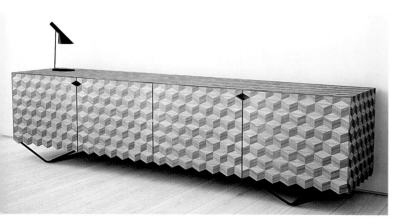

Figure 46. Necker Cube Cabinet, Pieter Maes, Netherlands, 2009. The Necker Cube is an optical illusion, first published in 1832 by the Swiss crystallographer Louis Albert Necker, based on an ambiguous line drawing that could be read in two ways and then adjusted to an isometric view.

Oblique view

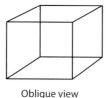

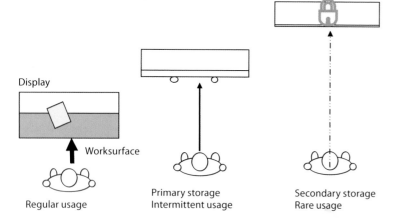

Display

Worksurface

Regular usage

Primary storage
Intermittent usage

Secondary storage
Rare usage

and form is given to fit in with the plan of the enclosure and the circulation of the user. The third consideration is whether this is to be a single entity or a repeated component of a scheme.

FEATURES

Storage and display products have various possible relationships to an interior space. They may be fixed to a structure, moveable (by lifting), or mobile (on casters or wheels). They could be freestanding (on a ground plane, by gravity), cantilevered (from a wall), or suspended (from a ceiling).

For the display form, you need to be able to use the worksurface and to display objects that inform, remind, entertain and secure admiration. The display furniture may be open to reveal the object in its internal space, enclosed but allowing the object to be seen (e.g. use of glass), supported by a horizontal surface, or held by a special fixing.

In primary storage, the container usually separates the stored object from view. You need to be able to access it by opening a door, shutter, tambour, fabric or lid; or by operating these by sliding, a hinge, rollers or a pivot. The container may have handles, a recess grip or locks. In secondary storage, the important thing here is to have an appropriate size and good access, usually unseen, to the major interior space(s).

RELATIONSHIP WITH PEOPLE

Having examined different types of storage and their functions it is as well to consider the relationship of these items with the people who use them.

Norberg-Schulz[15] refers to Parson's (1951) theory of the three kinds of relationship we have with objects:

1. *Cognitive attitude* – Consists of trying to classify and describe an object.
   This confirms that we need to identify with the objects around us.
2. *Cathectic attitude* – A spontaneous reaction to an object according to the gratification it offers us.
   This confirms that we have a desire to be pleased with objects around us.
3. *Evaluative attitude* – Where we try to establish 'norms' without letting ourselves become attached to an object.

We also have an inbuilt categorisation process in assessing the degree of attachment we have to the object.

ELEMENT 8: DECORATION

HISTORICAL DEVELOPMENT

Through the processes of painting and carving, humans adorned early structures with images, colours and shapes that had some sort of attachment to the environment. In the 5th century BC, the Chinese painted on silk and paper scrolls and the Ancient Egyptians painted on linen – these are some of the earliest examples of portability in art. In monasteries and churches, examples of decorative elements could be found in the form of frescoes, icon paintings, mosaics and illuminated manuscripts. From the early Middle Ages, wooden panels were used for painting and stained-glass windows became an art form in their own right. Art gradually became more personalised and under individual ownership, commissioned by the influential religious and wealthy landowners of the day.

Decoration became more sophisticated as societies progressed. The term 'graphic' was used to distinguish decoration as a more commercially applied skill that was designed to market or sell a product or service, as opposed to fine art. The term 'visual communication' was coined to describe a huge discipline covering all the graphic arts, graphic design, photography and interior decoration. It also distinguished between the still and moving image, by embracing films. We now have that meaningless generic term 'media', which deals with 'communication' and which seems to cover so many subjects that it tends to confuse rather than inform. Decoration in interiors expanded over time from painting to embracing all surface finishes, and eventually furnishings.

In modern interior design practice, the notion of leaving decoration out of the conceptual stages of the design process, and considering it as a last-minute tactic 'to fill an empty space' is not the correct way to ensure an integrated design solution. It is not an 'add-on'. Interior designers should be used at the commencement of a new architectural project and not near the end, for 'finishing off'. This approach undermines the role of the interior designer, and devalues his or her contribution to the architectural design process. Let us consider the following classifications for describing types of decoration: gestural, entertainment, communication, commemorative, directional, or related to a building's geometry (either in opposition to it or in harmony with it).

TYPES OF DECORATION

Gestural

Since the beginning of time, it has been a natural urge for human beings to mark their environment for the following reasons: as respect for, or in awe of what they have seen – leading to religious convictions, or to identify themselves with their environment.

Figure 47. Cave painting from the Lascaux caves. Courtesy of Mimenta.com.

Entertainment

Decoration may feature as a means of entertainment – to give pleasure.

Figure 48. Laminated mural at Westfield Shopping Centre, London. Lynne Hollingsworth, 2007.

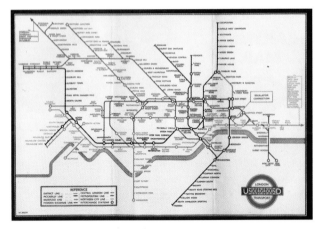

Figure 49. The London Underground map, created by Harry Beck in 1933. Laminate from the London Transport Museum's collection. © TfL. This could also go into the category of Element 9: Information.

Figure 50. Mural on Charing Cross underground station. David Gentleman, 1979. Wikimedia Commons. Author: Sunil Prasannan.

Communication
Decoration may be used to communicate messages and inform people.

Commemorative
Decoration may confirm an event historically or celebrate an event.

Directional
Decoration may be used for directional emphasis.

Figure 51. Café bar and foyer space, carpeted, Manchester Library Theatre, 2009. Photo courtesy of the Theatres Trust Image Library.

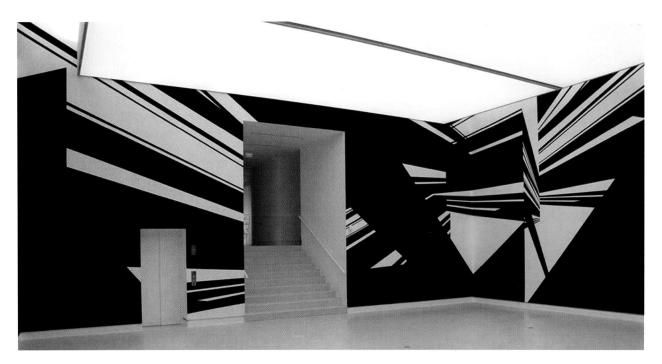

Figure 52. *Dead Reckoning, Room Drawing* (detail), Kunsthalle, Mainz (Germany). Christine Rusche, 2008–9. PVAC wall paint in matt black. Size: 12 x 12.5 x 6.3 m. © Christine Rusche. Courtesy of Gallery Marion Scharmann, Cologne.

Figure 53. *Right.* Lounge in an apartment, New York. Jennifer Post Design, 2009.

Related to a building's geometry

Decoration may be created to oppose a building's geometry, such as Christine Rusche's artwork, *Dead Reckoning*, on the walls of an art gallery. Alternatively, it may integrate with a building's geometry, such as the lounge in an apartment shown in Figure 52. This apartment reveals a clear, geometric style on a dark brown and white theme, which is well balanced with large areas of white and brown combined with brown linear elements. The translucency of the window fabric is non-assertive and allows the peaceful ambience to pervade.

PROPERTIES AND FEATURES

Decoration using colour and texture may consist of abstract patterns, figurative work, identifiable images, letter and number forms, or pattern that is integral with the material used.

There are two different kinds of decoration: applied decoration, and decoration that is integral with the primary or secondary structure.

Applied decoration

The primary or secondary structures may receive decorative treatment applied directly on-site or applied as factory-prepared products in the form of:

■ **Coatings** – Liquid, film or plaster; applied by brush, trowel or spray.

■ **Flexible membrane** – Paper (wood-based product), plastic, fabric, carpet, veneer or sheet; applied by glue or stretched and pinned.

■ **Cladding** (rigid) – Panels/tiles of wood-based products, metal, plastics, fabric, glass, mirror, ceramics, marble, stone or rubber.

Figure 54. Ancient Egyptian decoration is noted for the abstracted geometric representation of plant and feather forms. Wikimedia Commons. Author: Lepsius-Projekt Sachsen-Anhalt.

Figure 55. *Mandala of Vajradhatu.* Tibetan Buddhist thangka painting. The outer form of these holy circles is a geometrical diagram – a mandala – and each detail of its construction has symbolic meaning. To view this was to help contemplate the goal of one's existence. Wikimedia Commons.

Decoration integral with primary or secondary structure

- Wood grain texture on concrete, produced by timber shuttering.

- Pattern from brick and blockwork.

- Wood grain.

- Anything cast into liquid concrete or plaster.

- Instances when the structural form itself and its connections become decorative.

Ornament

One word, used throughout history, and which impacts on decoration, is 'ornament'. To expand:

■ **An ornament** (noun) – An object that contributes towards the decoration of a space. Its positioning is vital with regard to its own effect as well as its effect on the balance of the interior.

■ **To ornament** (verb) – To apply ornamental features that may not depend on one object but can be ascribed to a larger part of the interior in terms of an intense and involved content.

■ **Ornamental** (adjective) – Describes the effect of an interior.

Measurement and control

The ability to quantify decorative content is something that grows with the general conceptual design process. You will gain an awareness of controlling the dualities of decoration: loud effect or quiet effect, hot or cool areas, constrained or free areas, inviting or uninviting spaces, sociable or unsociable purposes, formal or informal effect.

COMMENT ON EDUCATIONAL PROVISION

I believe that the study of historical decoration within interior design degree courses has been undermined, over the past 40 years, by educational ideologies that are highly influenced by fashionable trends and technological wizardry. Due to cutbacks in higher education, the teaching programmes in British universities hardly have time to cater for this important subject in their tightly modularised and underfunded units. A return to the Beaux-Arts[16] tradition of teaching might well be welcomed in this starved educational scenario.

ELEMENT 9: INFORMATION

In everyday language we speak of signals, signs, symptoms, representations, copies, pictures, symbols and expressions as separate phenomena, even if there is not always a clear idea of the lines of demarcation between the concepts designated in this way.[17]

Sven Hesselgren

TYPES OF ENVIRONMENT

This element covers any pattern, sign, symbol or graphic image (2D or 3D) that is conveying information or an instruction to warn, inform or advise. The areas of design that are mainly concerned with this element are those of exhibitions, museums, transport stations and airports, events, hospitals and interactive media.

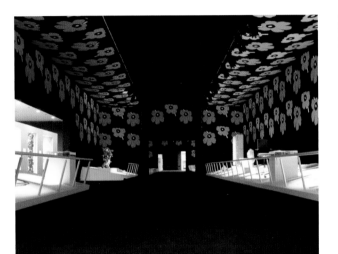

Exhibitions
Figure 56. *Design Anatomy*, 'Interieur' fair in Kortrijk. James Irvine, 2004.

Museums
Figure 57. Canadian War Museum, Ottawa, Canada. Haley Sharpe, 2005.

Transport stations/airports
Figure 58. St Pancras International Station, London, 2008. Courtesy of James Lisney, Infotech.

Events
Figure 59. British Airways corporate event at a Gatwick aircraft hangar, 1988. Courtesy of Imagination, London.

Figure 60. Sign in the Whittington Hospital, Archway, London. Enterprise IG, 2009. Manufactured by Rivermeade Signs.

Hospitals

Communication, therefore, is based upon common symbol systems, which are attached to common behavioural patterns or 'forms of life'.
Christian Norberg-Schulz, *Intentions in Architecture*

Interactive media
Figure 61. The Futures Gallery at Thinktank, Birmingham Science Museum. Land Design Studio, 2003.

PROPERTIES

Let us examine the various terms that define information in the environment:

- *Communication* – The means by which information is conveyed; the medium.

- *Transmitter* – The source of information; the message.

- *Receiver* – The audience; the observer.

This list is similar to the essential elements of the communications channel in a description by Shannon and Weaver[18] (1949): information source (transmitter) vs. communications channel (communication) vs. information destination (receiver).

How well a piece of information is understood, absorbed and acted upon depends on certain conditions: how clear the means of communication[19] is, how clear the transmitter is, and whether the observer is familiar or unfamiliar with the means of communication and the transmission. Whenever something does not work as planned or receives adverse criticism, it is usually to do with information breakdown. It is helpful to try and analyse why it happened. So let us permutate the above conditions using the terms clear, unclear, familiar and unfamiliar as follows:

Transmitter	Communication	Receiver	Result
clear	clear	familiar	✓
clear	clear	unfamiliar	✗
clear	unclear	familiar	✗
clear	unclear	unfamiliar	✗
unclear	clear	familiar	✗
unclear	clear	unfamiliar	✗

The table above illustrates how there is only one set of circumstances in which a full, clear understanding is possible. You can apply this analysis to any situation in order to ascertain why communication breakdown exists.

The medium is the message.[20]

H. M. McLuhan

The field of the communication of information is also known as the media. Edmund Carpenter,[21] anthropologist and communications consultant, wrote:

We don't read a newspaper: we step into it the way we step into a warm bath. It surrounds us. It environs us in information. We wear our media. They are our real clothes.

Radio and TV bombard us with images, cover us tattoo style; … asked if she had anything on when posing for nude calendar shots, Marilyn Monroe replied, 'The radio'.

DESIGN CONCEPTS

Design concepts form part of the design process, as mentioned in the diagram at the end of Chapter 1 (see p.25). A concept is an idea, usually original, which tends to offer a solution to a problem. A design concept will offer a strategic approach as well as a potential solution based upon a theoretical and philosophical stance. In interior design, there are many issues that determine a solution or a final design scheme. When explaining a scheme, the designer will refer to the concept behind the scheme; in other words, the leading spirit or motivating factor that gives the design its particular character or selling point. This will harness the use of the nine interior design elements listed earlier in this chapter.

Before a major concept is defined, there are eight minor design concepts of interior design to consider (requiring a conceptual understanding of principles and methods), which should either intertwine with the dominant design concept of a scheme (if there is one) or allow for one to grow out of the interconnections and analysis that will take place. A final design scheme will then emerge, which can be presented to the client. The eight concepts are described below. Other writers' views are also shown here to ensure a balanced coverage.

EIGHT MINOR DESIGN CONCEPTS

There are four organisational concepts: planning, circulation, lighting and services; and four concepts relating to form: 3D, construction, material and colour. These eight must all be developed in order to form the main design concept. It is important to emphasise that designers should adopt an equal approach to the minor design concepts in a project, without having a bias towards one single element that allows it to hold sway over the others. There is of course a processional sequence of designing, where planning is a generating concept, but more confidence is gained if a scheme can be deemed to have been arrived at democratically,

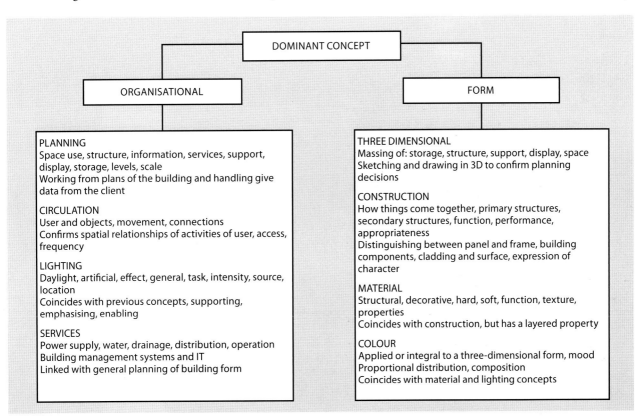

with all concepts having been considered fairly and in proportion to their input.

Kilmer and Kilmer, in their book *Designing Interiors*, give their version of the elements of design and principles of design as being part of a design language vocabulary, which they describe as being part of 'basic design compositional theory'. These elements are listed below, with detail as to how they relate to the contents of this book.

Elements of design

- **Space**   One of this book's stated elements.

- **Line**   Comes into Chapter 4 on geometry (see p.76).

- **Form**   Dealt with in Chapter 7 (see p.123) under the generation of 3D form.

- **Shape**   Covered in many sections of this book.

- **Texture**   This term is more closely related to materials, not covered here in any depth.

- **Time**   Mentioned in Chapter 1, under Lifespan (see p.16).

- **Colour**   Included in Element 8: Decoration (see p.49); also mentioned in Chapter 7 (see p.124).

- **Light**   One of this book's stated elements.

Principles of design

- **Balance**
- **Rhythm**
- **Scale**   } All listed under 'Glossary of descriptive terms' in Chapter 7 (p.136)
- **Harmony**
- **Emphasis**
- **Unity**

- **Proportion**   Dealt with in Chapter 4 (see p.77)

Malnar and Vodvarka, in their book *The Interior Dimension*, suggested a concept-forming structure (shown opposite; reprinted with the permission of John Wiley & Sons). Some headings are not too dissimilar to those of the Kilmers, and they propose three concepts that form the major one. 'Materials', 'structure' and 'colour' occur within the concept headings we have used here. The difference between these two sets of headings for concept development could not be greater. Malnar and Vodvarka's 'visual elements' are included within our concept heading of 'three-dimensional

Example of a typical exploratory concept sketch of a space. It indicates the content of the space, whilst searching for a composition that deals with emphasis, balance and visual connections. All other minor concepts are developed alongside with mutual interaction.

form' (see p.55), and their 'principles of organisation' is included in Chapter 7, within a section called 'Glossary of descriptive terms' (see p.136).

There is a huge gulf of understanding between British and American thinking on the subject of design. The American Roberto Rengel, in his book *Shaping Interior Space*, again produces a different definition for what a concept is and makes two groups – organisational concept and character concept – as shown opposite ('planning' and 'circulation' match the concepts used in this book).

Tiiu Poldma[22] has a very small section in her book *Taking up Space – Exploring the Design Process* under the heading of design concept evolution, which lists three-dimensional development, colour, material and lighting. She also defines three concepts that are part of the design process: the analysing of information, the creation of design ideas and the design solution.

Susan J. Slotkis,[23] in her book *Foundations of Interior Design*, describes rather loosely that a design concept stems from programming and that it is 'a plan or system by which action may be taken towards a goal. A who, what, when, where and how of the design project'. She then goes on to talk about 'schematics' in terms of the design process and the procedures through which the design is produced. She lists her design principles ('proportion' and 'balance' are the same as Malnar and Vodvarka's 'principles of organisation') as being:

- Proportion
- Balance
- Rhythm
- Contrast
- Emphasis
- Harmony

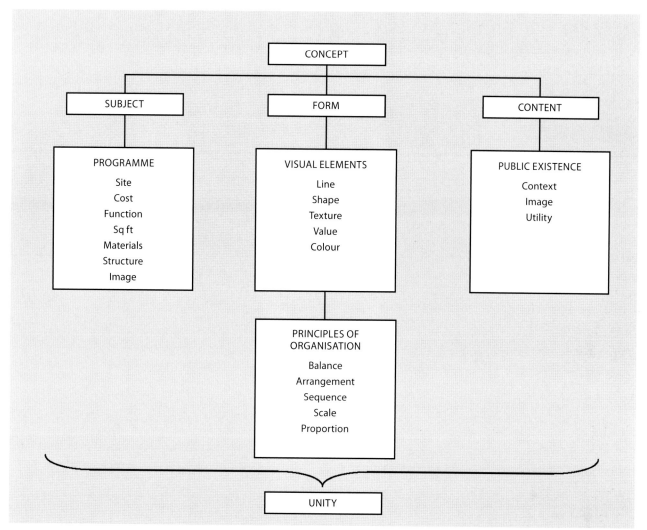

Malnar and Vodvarka concept structure.

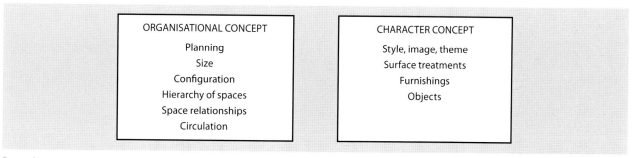

Rengel concept structure.

Clive Edwards,[24] in his book *Interior Design – A Critical Introduction*, only refers to design concepts as part of the survey of a property and then later as part of the design presentation to a client – he mentions the rather old-fashioned 'concept boards and mood boards'. Under 'interior design process', he lists the sequence of programming a contract from formulation to completion/evaluation. He then expands the topic by listing the following principles of interior design and the elements of it, on similar lines to those stated by Kilmer, and Malnar and Vodvarka:

Principles of interior design

- Proportion
- Balance
- Symmetry
- Axis and alignment
- Rhythm and repetition
- Contrast and opposition

- Unity
- Harmony

Elements

- Line
- Shape or form
- Texture
- Pattern context

My summary diagram

This outlines the elements, concepts and theoretical basis that make up a design methodology (see Chapter 7, p.122–123). The following diagram shows how concepts are formed using the elements to be manipulated, which are justified by theoretical and philosophical reasoning.

Refer back to the diagram at the end of Chapter 1 for the location of concept development in the project sequence of working (see p.25).

The act of planning can use all of the elements, in different stages, until a planning concept (see Chapter 7,

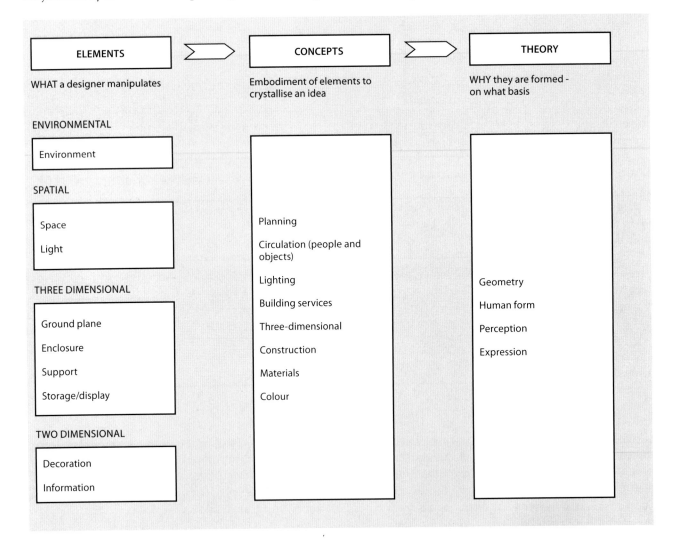

p.129) emerges, which will be based upon certain theoretical notions as listed here. There is no strict mechanical sequence because the process of designing needs to be governed by inspiration as well as by informed technical subject matter. It is not difficult to see how the other concepts will use different elements as and when required. This will begin to make more sense to the reader later in the book.

Another way of looking at this process is by describing it as moving from content to implementation devices to rationale. It could be argued that all of the elements listed in this table could also be described in conceptual terms, and, if this is the case, designers will have to prioritise what the main driving forces of a project are. In my own experience, I have found the above breakdown very helpful in organising my own thoughts and decision-making process.

DESIGN RATIONALE

The rationale behind a design will involve much soul-searching into the semantics and sometimes the morality of art, style, aesthetics and other motivational subjects that influence our visual judgement and decision-making, but it is beyond the scope of this book. Chapter 6 (p.114) explains that part of the act of expression dealing with one's own design philosophy – the designer's intent. In the past, certain theories have been expressed that have influenced much debate and action to such an extent that they have inspired artists and designers to produce work resulting from those theories. Included below is a selection of quotes from some of these key writings.

> *Well building hath three conditions: firmness, commodity, and delight.*
>> Vitruvius, from *De architectura*, as translated in Sir Henry Wotton's *Elements of Architecture*, 1624

This statement has been inspirational to architects since it was written, and was seen as a useful summary of all the noble aspirations that would ensure good building design. It became open to interpretation to produce diverse theories.

The following two texts emphasise that a copy of something is a cheaper solution and therefore not the 'real' thing; one should be true and honest to materials. Firstly, the John Blake article from *Design* magazine quoted from in Chapter 1 (see p.19) serves to illustrate the absurdity of coal-effect fires. And secondly, *Design*

for the Real World, by Victor Papanek,[25] published in 1971, reveals the author's views on ecology, recycling and the social effects of design, which were truly ahead of his time. He also condemned imitation and the absurdity of items such as the electric toothbrush.

> *Imitation is the worst enemy of art.*
>> Rioux de Maillou, *The Decorative Arts and the Machine*, 1895

> *Architectural Deceits: The painting of surfaces to represent some other material, other than the true one …*
>> John Ruskin,[26] *Seven Lamps of Architecture*, 1907

The next statement helped to strip away the unnecessary adornment and superfluous decoration inherited from the 19th century, and also helped designers of structure to become more expressive of their materials and forms. It coincided with huge developments in technology and culture.

> *Form follows function.*
>> Louis Sullivan

C. R. Ashbee wrote the following in support of the Arts and Crafts Movement, and it exposed the tension that continues to this day between machine-made and hand-made goods. The advance of computers has fed factory processes and helped to speed up production whilst attaining levels of economic viability. This in turn has made handcrafted products become almost financially unattainable by the common population, and these products survive only because the wealthy buy them.

> *Modern civilisation rests on machinery, and no system for the endowment, or the encouragement, or the teaching of art can be sound that does not recognise this.*
>> C. R. Ashbee, *A Chapter of Axioms*, 1911

David Watkin is a traditionalist rather than a modernist, and his stance exposes another tension that exists in design, which concerns the reproduction of styles. Not everyone in society accepted the ideals and zealousness of the modernism movement, and to this day we are surrounded by 'repro' products in all the arts. These products are made as an imitation of a past style such as Gothic, Georgian or Baroque, but not necessarily using identical materials or the methods of making of that time.

... the morally insinuating and widely disseminated argument that modern architecture exercises some special unassailable claim over us since it is not a 'style' which we are free to like or dislike as we choose, but is the expression of some unchallengeable 'need' or requirement in the twentieth century with which we must conform.

David Watkin,[27] 1977

Lewis Mumford penned wise words that advised caution, especially with regard to the cultural and technological explosions society was witnessing as the twentieth century unravelled. The following was written during what Mumford described as a 'Time of Trouble':

Law, order, continuity: these conditions are fundamental to freedom, variety, and novelty, and are thus the very basis of social creativeness: for freedom without law is irresponsible anarchy, variety without order is chaos, and novelty without continuity empty distraction.

Lewis Mumford, *The Condition of Man*, 1944

REVIEW

This chapter has outlined the core of a designer's thinking, which consists of the elements, concepts and theoretical reasoning. It is very easy, when working in the design profession, to be led or influenced by factors that do not necessarily give you the proper time to consider everything described in this chapter. Commercial pressures on your time can sometimes force your hand in making decisions for reasons of expediency and to satisfy profit margins.

During the course of a designer's working life, certain procedures are developed, which are the result of experience and are proven to have worked. Outside the confines of work on a contract, designers should be doing the equivalent of exercising in the gym, such as research and preparation that involves sourcing ideas, materials and products; these exercises are not necessarily related to a particular job, but are part of one's basic instinct as a 'hunter and gatherer' for survival. It is part of being prepared for the professional duties assigned to you.

PART TWO

THE BODY AND MEASUREMENT

3: THE HUMAN FORM

ABOUT THIS CHAPTER

This chapter is a summary of the kind of information that a designer should have access to in order to understand the body as a biological specimen and also in terms of a person's characteristics, qualities and needs. We are designing for people who use our spaces, for clients who commission the work, and for contractors to build and make what we have designed. Therefore it is critical that we know as much about human beings as possible in order to be able to come up with solutions that work and which satisfy all concerned. So, we will examine where things have gone wrong and do not work. We will examine the progress of living matter and how important this has been as a design source. And we will refer to leading scientists and philosophers, whose theories have become an important source for design.

DESIGN AND THE HUMAN BODY

In the chart below, I have selected information on the human form's functions and properties, from a variety of sources, that is usefully relevant to a designer. See Hochberg[1] and Fletcher[2].

The thirteen human capabilities listed in the chart use a combination of our physical, mental, emotional and spiritual characteristics, identifying what makes us human compared to other living species. The list could be endless, but I have concluded that these capabilities are the main ones that help to define our species.

What we are	The senses according to Hochberg	Human types – shape	Human ethnic groups	Social groups
Male, female, different ages	Distance senses (seeing, hearing)	Endomorph – plump	Caucasian	National
Structure – anatomy	Skin sense (touch, taste, smell)	Mesomorph – well proportioned	Mongoloid	Geographic
Body – biology	Deep sense (kinaesthetic – muscles, joints; vestibular – equilibrium; internal organs – functions)	Ectomorph – thin	Asian	Political
Workings – physiological			Native American	Linguistic
Mind – psychology			African	Religious
Groups – sociology				Cultural
				Basic needs (see Fletcher)

Primary instincts	General instinctive tendencies	Human capabilities		Eleven major body systems
Breathing	Pleasure	Explore		Circulatory or cardiovascular
Eating	Pain	Be a hunter-gatherer		Respiratory
Drinking		Orient to objects		Skeletal
Sleeping	**Postulations by others**	Communicate		Muscular
Excretion	Attachment/ avoidance	Respond to stimuli		Nervous
General activity	Positive/negative ego	Invent/create		Reproductive
Sexual activity		Compete		Digestive
	Biorhythms	Make		Urinary
	Peaking every 23 days – physical endurance	Organise		Immune or lymphatic
	Peaking every 28 days – feelings/intuition	Learn		Endocrine
	Peaking every 33 days – reasoning power	Solve problems		Integumentary system (skin, hair and nails)
		Control instincts		
		Formulate abstract concepts		

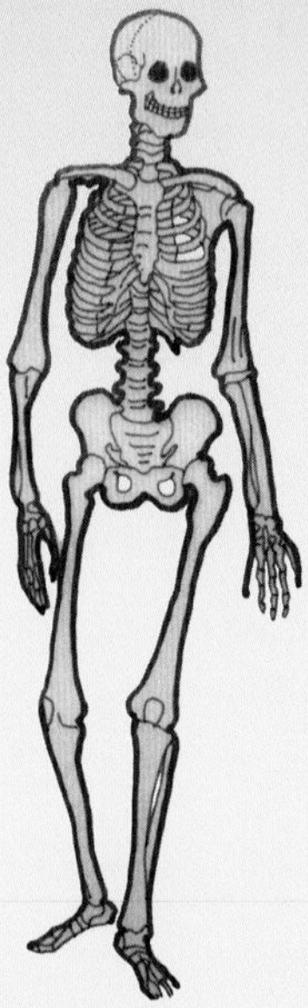

Figure 62a. Human skeleton. Drawing by author.

DESIGNING FOR PEOPLE

There is an area of study that helps designers to understand how people respond to their environment, called environmental psychology.[3] It concentrates on the environmental influences on mood and behaviour. We shall not dwell at length on this subject, except to examine how things have gone wrong in certain places. It is vitally important that we know the people we are designing for: their customs, habits and learning capabilities. This is so that we can make informed choices and decisions, and nobody will be surprised or confused by what we have done.

As designers, we have to be sensitive to the very many types of people who use our spaces. They will have a label according to their job, or they may just be members of the public. We have two user groups, as mentioned in Chapter 1 – occupiers and visitors. Every person entering an interior has to be catered for, whether as an individual or as a group. Designers need to take the following factors and people into account:

- Male, female (consider age)
- Social status (corporate or civic, if relevant)
- Job title (if relevant)
- Disabled people
- People carrying shopping
- People carrying umbrellas
- Tradespeople performing a task within the building
- Representatives delivering goods
- Security personnel
- Emergency services
- Messengers/couriers
- Maintenance staff

THINGS THAT DON'T WORK

There are many irritations in interior design: things that do not really work or that are ill-considered. The following is a personal account, and serves as an example of something all designers should do, in recording feedback from the many design faults experienced. We all learn from mistakes, but some mistakes can easily be overlooked.

IMITATION

Figure 62. City-centre café. Photo by author.

The café above has false bamboo (metal) backs to the seating and painted curtains on the windows. It is an extremely popular city café serving a reasonably priced menu. With the garish exposed fluorescent light fittings, it has a kitsch appeal. It is not so much an example of designer error, but rather an example of anti-design.

There are many examples of products being manufactured to imitate the real thing, and these have remained taboo items for designers of worth and integrity. The difficulty is that these products sell very successfully because they are cheaper for the public to buy than the originals, but still vaguely look the same; they are also cheaper for a factory or workshop to make than the original item. However, the result is that items become easily disposable or replaceable because of their cheapness.

With the increase in popularity of fake products, the danger is that the original product becomes devalued and the public's level of appreciation becomes debased. John Blake wrote in *Design* magazine in 1979:

> *But closer examination of the coal-effect fires and the neo-Georgian cabinets and chairs reveals a frequent lack of skill in both the conceptual and the detail stages of the design. Scale, proportion seem ill-considered, decorative motifs inappropriate, materials poorly used and construction entirely unconvincing to the eye.*

WEAK LINKS

A lively, revitalised market area marred by a balustrade lacking in character and relevance to the existing architecture. The continuous handrail is not necessary. Its harsh horizontality conflicts with the existing curved structures and the human form. My proposal, in the right-hand picture, improves that relationship.

Figure 63. *Left.* Existing indoor market. Photo by author.

Figure 64. *Right.* Proposed alterations to indoor market. Drawing by author.

Both images show a public space. The left-hand image shows an internal bridge that effortlessly glides from one form to another, whilst the right-hand image shows a bridge that is glaringly misplaced and unsuited to its environment.

Figure 65. *Left.* Bridge link – good. Courtesy Foster + Partners.

Figure 66. *Right.* Bridge link – bad. Photo by author.

POORLY THOUGHT-OUT EATING AND DRINKING AREAS

Figure 67. 'Goldfish bowl' café. Photo by author.

Figure 68. Cramped café. Photo by author.

Figure 67 reveals the goldfish bowl syndrome, where so many things are wrong:

- What were once shop windows for viewing goods now allow the public to stare in, making the customers uneasy and the viewing public embarrassed.

- Interestingly, it appears that the customers with their backs to the windows are mostly male, allowing the females to be distracted from their partners by watching the world go by. This is an uneven duality (male and female being the duality in this case; see Chapter 7 on Planning Concept

p.128). The males' faces will be difficult for their partners to see against the brightness of the daylight. A better layout would be for the couples to be sideways on to the window.

In Figure 68, we see a space that is intended for relaxing in with coffee, but in fact it is a space full of tension, for example:

- The space is too small for counter service, the queuing public and scattered furniture.

- The staircase invades the café, with a feeling that it belongs to some former use.

- The full glass frontage exposes the front part of the interior to viewers outside, but at the risk of an imbalance of daylight inside. The gradient of lighting levels from the bright frontage to the dark interior is too much of a contrast.

INVISIBLE ENTRANCES

Figure 69. London University building. Photo by author.

Where is the entrance? The architects of many modern buildings are so preoccupied by the overall structural form that to express the entrance would destroy the integrity of that structure for them. Unfortunately, the result is that confusion abounds for the visitor.

The entrance to the London University building in Figure 69 is not expressed as being of any importance and is lost within the modular structure. My chapel conversion overleaf, however, Glendower House (Figure 70), identifies the entrance in a typically classical manner. Symmetry, columns and piers by the road all contribute to a clear route to the door.

Figure 70. Glendower House (chapel conversion, 2002). Designer: Anthony Sully. Architect: Graham Frecknall. Photo: Ken Price.

LACK OF PLANNING FOR QUEUES

Queues are a British passion. We form an orderly line respecting the 'first come, first served' principle, and we wait our turn. But there are many instances where these queues can interrupt a space because the designers have not allowed enough room for them. It is not as though queues are a desirable visual gathering, or that people enjoy waiting in a queue, but they exist due to the nature of the service being offered. They can also block people's access to doorways, display notices or other through routes.

CONCEALED LIGHTING

Concealed lighting can be installed behind the edge of a suspended ceiling, producing a floating effect for the ceiling and a cascade of light down the walls' surface. But this can be spoiled by catching sight of the light fittings at certain viewpoints – akin to seeing parts of a stage setting that are not supposed to be seen.

PROBLEMS IN DOMESTIC INTERIORS

My focus is on the provision of homes for the main body of the public. In the UK today, builders work according to cost yardsticks that stipulate a level of impoverishment contrary to the standards expected of modern life. The following items, I believe, need some serious attention:

■ **Bedrooms**. There is no such thing as a bedroom anymore in the sense that it is just for sleeping. This space has popularly become a 'bedsitting' room, especially as far as young people are concerned, being used as a study as well as a living space. Houses are still designed based on traditional norms without accommodating these changes in living style. Spaces become very restricting and can cause unhappiness within the home.

■ **Soundproofing** between rooms is often so poor that it can be a powerful contributor to family conflicts and lack of privacy.

■ **Lack of storage space** is a critical social problem. How many people actually put their cars in the garage? The garage often doubles up as a workshop, garden shed, utility space and store, indicating a shortfall in those areas. The loft space, which forms an insulating break between living spaces and the roof, has always been an important storage area. Storage space needs to be properly allocated in the quantifying of space-use in our homes, and it should not be left to the homeowner to ingeniously solve a problem that should have been attended to by the designers.

■ **Front/back entrance**. The outdoor activities of families (especially those with pets) are numerous and frequent. There is never enough space for hanging coats, hats and scarves or storing shoes and wellingtons, never mind accompanying equipment such as walking sticks, torches, maps, rucksacks, picnic boxes and so on.

■ **Staircases**. These are a major source of accidents and need real design attention. Why have such a steep rise? Why not break them with a landing every three steps? This of course negates the compact planning and occupation of a staircase, and hence could increase the cost of the project. Cost concerns should not override human safety and comfort.

■ **Doors**. These are another source of accidents, especially for children who can trap their fingers. Also, they are noisy when slammed. If you think about a heavy panel, 2 m x 80 cm (6½ ft x 31½ in.), swinging round in an arc, it can be quite a lethal object. More design attention is needed.

- **Glass**. Toughened glass should be used throughout, as ordinary glass has been the cause of many accidents in the home. In many cases, ordinary glass is used as a design or fashion statement rather than the more solid alternative, and this is the worst reason for such use.

- **Bathrooms**. My main plea here is that wall urinals should be in every house occupied by men. For a man to stand and pee into a WC is unhygienic. If a urinal is not installed, then social pressure should be exerted upon men to sit on the loo just as women do.

- **Kitchen**. This is the most dangerous room in the house. The way kitchens are designed as showrooms for the manufacturer is totally contrary to the real needs of the space. See the recommendations below.

RECOMMENDATIONS FOR KITCHENS

The whole area of the domestic kitchen needs a radical overhaul. Children should not be able to touch anything hot. All hobs should be designed with cooking utensils in mind, so that they fit into a contained structure with no fear of the utensils being knocked over.

All cupboard storage should only be 350 mm (13¾ in.) deep and 500 mm (19½ in.) from floor level. To access goods at the back of deep shelves is difficult. Why have storage at ground level that forces people to bend down to take things out of it, and which is accessible by young children and babies?

The original 'fitted' kitchen was the 'Frankfurt kitchen', which was properly designed as a whole unit of space in 1926 by the Austrian architect Margarete Schütte-Lihotzky, for the social housing project Römerstadt in Frankfurt, Germany, of the architect Ernst May. It was very functional and compact, based on observations from a work study, and designed to be an efficient machine for cooking and food preparation, reducing circulation to a minimum of 18 basic movements. Margarete was inspired by the kitchen galleys on railways, and was impressed by how much could be done in such a confined space. The design was also in response to a need for women to reduce their time in the kitchen so that they could have more time for factory work. It was also in recognition of the emancipatory movement for women, providing a liberating, purpose-made space that was considered a woman's domain. It was the forerunner of all the fitted

Figure 71. Reconstructed 'Frankfurt kitchen' designed by Margarete Schütte-Lihotzky in 1926. Wikimedia Commons. Photo: Christos Vittoratos.

kitchens that are produced today. Unfortunately, people began to dislike this model because it was too clinical, lacked warmth and was too small.

This professionalisation and revaluing of work in the home began to be seen as the confinement of women to the kitchen. Many of the cold, bare style characteristics of the modernist movement were also rejected for being too austere and lacking in humanity. This serves as an example that human beings do have natural instinctive desires for certain types of spaces, and it is the designer's job to understand what these are, rather than to impose some ideology which is foreign to these basic needs.

ANTHROPOMETRICS

Anthropometric data about human beings is a critical resource for the designer. The figure is drawn from different viewpoints, including a plan view, and dimensions are added to provide the designer with the necessary data. The design of interior spaces cannot be carried out without this knowledge. This information, allied with calculations of body movements, enables the activities of users within an interior to be calculated

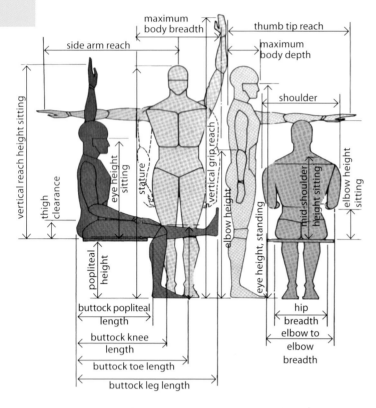

Figure 72. 'Body Measurements' Reproduced from J. Panero and M. Zelnik, *Human Dimension and Interior Space*, 1979, p.30. Courtesy of Julius Panero and Martin Zelnik.

using the elements listed in Chapter 2 (see p.29). The field of ergonomics, which is the study of human beings and their responses to various working conditions and environments, also enters the picture. This field of study is dealt with by specialist ergonomists, who usually provide detailed information for designers of driveable machines and specialist furniture.

MAPPING OUR PHYSICAL ENVIRONMENT

People, as well as the spaces around them, are measured in order for planning and detail design to take place. In order to carry out this process, grids and co-ordinates are applied to our buildings, as explained in chapter 7 (p.128). The following ideas of mapping the space immediately around the human figure are an extension of this, and help certain scientific specialists to organise space in relation to the physical and physiological properties of the figure.

Bloomer and Moore[4] quote Hartley Alexander[5] as referring to the seven points described by the psycho-physical coordinates (that is, man's sensory responses to the environment) as a sacred number representing man's primary projection into the universe as his world frame or world abode. On a horizontal plane, this is front/back/right/left. On a vertical plane, it is up/down. The seventh point is the central one. Figure 73 shows six useful points to sum up the 3D space configuration.

When describing parts of the body, the medical profession uses terms to define position and direction. An organ or the entire body can be described by three planes known as the sagittal, frontal and transverse planes (see Figure 74).

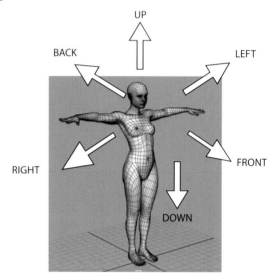

Figure 73. Body planes. Base mesh courtesy of Joel Mongeon (www.joelmongeon.com/4.html).

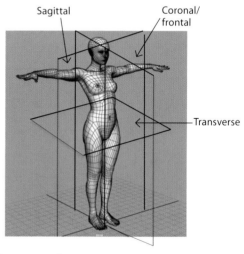

Figure 74. The sagittal, frontal and transverse body planes. Base mesh courtesy of Joel Mongeon (www.joelmongeon.com/4. html). Overlaid drawing by the author. This method of mapping is used by the medical profession.

ANALYSIS OF HUMAN ACTIVITY

	DESIGNER Plus consultants	BUILDER Plus others	BUILDING USER Occupier	BUILDING USER Visitor	CLIENT Commissioning agent
Main title	Interpreter of client's requirements	Fabricate Install Fit-out	Operator/worker Service	Customer	Building owner or occupier or patron
Main role	Researcher Creator	Tradesmen Craftspeople	Constant residency	Short term visit	Funding project
Duration	Project time	Project time	Employment contract	Appointment booked time	Permanent interest/temporary interest
Responsibility	Design suitability Supervisory	Safety Good working order Standards	Efficiency Productivity Service	Co-operative Attentive Searching	Supportive
Designer's main task to the others	Design and project supervision	Provide drawings and specifications	Planning Ensure good working conditions Building maintenance	Planning Directional guidance	Satisfy budget
Usual job provider	Client	Designer	Client	External	Self
Residency during project	50%	100%	10%	0%	30%
Residency after completion	0%	0%	100%	30%	5%

It is the designer's responsibility to develop methods of observation, recording and analysis of people engaged in the various activities within our buildings. This work results in providing the designer with statistical information about the human form, which is required prior to design activity taking place. As an example I have chosen a selected group of main players involved in a design contract. I have produced a chart above, containing minimal data, which may appear obvious but which serves as an example of an analysis of people working together in a job role. The leading players I have selected are: Designer, Builder, Building User (Occupier, or user of the building), Visitor, and Client/Commissioning Agent. Note: percentages are estimates. This chart can be extended and developed by designers to include more information that is deemed helpful.

PROGRESS OF LIVING MATTER

It is important for designers to appreciate the evolution of man in relation to scale and time. The writings of experts in the fields of science and philosophy can and should be inspirational, because they are about the formation of life on this planet. The more doors and windows that are open to the world, its history

Life's beginnings	4,600 million years	3,500 million years	543 million years	1 million years	500,000 years
	Earth's crust	First organic life	Cambrian period	First evidence of human life	Modern human

Progression of living matter

Plants ⇨ Fish ⇨ Amphibians ⇨ Winged insects ⇨ Mammals ⇨ Humankind

and its current state, the greater the pool of reference for designers. Why put a cap on the way that ideas and information are resourced? Calling on all the sciences for evidence, such research explains *how* the Earth evolved, *what* it is and *who* we are. The question of *why* we exist prompts more religious and philosophical enquiry.

Our primeval ancestors and early tribes paid homage to the wonders of the Earth and sky because they were humbled by them. They could not reason out the existence of things in the way we can now. In our present society, because we have made discoveries and acquired knowledge over the centuries, we have become desensitised in comparison with those feelings of awe experienced by early societies.[6] Not until we are caught in an earthquake or other natural disaster do we tremble with fear. But that fear results because of a threat to our own existence, not a fear of the unknown. Human progress, due to the need for survival, has been made through the development of two major characteristics:

1. The ability to make things for everyday practical use: what we now call science and technology, commerce and industry.
2. Thought processes to produce mental and spiritual wellbeing: these have given us the arts, community, law and politics.

Aristotle,[7] in his book *Physics*, which is concerned with change within natural beings in terms of place, movement and lifespan, states that a human being is designed by nature to find happiness in a certain kind of 'being and doing'.

> *In biology, the fundamental role of geometry and proportion becomes even more evident when we consider that moment by moment, year by year, aeon by aeon, every atom of every molecule of both living and inorganic substance is being changed and replaced. Every one of us within the next five to seven years will have a completely new body, down to the very last atom.*[8]
>
> **Robert Lawlor**

The process of living through time concerns designers because we have a duty to understand:

- The origins of the materials we use and their sources;
- Their strength, properties and characteristics;

- That their selection enhances healthy living, and does not disturb any ecosystems;
- Their lifespan when in use – the wear and tear factor;
- The planned or expected use of the interiors we create;
- The changes that take place over time – space usage, personnel, building services and artefacts.

THINK SMALL

> *Small is beautiful.*[9]
>
> E. F. Schumacher

> *It has been biology, out of all the sciences, to which architectural and design theorists have most frequently turned.*[10]
>
> **Philip Steadman**

Everything we deal with is down to a question of scale, size and proportion. We should be aware of the smallest identifiable mark or material in relation to the large-scale components of our interiors. The following examples are the beginnings of structure in life; they have a centre and a shape. Cells vary in shape according to the particular living species.

The atom:
Smallest particle of living matter.
One human = 1,000 million atoms

Electrons
Nucleus

The molecule:
Smallest particle of any substance that retains the properties of that substance.
Organic and inorganic.

The cell:
Unit mass of living matter. The human body has 1000 million[2] cells. Capable of reproducing itself and utilising raw material.

Plasma membrane
Nucleus
Cytoplasm

Claude Bernardi[11] a 19th century French physiologist propounded that all organisms are composed of cells which suit their environment by random chaotic movements.

Out of the three examples above, the term 'cell' has been used in design language – to describe 'cellular offices', for example (offices defined by some sort of enclosure as opposed to those that are open-plan). In nature, the honey bee makes a formation of cells in the construction of honeycomb:

Honey bees construct wax combs inside their nests. The combs are made of hexagonal prisms – cells – built back to back, and are used to store honey, nectar, and pollen, and to provide a nursery for bee larvae. The combs are natural engineering marvels, using the least possible amount of wax to provide the greatest amount of storage space, with the greatest possible structural stability.[12]

Darwin Project

Bees making wax cells against each other | The hexagonal result | Final honeycomb

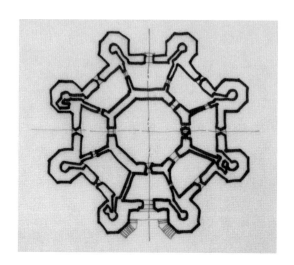

Figure 75. Diagrammatic plan of the Castel del Monte, Italy, *c*.1240. Drawing by author.

The forms of the hexagon and octagon have inspired architects and designers through time. Two 13th century buildings provide good examples of the use of the octagon. The Castel del Monte in southern Italy, built for Frederick II, is undoubtedly a unique early example of an octagonal plan for a whole building. The architect Arnolfo di Cambio designed the Cathedral of S. Maria del Fiore in Florence, and later, in 1420 Brunelleschi designed its wonderful octagonal dome. We shall see, later in the book, that geometry is an important generative device for design and planning.

Figure 76. *Right.* Cathedral of S. Maria del Fiore, Florence. Shutterstock. Author: Circumnavigation.

Matter as such produces nothing, changes nothing, does nothing; and however convenient it may afterwards be to abbreviate our nomenclature and our descriptions, we must most carefully realise in the outset that the spermatozoon, the nucleus, the chromosomes or the germ-plasma can never act as matter alone, but only as seats of energy and as centres of force.

D'Arcy Thompson, On Growth and Form

ANALOGIES

The following people are noted for their theoretical notions that living organisms are a source for ideas in design and architecture.

ARISTOTLE

Aristotle, Greek, (384 BC–322 BC) was a philosopher and mathematician. His view was that 'wholeness' meant unity of structure and coherence in nature, and that this served as inspiration for artists. Visual appearance and function were interrelated. He referred to the workings of biology as analogous to mechanical parts.

DESCARTES[13]

René Descartes, French, (1596–1650) linked the organs of the body with mechanical working parts.

CUVIER[14]

Georges Cuvier, French, (1769–1832) was a naturalist and zoologist, and an important source for designers. He studied the relationship of the organism to the environment. His famous principle of the 'correlation of parts' led to concepts of coherence and unity. His writings served as models of study for the analysis of buildings by the famous nineteenth-century architects Viollet-le-Duc and Semper.

> *Francesco di Giorgio demonstrates by means of the inscribed human figure how to weld together organically the centralised and the longitudinal parts of such a church design. The centralised eastern end is developed from the basic geometrical figures of circle and square.*[15]
>
> Rudolph Wittkower

LE CORBUSIER

The Swiss architect Le Corbusier, born Charles-Édouard Jeanneret-Gris, stated for the first time in *My Work* (1960) that body parts were analogous to architecture:[16]

Breathing	=	Ventilation
Nervous system	=	Power supply
Bowels	=	Drainage, refuse systems
Drinking	=	Water supply
Blood circulation	=	People

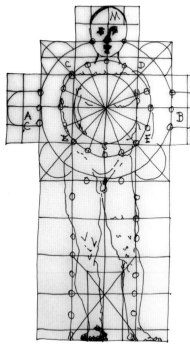

Figure 77. Drawing originally by Francesco di Giorgio, c.1470. Figure of a man inscribed in an ideal church. The components of the human form became highly influential in the planning of religious buildings. Copy drawn by author.

USEFUL THEORIES AND PHILOSOPHIES

Designers and architects produce designs based upon certain theoretical and philosophical principles. They are inspired by many different sources, as this book attempts to explain. The following examples show just some of these principles.

JAN PIAGET

This Swiss-born child psychologist (1896–1980) concluded that children adapt to the world through assimilation and accommodation. Assimilation is the process by which a person takes material into their mind from the environment, which may mean changing the evidence of their senses to make it fit. Accommodation is the difference made to one's mind or concepts by the process of assimilation.[17]

RATIONALISM

Proponents of some varieties of rationalism argue that, starting with foundational basic principles, like the axioms of geometry, one could deductively derive the rest of all possible knowledge. Further reading: Socrates, Descartes, Spinoza and Liebniz.

EMPIRICISM

The empiricist view holds that all ideas come to us through experience, either through the five external senses or through such inner sensations as pain and pleasure, and thus that knowledge is essentially based on, or derived from, experience. Further reading: John Dewey,[18] William James, John Locke, George Berkeley and David Hume.[19]

BEHAVIOURISM

Behaviourism is a philosophy of psychology based on the proposition that all things that organisms do – including acting, thinking and feeling – can and should be regarded as behaviours. Further reading: B. F. Skinner, J. B. Watson.[20]

GESTALT

Gestalt psychology of perception, or isomorphism, as it is defined, is about the study of the essence or shape of an entity's complete form. It is about distinguishing the 'part' from the 'whole'. The 'gestalt effect' refers to the form-forming capability of our senses, particularly with respect to the visual recognition of figures and whole forms instead of just a collection of simple lines and curves (see Chapter 5, p.91, for further discussion). For further reading of leading theorists on gestalt: Max Wertheimer,[21] Kurt Koffka – German psychologist(1886–1941) Wolfgang Kohler – German/American psychologist (1887–1967), Immanuel Kant – German philosopher (1724–1804) Ernst Mach – Austrian Physicist and philosopher (1838–1916)

PROXEMICS/HUMAN COMMUNICATION

Proxemics was introduced by anthropologist Edward T. Hall[22] in 1966. It is the study of set measurable distances between people as they interact. Body spacing and posture, according to Hall, are unintentional reactions to sensory fluctuations or shifts, such as subtle changes in the sound and pitch of a person's voice. Social distance between people is reliably correlated with physical distance, as are intimate and personal distance, according to the following delineations:

■ **Intimate distance** – for embracing, touching or whispering. Close phase – less than 15 cm; far phase – 15–46 cm.

■ **Personal distance** – for interactions among good friends or family members. Close phase – 46–76 cm; far phase – 76–120 cm.

■ **Social distance** – for interactions among acquaintances. Close phase – 1.2–2.1 m; far phase – 2.1–3.7 m.

■ **Public distance** – used for public speaking. Close phase – 3.7–7.6 m; far phase – 7.6 m or more.

Albert Mehrabian[23] is known for his pioneering work in the field of non-verbal communication (body language). His theoretical work and experiments helped identify the non-verbal and subtle ways in which one conveys like or dislike, power and leadership, discomfort and insecurity, social attractiveness, persuasiveness, and ways to detect when others are being deceptive in communication. Communication and leadership trainers and political campaign managers have often relied on these findings.

Professor Mehrabian's major theoretical contributions include a three-dimensional mathematical model for the precise and general description and measurement of emotions. His emotion scales are used to assess consumer reactions to products, services and shopping environments. Additionally, the scales can be used to assess the emotional impact of a workplace, an advertisement, a website, or a medical or psychotropic drug. His parallel three-dimensional temperament model is a comprehensive system for describing and measuring differences among individuals (e.g. anxiety, extroversion, achievement, empathy, depression, hostility and cooperativeness). Further reading: Etienne Jules Marey,[24] Eadweard Muybridge,[25] Robert Sommer[26] and David Canter.[27]

GENETICS

The biologist Richard Dawkins gives a wonderful explanation of our hereditary and ever-lasting personal characteristics that continue to survive through the ages:

Was there to be any end to the gradual improvement in the techniques and artifices used by the replicators to ensure their own continuance in the world? There would be plenty of time for improvement. What weird engines of self-preservation would the millennia bring forth? Four thousand million years on, what was to be the fate of the ancient replicators? They did not die out, for they are past masters of the survival arts. But do not look for them floating loose in the sea; they gave up that cavalier freedom long ago. Now they swarm in huge colonies, safe inside gigantic lumbering robots, sealed off from the outside world, communicating with it by tortuous indirect routes, manipulating it by remote control. They are in you and in me; they created us, body and mind; and their preservation is the ultimate rationale for our existence. They have come a long way, those replicators. Now they go by the name of genes, and we are their survival machines.[28]

Pallasmaa echoes how important it is to connect to the origins of our life on this planet (see Chapter 2, Element 1: Environment) as well as confirming that our senses play a vital role in the process.

Architecture is the art of reconciliation between ourselves and the world, and this mediation takes place through the senses.[29]

Juhani Pallasmaa

UNDERSTANDING THE NEEDS OF THE USER

Designers need to ask questions to help make design decisions. They need to place themselves in the position of the user of the building and imagine their needs and the sort of questions they would ask. This illustration is intended to give you an idea of some of the basic considerations that a designer must address.

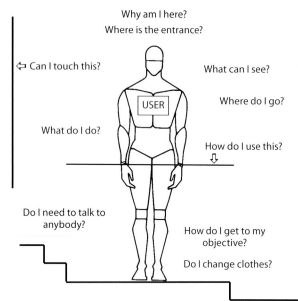

How do I see where I'm going?

Why am I here?
Where is the entrance?

Can I touch this?

What can I see?

Where do I go?

USER

What do I do?

How do I use this?

Do I need to talk to anybody?

How do I get to my objective?

Do I change clothes?

REVIEW

How useful is the information in this chapter for designers? The research will serve as an aid to designers on all project work. Designers should establish their own personal research file for the continual gathering, scavenging and collecting of anything that they think may be useful in the future. The efficient collation and organisation of this work is essential for careful progress to be made. Research for specific design projects will require you to call upon your own personal research file as well as being directed to task-specific activity. The following list details how useful this chapter should be for the designer in relation to working with or for the design team, the client, the building users, and the builder/installer.

THE DESIGN TEAM

- It will provide you with insight about each individual's performance.
- It will help you understand others' viewpoints.
- It will help with assessment of character and attitudes.
- It will fuel a cooperative spirit.
- It will help with refining your own philosophical and theoretical stance.

THE CLIENT

- It will advance your interpretive skills and analysis of the brief.
- It will boost your confidence with the client in all meetings.
- It will strengthen your design and presentation skills.
- It will give substance to your design strategy.
- It will enhance your management skills.

USERS OF THE BUILDING

- It will provide you with the sensitivity and knowledge of human needs that you require in order to be able to focus on project-specific needs.
- This information will enable you to match technology to user activities.
- You will be able to define and allocate space in accordance with the client's brief.
- You will be skilled in knowing the effect that your design will have on the users.

THE BUILDER/INSTALLER

- You will realise the importance of good communication of information.
- You will be a better team player.
- Your demands and instructions will be applauded for their clarity and appropriateness.
- Project monitoring and supervisory skills will be enhanced.

4: GEOMETRY AND PROPORTION

ABOUT THIS CHAPTER

This chapter examines definitions, measurement, numbers and theories showing the influence of geometry in design, and the proportional systems that have been developed. It begins by tracing the development of the geometrical shapes that have been used by designers over the centuries, from the tree of life to the Platonic solids. It also explores sacred geometry and how certain shapes exist in natural form. We will look at proportional theories, from ancient times, such as the classical orders, through to architects such as Serlio and Palladio, and the work of Frank Lloyd Wright and Le Corbusier.

SHAPE AND RHYTHM

The construction of shape is made through geometry and measurement. The *composition*, as a collective with others, is judged on the basis of proportion: size, width, height, balance and rhythm. There are two laws of *balance* involved: symmetry and asymmetry.

Symmetry

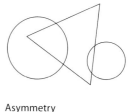

Asymmetry

RHYTHM

If you feel that a line is rhythmic it means that by following it with your eyes you have an experience that can be compared with the experience of rhythmic ice-skating, for instance. Often the man who forms architecture also works rhythmically in the creative process itself.[1]

Steen Eiler Rasmussen

In interior design, rhythm can be suggested by a sequence of forms or shapes such as a row of components and the spaces in between them. The actual spacing will determine how quickly the experience is felt. The sequence can be designed by repetition of the same component, or by jumping between different components that have a common link such as colour or material. Music is a classic example of varied rhythms. A drumbeat is the repetition of the same sound (or beat), whereas other instruments produce an arrangement of varied notes hanging on a particular rhythm. The spacing between the beat has a similar effect to the visual spacing of components in an interior. Have a look at the many illustrations in this book to see what degree of rhythm exists.

THE BEGINNING

An interior designer uses drafting as a means of drawing accurate measured drawings that describe an interior project in terms of plans, sections, elevations, construction details, and various types of three-dimensional drawings such as axonometrics and isometrics. The buildings we work on are designed on some kind of geometric basis, and our proposals for the interior will also be constructed using geometry and proportion – either blending with it, or acknowledging the existing geometry but creating a new discipline. This geometric pattern has two sequential functions:

1. It is a composed geometric structure of shape within a grid, using lines that may be broken down into parts, and helps to give *position* and *place* to points, edges, lines and planes in an holistic arrangement – in 2D or **3D**.
2. To transmute those lines into structure, surface, object and material.

The design of the geometric arrangement will usually begin by referencing inherited shapes that have been passed down through history, and which have been used many times in various modes. These shapes can have symbolic associations as well as origins in natural forms. As explained in Keith Critchlow's[2] seminal book *Order in Space*, the beginning sequence of drawing in two dimensions is as follows:

A plane is a two-dimensional shape made of straight lines. The most economical enclosed shape made using straight lines is the equilateral triangle, 'the symbol of the fiery trinity of active creation'.[3] The next move from this, the creation of a three-dimensional form, results in the first prime solid, a tetrahedron. This is done by extending a vertical line from the centre of the triangle to a point whereby each of the new faces is an equilateral triangle.

In addition to the equilateral triangle, the other two inherited shapes that have had common usage are the square and the circle.

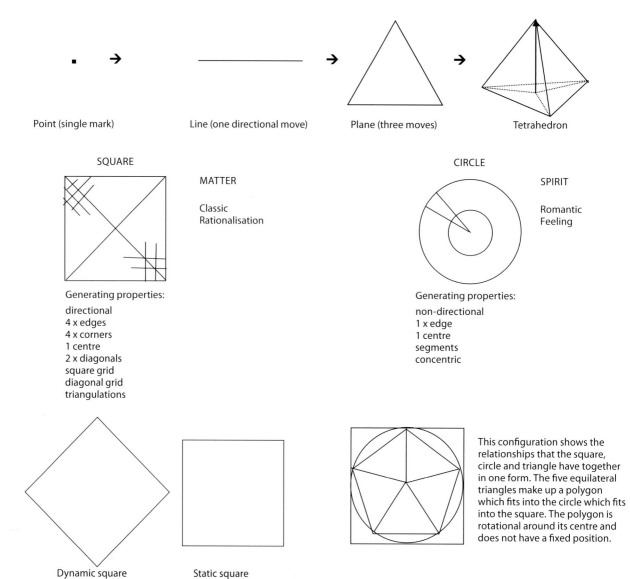

Point (single mark)

Line (one directional move)

Plane (three moves)

Tetrahedron

SQUARE

MATTER

Classic
Rationalisation

Generating properties:
directional
4 x edges
4 x corners
1 centre
2 x diagonals
square grid
diagonal grid
triangulations

CIRCLE

SPIRIT

Romantic
Feeling

Generating properties:
non-directional
1 x edge
1 centre
segments
concentric

Dynamic square

Static square

This configuration shows the relationships that the square, circle and triangle have together in one form. The five equilateral triangles make up a polygon which fits into the circle which fits into the square. The polygon is rotational around its centre and does not have a fixed position.

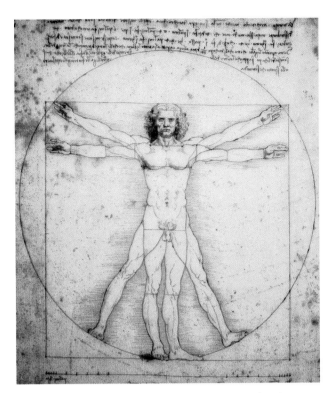

Figure 78. Leonardo da Vinci, *Vitruvian Man*, 1487. The drawing relates the figure to the square and the circle. Shutterstock. Photo by Reeed.

The *Vitruvian Man* is a world-renowned drawing created by Leonardo da Vinci in around 1487. It is surrounded by notes based on the work of the famed Roman architect, Vitruvius. The drawing, which is in pen and ink on paper, depicts a male figure in two superimposed positions, with his arms and legs apart and simultaneously inscribed in a circle and square. This image has become an icon, inspiring designers through the ages.

The Chinese (and Japanese) religion of Zen Buddhism is a school of Mahāyāna Buddhism; 'zen' means 'meditation'. It has a description of creation which uses first the unity of the circle, then the triangle to finally the manifest form of the square, overlapping and reading from right to left:

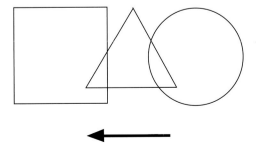

SOME DEFINITIONS AND QUOTATIONS

Designing involves measuring and calculating the forms we create, and our ideas stem from theories and beliefs inherited and acquired. It is useful to note the origins of the tools we use:

■ **Geometry** – The first sign of humankind's method of dividing up/measuring the land for agricultural purposes. A geometer was such a person.[4]

■ **Mathematics** – From the Greek word *mathesis*, meaning reminiscence. Pythagoras believed that wisdom is the bringing out of such laws, which are latent within us.

■ **Theory** – From the Greek word *theos*, meaning the ability to look within oneself as well as without.

■ **Religion** – From the Latin word *ligare*, meaning to connect ourselves to what underlies our existence.

■ **Aesthetics** – From the Greek word *aestheticos*, meaning sense of perception.

Geometry is the study of spatial order through the measure and relationships of forms.[5]

Robert Lawlor

Geometry is the heart of shape, and number the heart of geometry.[6]

Lawrence Blair

Geometry is the mother of invention.[7]

Louis Khan

Geometry is our greatest creation and we are enthralled by it.[8]

Le Corbusier

THEORIES OF GEOMETRY AND PROPORTION

THE TREE OF LIFE

The tree of life appears in various ancient beliefs and rituals, as explained in Roger Cook's book, *The Tree of Life*.[9] It is symbolised by a centre of growth, usually in the form of a tree, which penetrates the three zones of heaven, Earth and the underworld. This vertical cosmic axis appears in the form of three popular images: the pillar or pole, the tree and the mountain.

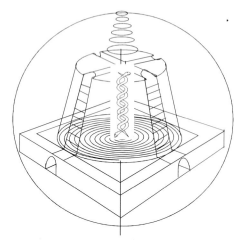

This cosmic mountain is represented as circular with a square base. The central axis is known as the axis mundi, which grows out of a spiralling base, as well as intertwining serpents forming a double helix reminiscent of the helical DNA spiral. The tree of life is also known as a symbol of unity and love.

Verticality, inspired by the male phallus, is common in the design of our environment, confirmed by global competition to see who can build the tallest building in the world. It remains a powerful and symbolic ingredient in design.

NUMBER

We use numbers for measurement and calculation. All numbers from zero to ten have symbolic associations and the most interesting I have found[10] are as follows:

0. Nothing – infinite light of chaos – zero
1. Vertical – I am – the phallus – unity – beginning – Single entity
2. Duality – I know that I am – confirmation of opposites
3. Trinity – wisdom – harmonious stability – perfect number of Pythagoras because it has a beginning, a middle and an end – third dimension – three wishes – three witches
4. The Earth – stocktaking – measurement – solid – North, East, South and West – four elements (earth, air, fire and water)
5. Dominant in living forms – laws – memory and experience – five senses
6. Triad of dualities – symmetry – most productive – luck – love – health – beauty
7. Sacred – mysterious – victory – days in a week – colours in a spectrum – wonders of the world – intervals in a musical octave – security – Venus
8. Vertical sign of infinity – perfect rhythm – regeneration
9. Tripod of threes – goal of endeavour
10. Return to one – completeness

Other associations are that the numbers six and eight are dominant in inorganic structures such as crystals, whose forms are based upon polyhedral shapes such as the cube, hexagon and octahedron.

The content of our experience results from an immaterial, abstract, geometric architecture which is composed of harmonic waves of energy, nodes of relationality, melodic forms springing forth from the eternal realm of geometric proportion.[11]

Robert Lawlor

Quoted above, from his book *Sacred Geometry*, Lawlor describes the hidden sources of geometry and proportion.

FLOWER OF LIFE

The flower of life is the modern name given to a geometrical figure composed of multiple evenly spaced, overlapping circles that are arranged to form a flower-like pattern with a six-fold symmetry, like a hexagon. This is similar to the honeycomb structure discussed in Chapter 4 (see p.71). The centre of each circle is on the circumference of six surrounding circles of the same diameter. The earliest known evidence of the figure is from 6th century Egypt. Further research has shown that Leonardo da Vinci worked on the same pattern. Designers through the centuries have been inspired to make jewellery and other decorative products using this pattern as a basis. The Kabbalistic 'tree of life' is embedded in this pattern, as well as codes of certain alphabets.

behind many designs in the field of product design and have served as a source of inspiration for designers such as Richard Buckminster Fuller and Keith Critchlow. The Platonic solids give two-dimensional patterns that can be used for planning purposes, and three-dimensional forms for resolving three-dimensional structures.

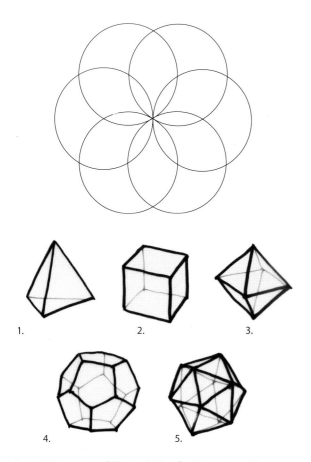

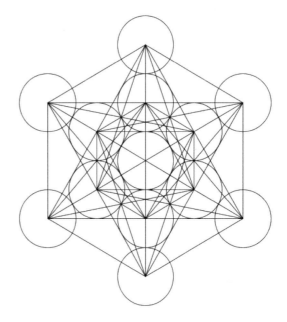

Metatron's Cube

Figure 79. The seed of life (top); The five Platonic solids (bottom): 1. Tetrahedron, 2. Cube, 3. Octahedron, 4. Dodecahedron, 5. Icosahedron. Drawing by author.

The seed of life is a figure formed from seven circles placed with six-fold symmetry, creating a pattern of circles and lenses, which acts as a basic component of the flower of life. The Platonic solids (tetrahedron, cube, octahedron, dodecahedron and icosahedron) all fit within this hexagonal framework.

The Platonic solids are delineated by a sacred geometric template called Metatron's Cube. It contains a centre circle bounded by six equally sized circles, which in turn have six more circles outside them. The centres of these outer circles create a hexagon when joined up. As the diagram expands, the cube and hexagon are continually replicated. The whole figure relates to the seed of life drawing, above. In geometry, a Platonic solid is a convex regular polyhedron, a three-dimensional analogue of a regular polygon. The name of each figure is derived from the number of its faces: respectively 4, 6, 8, 12 and 20. Due to their aesthetic beauty and symmetry, the Platonic solids have been a favourite subject of geometers for thousands of years. They are

THE CHAKRAS IN YOGA

Yoga is a meditative form of exercise, and chakras are points of energy that spiral through the body. What makes them interesting for designers is the fact that they are positioned in the same places on the human body as the five Platonic solids.

The five Platonic solids

- Dodecahedron (12 faces)
  Crown chakra
  Element: aether
  Colour: gold

- Octahedron (8 faces)
  Heart and throat chakra
  Element: air
  Colour: yellow (represents the intellect)

- Tetrahedron (4 faces)
  Solar plexus chakra

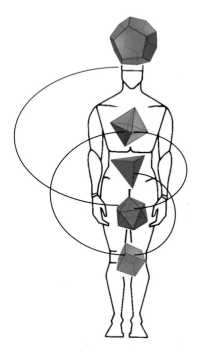

THE CHAKRAS IN YOGA
The five Platonic solids

1. DODECAHEDRON
   Crown chakra
   Element of Aether
   Gold

2. OCTAHEDRON
   Heart & throat chakra
   Element of Air
   Yellow – Intellect

3. TETRAHEDRON
   Initiator of the spiral
   Solar plexus chakra
   Element of Fire
   Red – Spirit

4. ICOSAHEDRON
   Generative chakra
   Element of Water
   Blue – Emotion

5. CUBE
   Foundation chakra
   At root of spine
   Element of Earth
   Green or black – Physical

Element: fire
Colour: red (represents the spirit)

- Icosahedron (20 faces)
  Generative chakra
  Element: water
  Colour: blue (represents emotion)

- Cube (6 faces)
  Foundation chakra (at root of spine)
  Element: earth
  Colour: green or black (represents the physical)

YIN AND YANG

The beautiful Chinese Taoist symbol of yin and yang refers to the complementary opposites within a greater whole. Everything has both yin and yang aspects, although yin or yang elements may manifest more strongly in different objects or at different times. Common dualities are male/female, left/right, day/night, and so on.

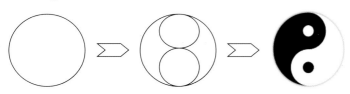

SACRED ROOTS

Sacred roots fall within the study of sacred geometry which is an area of philosophical, scientific and mathematical exploration into life on this planet. Robert Lawlor describes the following roots with the sides of each square being 1:

> *The two principal elements of sacred geometry, circle and square, in the act of self-division give rise to the three sacred roots. The roots are considered as generative powers, or dynamic principles through which forms appear and change into other forms.*
>
> Robert Lawlor

GOLDEN RATIO

> *Geometry has two great treasures: one is the Theorem of Pythagoras; the other the division of a line into extreme and mean ratio. The first we may compare to a measure of gold; the second we may name a precious jewel.*[12]
>
> Johannes Kepler

The discovery of this proportion is not entirely clear, but Ancient Greek mathematicians first studied what we now call the golden ratio because of its frequent appearance in geometry and in nature. They denoted it by the Greek letter *phi* (φ). The golden ratio or golden section, i.e. the division of a line into 'extreme and mean ratio', is important in the geometry of regular pentagrams and pentagons. Biologists, artists, musicians, historians, architects, psychologists, and even mystics have pondered and debated its origin and appeal.

The golden ratio also exists as a proportional system:

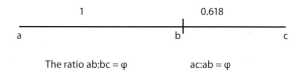

algebraically $\sqrt{5}-1$; numerically 8:5, or as a percentage, 61.8%:38.2%.[13] The ratio 8:5 is also part of the Fibonacci[14] series, which is a sequence of numbers that begins by adding the first two numbers together to create the third, then the fourth is created by adding the second and third numbers and so on: 0, 1, 1, 2, 3, 5, 8, 13. The uniqueness of this series is that it contains the golden

SACRED ROOTS

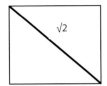

Generative

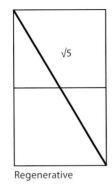

Regenerative

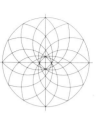

The centre of this sunflower shows the seed pattern in two interlocking spiralling shapes. The overall pattern is created by a series of proportionally related squares arranged concentrically around a central point. The proportional relationship of one square to the next as shown in the drawing is in the golden ratio.

gold   silver

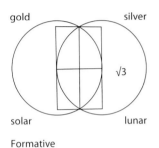

√3

solar   lunar

Formative

Two circles cross forming a Vesica Pisces eye shape. Two squares are placed along its length. The vertical centre line is now √3.

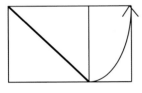

Root 2 rectangle with sides of square being 1.
Formed by drawing an arc using diagonal as radius.
This proportion was adopted by *DIN* (Deutsche Industrie Normen) for the International 'A' paper sizes (A4 etc)

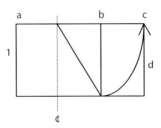

GOLDEN RECTANGLE

Take a square whose sides are 1 then bisect one side and place compass point on the bisection. Swing an arc to the extension of that side thus forming the length of the new rectangle ac. 1 ab:bc = φ ac:cd = φ

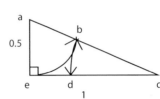

In a given 90° triangle with sides ae = 0.5 and ec = 1 as shown. Draw an arc eb. Draw a second arc bd. dc:de = φ

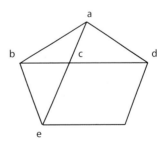

Divide a regular pentagon with two lines bd and ae. Where they cross creates golden ratios ac:ce and bc:cd.

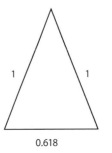

GOLDEN TRIANGLE

Golden triangle which is isosceles. The two long sides are 1 and the short side is 0.618

ratio with the numbers 5 and 8. This embodiment exists within the spiral form of the sunflower: the centre of the sunflower shows the seed pattern in two interlocking spiralling shapes. The overall pattern is created by a series of proportionally related squares arranged concentrically around a central point. The proportional relationship of one square to the next, as shown in the drawings, is in the golden ratio.

Using the same basis for constructing the golden rectangle, each rectangle reproduces itself in proportion to the golden ratio, growing larger.

The nautilus shell on the next page is an example of the existence in nature of the equiangular spiral.

EQUIANGULAR SPIRAL (GOLDEN SPIRAL)

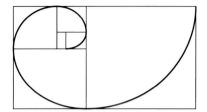

Nautilus shell

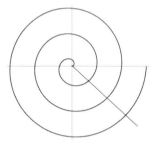

Archimedean spiral

ARCHIMEDEAN SPIRAL

The Archimedean spiral (also known as the arithmetic spiral) is a spiral named after the Greek mathematician, Archimedes. It is the locus of points corresponding to the locations, over time, of a point moving away from a fixed point, with a constant speed, along a line which rotates with constant angular velocity. It is very close to a series of concentric circles. If you take any line from the centre radiating outwards, you will see that each curve is equidistant from the next one.

THE SATURN SQUARE – DERIVATIVE OF THE MAGIC SQUARE OF MERCURY[15]

This is the smallest of the western occult series of magic squares which have been passed through the ages. The number five is the number of humankind, and goes into the centre. The 'feminine' even numbers are placed in the four corners starting from the top left. The 'masculine' odd numbers are placed around the remaining spaces, with the primal number one emerging from the abyss of

2	9	4
7	5	3
6	1	8

nothing at the base, and number nine placed at the top as the zero of transcendence, or goal of life. Whether you add up numbers vertically, horizontally or diagonally, they always add up to fifteen. Throughout history many religions have referred to mathematics, and specifically to magic squares. They have provided a constant source of inspiration for architects and designers.

APPLICATION OF GEOMETRY TO THE DESIGN OF DOMESTIC RESIDENCES BY FRANK LLOYD WRIGHT

The plans of these houses (Figure 80) all contain exactly the same number of rooms and Wright demonstrates by applying a different geometrical order to each one, such as square, circle and diagonal, how easy it is to produce a plan to offer to the client. Of course the solution to be built will rest on the client's choice as well as comparing in detail the advantages and disadvantages of each one.

PROPORTIONAL SYSTEMS

Theory is the ability to demonstrate and explain the productions of dexterity on the principles of proportion.[16]

Vitruvius

Arne Jacobsen[17] is noted for his sense of proportion. Indeed, he saw this as one of the main features of his work. In an interview he said: 'The proportion is exactly what makes the beautiful ancient Egyptian temples … and if we look at some of the most admired buildings of the Renaissance and Baroque, we notice that they were all well-proportioned. Here is the basic thing.'

The Italian architect Alberti[18] was a powerful influence on architecture in the 15th century. He wrote *Ten Books on Architecture*, which were inspired by those written by Vitruvius. He recommended the following proportional system to be used in the planning design of buildings:

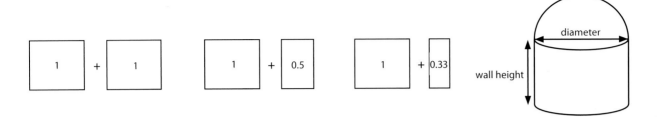

He also suggested that if a domed cylindrical space was required, then the ratio of wall height to the diameter of the circular plan should be either 1:2 or 2:3 or 3:4. These ratios comply with simple musical consonances because there is a sort of rhythm in any proportional method. Music consists of a language of notes, intervals and linking melody, which can also be expressed in design. He also said that beauty consists in a rational integration of the proportions of all parts of a building, in such a way that every part has an absolutely fixed size and shape and nothing can be added or taken away without destroying the harmony of the whole. This is a good test for any modern design, to ensure integrity and wholeness.

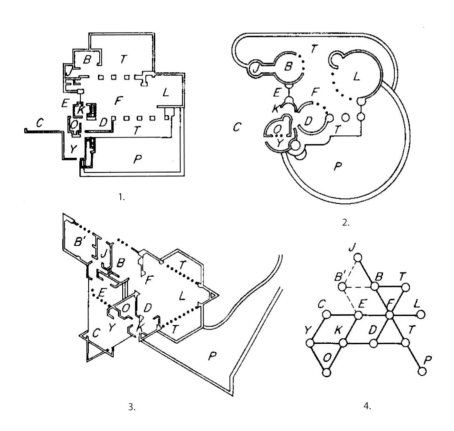

Figure 80. A house plan by Frank Lloyd Wright. There were variations for different clients, but with the same activity list, each following a different geometric basis. From *Geometry of the Environment* by Lionel March and Philip Steadman, RIBA Publications, 1971. Courtesy of Lionel March.

B	bedroom	F	family room	O	office
B'	Sundt bedroom	J	bathroom	P	pool
C	car port	K	kitchen	T	terrace
D	dining room	L	living room	Y	yard
E	entrance				

Figure 81. San Sebastiano Church, Mantua, northern Italy. This early Renaissance church was designed by Alberti. Wikimedia Commons. Photographer: Riccardo Speziari.

SAN SEBASTIANO

The Church of San Sebastiano in Mantua, Italy, by Leon Battista Alberti, demonstrates the first time that a church had the pediment of the front broken, in this case by an arch and window. Although the final result is a smoother facade, Alberti's original design was to have pilasters in place of columns.

The plan view is in the shape of a Greek cross, with three identical arms centring apses, under a central cross-vaulted space without any interior partitions. This plan grew out of churches built in the Byzantine period from about the 7th century AD. The Greek cross plan was widely used in Byzantine architecture as well as in St Peter's Basilica in Rome.

Churches based on the Latin cross are commonly associated with the Christian religion, and examples are seen in the great cathedrals of the Middle Ages, such as Salisbury Cathedral, below.

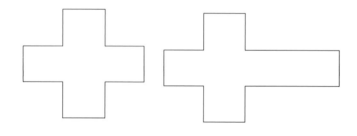

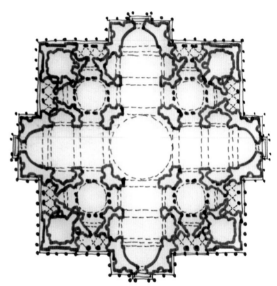

Figure 82. Plan of St Peter's Basilica in Rome. Drawing by the author.

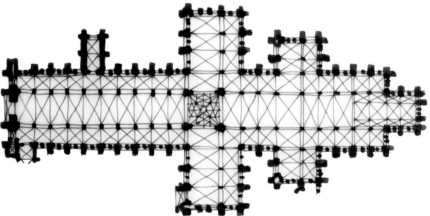

Figure 83. Plan of Salisbury Cathedral, UK, built in the 13th century. Drawing by the author.

SERLIO'S[19] DOORWAY DESIGN FOR A CHURCH

To reproduce Sebastiano Serlio's design for a doorway, proceed as follows. To construct the actual doorway (f-g-h-j on the diagram) first draw a square (a-c-e-d) to a height that allows for the door's architrave and pediment design. Draw diagonals as follows (a-e, c-d, b-d, b-e). Where they intersect (at f and g), this is the horizontal head of the door. The vertical lines drawn down from points f and g create the width for the door and reveal that the total shape of the door is precisely two squares. The golden ratio exists in df:fb as eg:bg.

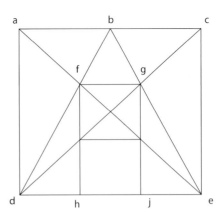

PALLADIO[20]

Andrea Palladio's Villa la Rotunda in Vicenza, built in the 16th century, was designed as a completely symmetrical building, having a square plan with four facades, each of which has a projecting portico. The whole is contained within an imaginary circle, which touches each corner of the building and the centres of the porticos. The name 'La Rotonda' refers to the central circular hall, which has a dome. It is curious to repeat such a noble entrance and facade four times, especially as there does not seem to be any variation between them to suggest different functions of use. The plan reproduces all four quarters precisely. It must be a headache for the postman! However, there are apparently subtle differences with regard to the approach and landscaping surrounding the villa, as Palladio considered orientation to be highly important. So the building does have a main approach and a main entrance.

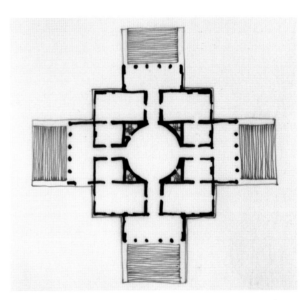

Figure 84. *Above*. Villa la Rotunda, Vicenza, Italy (1566–69) by Andrea Palladio. He recommended the following shapes as a planning basis: circle, square, square root 2, rectangle and golden rectangle. Diagrammatic plan drawing by author.

Figure 85. *Left*. Exterior of the Villa la Rotunda. Shutterstock. Artist: tswphotography.

CLASSICAL ORDERS

There are three distinct orders in Ancient Greek architecture, each with their own geometric principle – Doric, Ionic and, later, Corinthian – each characterised by the style of a column. These three orders were adopted by the Romans, who modified the capitals of the columns to make the Tuscan and the Composite orders. The Roman adoption of the Greek orders took place in the first century BC. The three Ancient Greek orders have since been consistently used in neoclassical European architecture. Callimachus,[21] the Greek sculptor, is credited with the invention of the Corinthian order.

The classical orders originated for use in the design of religious, military and civil buildings and they became, over the centuries, a standard way of designing buildings and have had an influence on architecture even to this day. The masculine Doric order was applied to fortifications, and the more feminine Corinthian order was applied to churches and palaces. The Ionic

Figure 86. *Above*. Classical columns, from an engraving in *Encyclopedie: Classical Orders*, Vol. 18 (18th century). Courtesy of the ARTFL Encyclopédie Project, University of Chicago. The classical orders shown are Tuscan (top left), Doric (top right), Ionic (middle left), Ionic Modern (middle right), Corinthian (bottom left) and Composite (bottom right).

DIAGRAM TO EXPLAIN BASIS OF AN ORDER

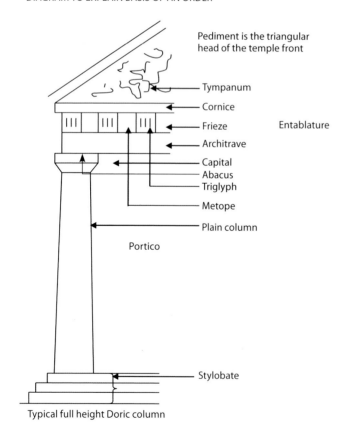

Pediment is the triangular head of the temple front

Tympanum
Cornice
Frieze — Entablature
Architrave
Capital
Abacus
Triglyph
Metope
Plain column
Portico
Stylobate

Typical full height Doric column

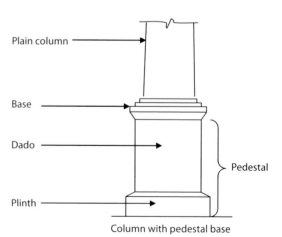

Plain column
Base
Dado — Pedestal
Plinth

Column with pedestal base

Figure 87. St Peter's Square, the Vatican, Rome. A line of columns forming a colonnade. Shutterstock. Author: Pavel K.

Figure 88. Senate House, Cambridge University, UK. Photo by author.

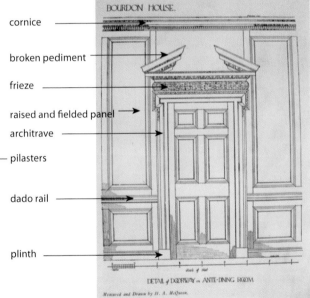

cornice

broken pediment

frieze

raised and fielded panel

architrave

pilasters

dado rail

plinth

Figure 89. Bourdon House, Mayfair, London. Georgian, 1720s. Ante-dining room wall panelling and doorway. This drawing was published in *Period Houses and Their Details*, first edition, edited by Colin Amery (London: Architectural Press, 1978), plate 153. Copyright Elsevier 1974.

order was used between these two extremes: it provided a means for making a three-dimensional structural design as well as presenting a noble entrance when used as a facade. The columns in each order were given strength and impact by building them in rows, almost giving the impression of a series of centurions guarding the building. These orders also became integrated into structural walls, creating 'pilasters', and were no longer a standalone structural item.

LE CORBUSIER'S *LE MODULOR*

Le Corbusier developed the two-volume *Le Modulor* (1948 and 1955) in the long tradition of Vitruvius, Leonardo da Vinci's *Vitruvian Man*, the work of Leon Battista Alberti, and other attempts to discover mathematical proportions in the human body and then to use that knowledge to improve both the appearance and function of architecture. Le Corbusier's system is based on human

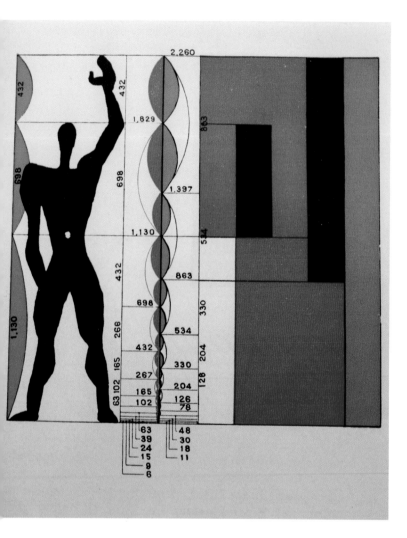

Figure 90. *Le Modulor* – an anthropometric scale of proportions devised by the Swiss-born French architect Le Corbusier (1887–1965). Published in 1948 by Birkhauser Verlag AG.

measurements, uniting the metric and imperial systems, Fibonacci numbers and the golden ratio.

Le Corbusier recommended that the ceiling height of a domestic residence should be measured as being the same height that an average man could reach by stretching one arm vertically upwards.

Proportion assumed metaphorical aspects millennia ago, and it is, in some sense, the most complex of the organisational principles. Practically, it simply serves to describe dimensional mathematical ratios such that pleasing qualities of mass and space result; and every society has evolved its own ideal system of proportion.[22]

J. Malnar and F. Vodvarka

REVIEW

This chapter provides designers with assistance in constructing designs according to chosen geometric principles, allowing them to assert control and order over planning and 3D design. It will strengthen the rationale of a design and add meaning to the forms created. It is important to appreciate the historic legacy of geometry and proportion, whilst at the same time realising the potential that exists for new configurations.

PART THREE

VISUAL UNDERSTANDING

5: PERCEPTION

ABOUT THIS CHAPTER

This chapter examines theories explained by Julian Hochberg (such as the 'gestalt' theory of perception) to assist in our understanding of what we see and how, as designers, we impose an ordered framework and solve three-dimensional form and space situations. The psychology of perception is explained with reference to the work of Sven Hesselgren and his analysis of the various factors that help us to categorise shape and pattern, and to the work of Keith Albarn and his analysis of the growth of pattern. Presented here are various exercises and illusions, including some tests.

> *It is not enough to see architecture; you must experience it. You must observe how it was designed for a special purpose and how it was attuned to the entire concept and rhythm of a specific era.*[1]
>
> Steen Eiler Rasmussen

> *Our perception of this world includes four elements: (1) light energy, the source of colour; (2) material and its response to that energy; (3) the eye, the receptor of light; (4) the brain, the interpreter of the received signal.*[2]
>
> Keith Albarn and Jenny Miall Smith

WHAT WE PERCEIVE

To perceive something implies that we understand what we are looking at. It is the process of attaining an awareness of, or the understanding of, sensory information. We reject chaos, instability and confusion, although certain forms of music and performance desire to use such themes for shock value. (This is fine because in a sense it is 'unreal' and there is a certain degree of safeness involved, as we are distanced from these performances as spectators.) With interiors, however, we are dealing with people of all ages who are engaging with the 'safe' physical aspects of a building as participators, and their lives must not be threatened. We 'read' the components of an interior usually in the following sequence:

- Anything moving – to ensure we are not in danger.

- Other people – people are fellow beings; they are of interest to us.

- The space perceived in terms of distance, size and scale.

- Large wall surface areas rather than small 'bits'.

- The light effect – whether daylight or artificial light.

- Large signage, if it exists.

- The floor.

- The ceiling.

In other words, we read it from large to small, from straight ahead to upwards and downwards. Bear in mind the fact that people can make misjudgements and pick up different messages from those the designer wanted to convey: they may go the wrong way, slip over or fall into an object, all of which will make them feel unhappy or disturbed, so designers must consider these aspects of human responses to interiors carefully when designing.

MAKING SENSE OF WHAT WE SEE

Some years ago, Dr Jonathan Miller[3] performed an experiment on British television whereby he painted random black shapes on a white background without any pre-planning. He then asked the audience to see if they could identify anything from these daubs of

Security cameras

Visually disruptive structure

Inconsistent book displays

Not enough space for seating

Clutter is also increased by additional promotional displays that were probably not included in the original designer's brief.

Figure 91. Bookshop, Cambridge, UK. By kind permission of Heffers of Cambridge.

paint. Many people said that they could see things such as a forest or a fence. The experiment illustrated how much people reject disorder and do not like chaos, and therefore try to find some pattern that makes sense, which they can identify with.

> *When a normally sighted person finds it difficult to identify the objects or events he perceives, he usually takes some steps to relieve himself of his doubt and uncertainty. No one likes such states, which are liable to cause anxiety and disquiet.*[4]
>
> **M. D. Vernon**

In interiors, people can suffer similar anxieties when they do not know where to go, or are unsure of how to use the facilities, or are presented with something that produces a confused state of mind. Sometimes lighting can be so bad that people cannot read instructions or recognise others. Some interiors are especially designed with low light levels in order to produce an intimate atmosphere, such as in a club or bar. That is fine as a major conceptual aim, but there should still be pockets of clear illumination to ensure some degree of clarity of vision. The same can be said of venues where the sound is too loud for conversation to take place.

Perhaps the provision for what I would call 'intervals of space', to allow for 'off-stage' dialogue or moments of contemplation to revive the brain, could be an added extra in such interiors.

Bookshops are renowned for being cluttered and confusing to use, despite the noble attempts of the staff to cover the place with signs. The shop in Figure 91, left, designed in the early 1970s, has suffered changes over the years, which the building's structure has not been able to respond to organically.

GESTALT THEORY

The gestalt (an organised whole perceived as more than the sum of its parts) effect, a term from a German school of psychologists, refers to the form-forming capability of our senses, particularly with respect to the visual recognition of figures and whole forms rather than seeing just a collection of simple lines and curves. It is about recognising the part from the whole and led to an explanation of how objects were to be perceived. The leading protagonists of this movement were Max Wertheimer,[5] Wolfgang Köhler and Kurt Koffka, with further developments by Julian Hochberg (see p.62).

The theoretical principles of gestalt are as follows:

■ **Totality** – The conscious experience takes into account all the physical and mental aspects of the individual simultaneously.

■ **Psychophysical isomorphism** – A correlation exists between conscious experience and cerebral activity.

■ **Biotic experiment** – The school of gestalt established a need to conduct real experiments, which sharply contrasted with and opposed classic lab experiments.

VISUAL ILLUSIONS

Some people say that the left-hand figure of the Müller-Lyer illusion (top right) reminds them of the internal corner of a room, and the right-hand figure reminds them of the external corner. This proves that we like to complete a so-called incomplete picture by adding more information to it. In the Müller-Lyer figure, the two long central lines are both of equal length, but the visual effect is that the drawing on the left has a longer central line than the other. Why is this? My analysis follows in the subsequent diagrams:

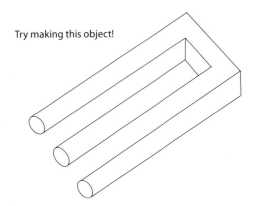

Try making this object!

MÜLLER-LYER ILLUSION

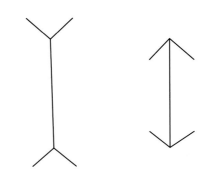

Directional lines

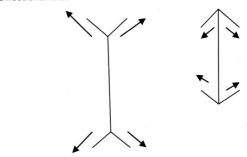

Stretches – makes it longer

Makes it shorter

But if we cut the vertical line into two parts we contradict this illusion.

Rotational

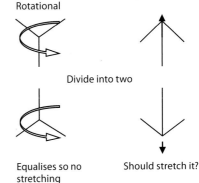

Divide into two

Equalises so no stretching

Should stretch it?

SOME VISUAL TESTS

As a way of testing your own powers of observation, have a go at solving the following visual perception tests. For the answers to the tests see p.97.

Test 1

The task here is to work out the quickest way of calculating the area of the uncoloured shapes. The drawing is comprised of two semicircles at either end, with a full circle of the same radius in the centre.

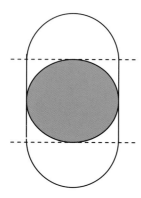

Test 2

These drawings represent a three-dimensional object. The third elevation is missing. The test is to find out what the 3D object looks like. All the information you need is in these two drawings. Remember, dotted lines on a drawing indicate something behind the exposed face; no such lines are necessary.

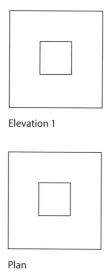

Elevation 1

Plan

Test 3

Connect all dots together in four straight lines without taking the pencil off the paper and without going over the same line twice.

Test 4

Wertheimer's 'experience factor': these three shapes make up … what?

RUBIN'S VASE

Rubin's vase (sometimes known as the Rubin face or the figure-ground vase) is one of a famous set of cognitive optical illusions developed around 1915 by the Danish psychologist Edgar Rubin. The viewer either perceives a vase, or two heads facing each other. It all depends on whether the observer sees predominantly white and therefore sees the vase, or if they see predominantly black, and therefore sees two heads. Eventually both shapes alternate for prominence.

THE FACTOR OF THE GOOD CURVE OR THE GOOD GESTALT
from Sven Hesselgren (see next section on factors)

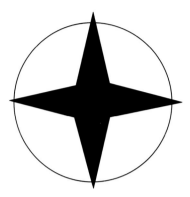

The circle is not perceived as absolutely round. The circle is perceived as a round gestalt. The star form crosses over the circumference of the circle and in so doing it seems to destroy this perfect circle by breaking the circle into four separate arcs.

SVEN HESSELGREN

PERCEPTION PSYCHOLOGY

The process of observation can be described in the following manner: some sort of physical energy reaches one of our sense organs, for example, the eye or the ear. From there, a sort of electro-chemical impulse is sent by a nerve to the brain. This impulse gives rise to the experience of something which is called either a sensation or a perception.[6]

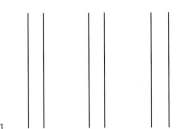

1.

When we see an object, we get a visual *perception* of it. When we discontinue seeing it, for whatever reason, a *conception* persists of the original perception. Wertheimer conducted analyses of many patterns in order to determine under what conditions the *form elements* combine to form gestalts. On the basis of these investigations, Hesselgren explains the formative factors of these gestalts as follows: the adjacency factor, the directional factor, the similarity factor, the symmetry factor and the closure factor.

THE ADJACENCY FACTOR (DIAGRAMS 1 & 2)

Components that are next to each other and repeated become identifiable as being adjacent. Designers must be able to see the total shape and be able to break this down by visual analysis as follows: both figures are symmetrical horizontally and vertically with a corresponding central axis. In Diagram 1 there are 11 identifiable units, and in Diagram 2 there are 20 (count each line as a unit and the space in between as a unit).

THE DIRECTIONAL FACTOR (DIAGRAMS 3 & 4)

An analysis of these rows of dots tells us that the main axis is horizontal. In Diagram 3 the lines are in pairs and in Diagram 4 the lines are in threes, with the horizontal spacing greater than the vertical spacing. In Diagram 3 and 4, the directional emphasis is made by slipping the bottom row(s) to the right. In Diagram 3 there are 45 units comprising 22 dots, 2 horizontal lines, 10 vertical pairs, 2 single dots, and 9 rectangles of dots. In Diagram 4, there are 67 units comprising 36 dots, 3 horizontal lines, 10 vertical threes, 9 vertical rectangles of six

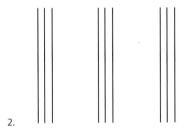

2.

3.

4.

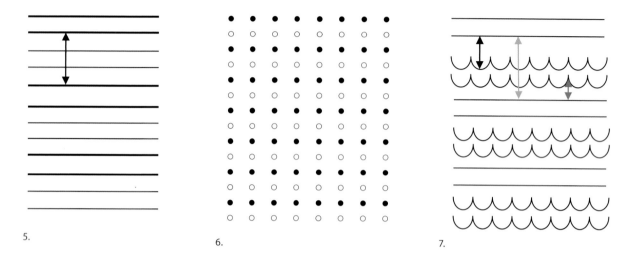

5.

6.

7.

Analysis: Similar units in perception become grouped together.

dots, 2 vertical twos and 2 single dots. The interesting visual fact here is that in Diagram 3 you should see the horizontal lines first, whereas in Diagram 4 you should see the vertical threes first because the vertical spacing is closer.

THE SIMILARITY FACTOR (DIAGRAMS 5, 6 & 7)

In perception, similar units become grouped together. In Diagram 5, there is a symmetrical vertical axis only. There are 36 units comprising 6 thick lines, 6 thin lines, 11 spaces between lines, 3 thick lined spaces, 3 thin lined spaces, 5 combined thick/thin line spaces, and 2 arrowed spaces.

In Diagram 6 there are 77 units comprising (horizontal lines of dots seen first over vertical ones because of similar adjacency) 7 horizontal black dots (seen first over white ones), 7 horizontal white dots, 8 vertical lines of alternating black and white dots, 6 horizontal spaces between black dots, 7 vertical spaces between black dots, and 42 rectangles of 4 black dots (vertical axis only).

In Diagram 7, there are 25 units comprising 6 horizontal lines, 6 curved lines, 3 spaces between lines, 3 spaces between curved lines, 3 black arrow spaces, 2 brown arrow spaces, and 2 blue arrow spaces (vertical axis only).

THE SYMMETRY FACTOR (DIAGRAM 8)

This factor is stronger than the similarity factor. The symmetry here is defined by the horizontal and vertical

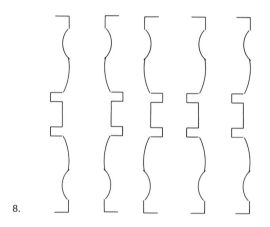

8.

Analysis: There are two groups of three and two similar profiles. There are two vertical axes and one horizontal axis.

axes. There are two groups of three and two similar profiles. There are two vertical axes and one horizontal axis. There is a total of ten units.

THE CLOSURE FACTOR (DIAGRAMS 9 & 10)

The closure factor overwhelms the adjacency factor. It has a 'containing' function. In Diagram 9 there are 18 units comprising 8 vertical lines, 6 short horizontal lines and 3 contained rectangles, with the whole form contained by end lines. In Diagram 10 there are 24 units comprising 8 vertical lines, 12 short lines at 45°, 3 contained spaces as indicated by the arrow, and the whole form is contained by end lines.

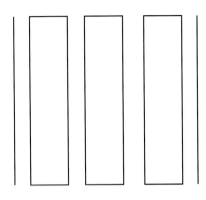

9.

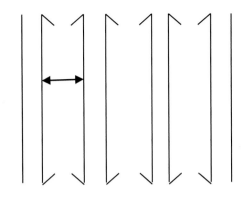

10.

Analysis: The closure factor overwhelms the adjacency factor. It has a containing function.

SUMMARY

All of these observations help us, as designers, to understand the visual relationships of forms and pattern when conceiving and planning interior spaces, through the capability to analyse structure and the relationship of components.

KEITH ALBARN

The grouped hexagons (page 98) are taken from Keith Albarn's book, *Diagram: The Instrument of Thought*, and in Figure 91a are initially based on a series of grid lines that are equally spaced and parallel to each side of the hexagons. The next stage was to make a variety of interpretations of this grid so that each hexagon shape looked like the surfaces of a cube, because the areas for change were on those cubic faces. The variations were realised in line thickness and dotted lines, and the reversal of what is line into space and vice versa, but with *no variation to the grid*.

In Figure 91b, whilst the top hexagon retains the grid of Figure 91a, the bottom two hexagons remove certain lines to emphasise a three-dimensional image. The left-hand image emphasises a 60° angled form, the right-hand image emphasises the vertical.

These diagrams represent similar variations that could be made on a building grid for an interior design project. In Chapter 7 (see p.128), I describe how grids are the ordering principle for planning, and how the organic process of designing involves variable adjustments to the layout, trying out one set of relationships compared with another, and so on.

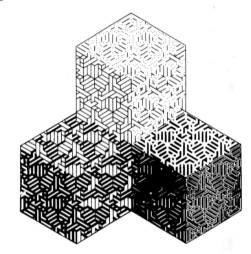

Figure 91a. From Albarn's *Diagram* book, p.52.

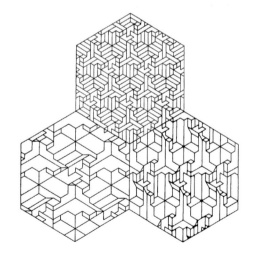

Figure 91b. From Albarn's *Diagram* book, p.53.

Figure 92. Natural forms. A pattern of branches may have provided inspiration for the design of the stained-glass window in Figure 93. Photo by author.

Figure 93. *Right*. Stained-glass window, Darwin Martin House, Frank Lloyd Wright, 1904. Getty Images.

Figure 94. Avenue of trees. We see here the undulating rhythm of light and shadow, perspective, columns and arches. In this case, the avenue of trees has been planted by humans, thus formalising parts of what nature has to offer us. Photo by author.

NATURAL REFERENCES

WHAT DO WE SEE?

Nature provides designers with plenty of inspiration simply by close examination and analysis of form, colour and texture. Frank Lloyd Wright's stained glass window is the result of formalising plant forms into a near abstract pattern. The photograph in Figure 92 is intended to show a connection with Wright's design.

VISUAL ASSORTMENT

These new offices for Google (see Figure 95) are designed to communicate a brightness and liveliness that matches the dynamic of a media company. Transparent walls play host to a series of brightly coloured dots, the colours of which are echoed in the enlarged graphic forms depicting the logo of the company. It has playful associations with a child's environment, perhaps helping to reduce the tension of a concentrated and demanding work environment. The magnification of the letterforms deliberately clashes with the building's structure, making the viewer wrestle with the 'reading' of the forms and the absorption of the 'message of intent' of the designers.

Figure 95. The reception at Google's London office, designed by Scott Brownrigg, 2010.

ANSWERS TO TESTS

Test 1 The drawing tells you that the circle is bound by a square. Therefore the answer is: area of square.

Test 2 From the square information given people generally presuppose that the answer is cubic in form. Wrong. This test demonstrates how much our preconceptions influence our judgement. A designer's training should reduce this kind of influence.

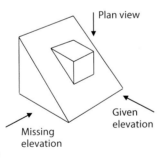

Test 3 The common failing here, as with Test 2, is that the image of the square dominates the observer's thought patterns and he tries to solve the task *within* the square, whereas the secret is to think *beyond* the square.

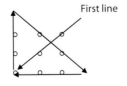

Test 4 This is an orientation issue. If you turn the page 90° clockwise it will be easier to recognise the capital letter 'E'.

REVIEW

The important point being made in this chapter is that visual understanding is paramount in a designer's skill base. Our capacity to see clearly and analyse what we are seeing informs our design capabilities. Apart from certain theories being propounded, the emotional value of what we perceive must be recorded.

A designer has to make visual judgements on:

■ Composition of form, colour, line and texture.

■ Scale and sizing of the elements of an interior relative to human use.

■ Adequacy of a space for the purpose of carrying out activities.

■ Effects of materials and lighting.

These skills cohabit with the many other skills necessary for designing an interior.

6: EXPRESSION AND MEANING

ABOUT THIS CHAPTER

This chapter questions how and why the minimalist movement tried to eliminate almost all inherited decoration from the past. It involves an abbreviated look at major design movements through history, to extract the essence and formal content of what is being expressed, so that we can understand and be objective about the present status of design. Building on this survey, I analyse what designers are expressing in their work, and suggest the main categories of expression that seem to encompass all building types. Finally, I examine how certain devices are underplayed in the design of our interiors, and how their positioning and presence is dealt with woefully.

INTRODUCTION

It seems to me if we wish to realise the ideal of a great and harmonious art, which shall be capable of expressing the best that is in us: if we desire again to raise great architectural monuments, religious, municipal or commemorative, we shall have to learn the great lesson of unity through fraternal cooperation and sympathy, the particular work of each, however individual and free in artistic expression, falling naturally into its due place in a harmonious scheme. Let us cultivate our technical skill and knowledge to the utmost, but let us not neglect our imagination, sense of beauty, and sympathy, or else we shall have nothing to express.

Walter Crane[1], *The Bases of Design*

The designed visual environment is an expression of the culture of that particular time in history. It is therefore an expression of attitudes and ideals and is reflective of the mood and technology of the day. The resultant effect upon people is an emotional one, and different emotions will be felt depending upon the type of interior. I will attempt to summarise the development of the design movements since the mid-19th century in order to establish where we are today, followed by a look at categories of expression and expression in detail. It is not my intention to dwell on the history of style in any great depth, nor the industrial, cultural and political movements that polarised their changes, as that is beyond the scope of this book. However, the legacy and sequence of past design movements, which affects the design of our environment, need to be understood before we can progress.

THE 19TH CENTURY

After the Great Exhibition of 1851[2] in England, Europe suffered from the constant reproduction of past styles (known as revivalism) such as the Gothic and Baroque, and the romanticisation of the Middle Ages. There was also great celebration of the arrival of the machine and mass production, simply because products could be made much more cheaply than before and on a greater scale, meaning that they reached a larger section of the public. Consumerism was born. This produced much common criticism of excessive decoration as 'bad taste', and interiors congested with artefacts and objets d'art were abundantly evident.

Figure 96. A typical Victorian domestic interior of 1900. Getty images.

Figure 97. Penthouse Marina Bolla in Monte Carlo. Claudio Silvestrin Architects, 2006.

FROM THIS …   … TO THIS: WHAT HAPPENED?

It is quite apparent that through economic necessity and profit-driven markets, aided by advances in technology and the pursuit of efficiency, a reductionist approach to making and designing has culminated in a mean environment, skinned by the vultures of consumerism. We now need to replenish our souls with an additive approach to our cultural wellbeing.

THE ARTS AND CRAFTS MOVEMENT[3]

This movement grew, towards the end of the 19th century, through people such as the writer John Ruskin and the designer William Morris.[4] They promoted rebellion against the 'machine aesthetic' and industrialisation, and called for a return to craft-based work, expressed through natural materials, and recognition for the vernacular. C. R. Ashbee and Ernest Gimson were also part of the movement in the UK. The Americans Henry H. Richardson (1838–86), Charles Sumner (1868–1954) and Henry Mather (1870–1957) also joined this movement. They sought to re-establish ties between the art of making and the worker. Decorative products continued to be produced at this time, but they had more originality and personal handiwork than during past revivalist movements.

Architects such as the Englishmen C. F. A. Voysey[5] and Sir Edwin Lutyens epitomised this period.

Figure 98. *Cabbage and Vine* tapestry. William Morris's first tapestry, woven at his home, Kelmscott Manor, in the summer of 1879. Wikimedia Commons.

Figure 99. *Left*. The Morris Room, café at the V&A Museum, London, 1866–68. Courtesy of the V&A, London.

Figure 100. *Right*. Voysey's design for a clock case for his house. Replica by Christopher Vickers (www.artsandcraftsdesign.com).

Figure 101. Voysey's own house, 'The Orchard', in Chorleywood, UK. Courtesy of the Three Rivers Museum Trust.

Figure 102. Interior of the Tassel House, Brussels, by Victor Horta, 1893. Getty Images.

ART NOUVEAU

The art nouveau movement, noted for its flowing lines and curves in interior and furniture design, grew out of the Arts and Crafts Movement in the 1880s. The Belgian designer Victor Horta[6] and the Czech painter Alphonse Mucha[7] were leading exponents of this movement. Its formal inspiration also came from organic and natural forms. Contemporary developments in iron manufacturing, such as the ability to cast curved forms, enabled the creations of designers such as Horta to be built.

Charles Rennie Mackintosh[8] was another influential exponent of art nouveau. He designed the Glasgow School of Art, which is one of the most important and influential art nouveau buildings in the world. Organic forms decorate this beautiful and unusual building. It has its own archive department, and still flourishes as an art college. He also produced the most beautiful drawings, not only of his design work, but which were works of art in their own right. His painting *La Rue du Soleil* reveals his compositional and textural skills, combined with an imaginative interpretation of the landscape. As discussed in Chapter 1, the skills used by a designer to express the environment artistically can be evident in that designer's 3D design work. The feeling for line, shape, colour and texture in 2D can be inextricably linked to a 3D vision.

Figure 103. Advertisement for F. Champenois. Lithograph by Alphonse Maria Mucha. Wikimedia Commons. Source: Art Renewal Center Museum.

Figure 104. *Right*. C. R. Mackintosh, *La Rue du Soleil*, 1926, watercolour. Courtesy of the Hunterian Museum, Glasgow.

Figure 105. The Willow Tea Rooms, Glasgow, seen today. Designed by C. R. Mackintosh in 1904. Wikimedia Commons. Author: Dave Souza.

Figure 106. The Daily Express Building, London, 1930–32. Architects: Ellis and Clarke with Sir Owen Williams, with interiors designed by Robert Atkinson. Wikimedia Commons. Authors: Rictor Norton and David Allen.

Figure 107. Glass vase by Emile Gallé, c.1900. Wikimedia Commons. Author: Goldi64.

ART DECO

From 1900 up until the 1930s, when it reached the peak of its popularity, this style was based on classical inspiration, sumptuous materials, and repeated geometric motifs derived from Cubism. Interestingly, art deco countered the sterility of the modernist movement (see below) and was led by leading French designers such as Ruhlman, Groult, Legrain, Lalique and Gallé,[9] the American Ralph Walker, and the Englishmen Oliver Hill and Robert Atkinson.

Despite the popularity of these beautiful decorative styles, the surging, questioning modernists, who retained purist ideals whilst pursuing mass-production techniques, were going from strength to strength. Combined with advances in technology with regard to materials, services and construction, buildings were being built using more glass than ever before, were more spacious and confirmed a desire for a healthier living environment.

THE MODERNIST MOVEMENT

The modernist movement, which was formed by the establishment and influence of the Bauhaus School[10] of design, the Dutch De Stijl[11] movement and the writings and work of Adolf Loos,[12] stripped away the excesses of Victorian style and Vienna Secessionist style, arriving at a more pure and truthful expression of what was summed up by the aphorism 'Form follows function.'[13] A key organisation that contributed to this movement was the Deutscher Werkbund (German Work Federation), a German association of architects, designers and industrialists founded in 1907 in Munich at the instigation of Hermann Muthesius. It spanned the ideals of the Arts and Crafts Movement as well as modernism as it developed during the 1920s.

Gillian Naylor, in her book *The Bauhaus*,[14] states: 'For the school set out, in a resurgence of optimism and idealism after the First World War, to train a generation of architects and designers to accept and anticipate the demands of the twentieth century.' There was a vision of a new kind of life – much healthier and responding to new forms of human behaviour.

Piet Mondrian[15] and Theo van Doesburg[16] were two giants of the De Stijl movement. They reduced abstract art to minimal geometric compositions, Mondrian with horizontal and vertical forms of expression and van Doesburg with diagonal forms of expression.

Figure 108. *Wassily Chair* by Marcel Breuer, 1925. It has qualities of floating and lightness, with a minimal use of materials. There are no 'legs' as such, but two long horizontal tubes. Courtesy of the Bauhaus Archive, Berlin.

Figure 109. Piet Mondrian, *Tableau I*, 1921, Reproduction of the painting, produced at the graphic print shop of the Bauhaus Weimar, Colour lithograph. A typical grid-like painting by Mondrian. Courtesy of the Bauhaus Archive, Berlin.

A cool, minimal and restrained style emerged, in which any excessive expression was removed. From 1900 onwards there were two world wars, the Depression of the 1930s, and a rapid expansion in communications technology. After 1900, the changes that took place altered people's lives beyond recognition. Mass production was now established as the means of producing goods for the mass market. The demands of industrialisation led to methods of standardisation and rationalisation. The pursuit of this industrialised purification continued after the Second World War,[17] and helped tremendously in catering for a war-damaged people through utility design solutions.

The Design Council[18] was founded in Britain in 1944 and together with the 1951 Festival of Britain, sought to revive a people suffering from post-war blues, bringing together the cream of architectural and design talent. It helped to establish reputations and a massive rebuilding operation was planned throughout Europe. Observers (see categories in Chapter 1, p.24) such as Nikolaus Pevsner,[19] Sigfried Giedion and Reyner Banham[20] describe in great depth how society grew to welcome such invention as displayed by architects such as Frank Lloyd Wright,[21] Mies van der Rohe,[22] Le Corbusier[23] and Walter Gropius (the founder of the Bauhaus[24]).

In Figure 111, Frank Lloyd Wright's Robie House,

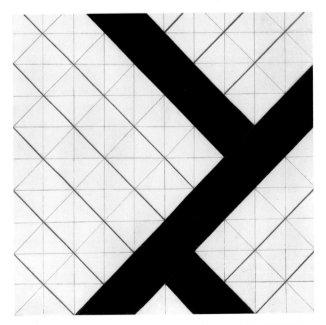

Figure 110. Theo van Doesburg, *Counter-Composition VI*, 1925. Wikimedia Commons. Source: www.maecla.it.

we can see how the strength of the horizontal understandably dominates the vertical due the proportional difference between the length and height of building. Wright's house blends into the landscape because of its organic qualities, such as the use of brick and the inter-layering mesh of varying spaces and forms. Mies van der Rohe's house (Figure 112), on the other hand, provides a stark and severe contrast with the landscape, and almost appears as though it belongs elsewhere. Van der Rohe's brilliant Barcelona Chair is

still produced as copies (Figure 113), and an analysis of the reasons for its success follows below.

The Barcelona Chair contains a wonderful simple duality of leather and steel, which combine to produce an object of grace. Its seductive flowing lines welcome the sitter, as well as presenting an object that is pleasant to look at. Because of these qualities, it has proved to be popular not only for reception areas in corporate offices, but also for domestic use.

Erich Mendelsohn's[25] Einstein Tower of 1921 in

Figure 111. Robie House, Chicago. Frank Lloyd Wright, 1909. Wikimedia Commons. Author: David Arpi.

Hugs you

Supports you

Grows out of the floor

Figure 113. 'Barcelona Chair', after Mies van der Rohe. Courtesy of Knoll International.

Figure 112. Farnsworth House, Plano, Illinois. Mies van der Rohe, 1951. Wikimedia Commons. Author Tinyfroglet.

Potsdam, Germany, with its plastic, curvaceous characteristics was way ahead of its time, and was probably considered appropriate as an expressionist memorial statement but did not seem to spawn any more buildings in that style. Mendelsohn left Germany for Britain in 1933, the year that Adolf Hitler became chancellor and Wells Coates[26] and others founded the MARS Group.[27] Within three months, he had won Britain's first explicitly modernist construction competition to design the De La Warr Pavilion, organised by the radical ninth Earl De La

Figure 114. *Right*. Einstein Tower, Astrophysical Observatory, Potsdam, Germany. Erich Mendelsohn, 1921. This is perhaps the most original building of the 20th century. Wikipedia Commons. Astrophysikalisches Institut, Potsdam.

Figure 115. *Below*. Diagrammatic plan of the Einstein Tower. Drawn by the author.

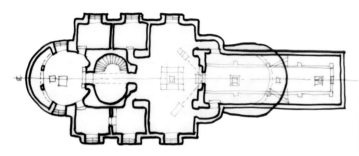

Figures 116 (left) and 117 (right). De La Warr Pavilion, Bexhill. Erich Mendelsohn, 1935. Serge Chermayeff was mainly responsible for the interiors. Figure 116 photo: Brian Hession. Figure 117 Shutterstock. Photo: Richard Donovan.

Warr, mayor of the small south coast resort of Bexhill, East Sussex. Mendelsohn's partner for the project was the Russian architect, interior designer and former ballroom dancer, Serge Chermayeff. Opened in 1935, the Pavilion's bars, restaurant, terraces and rooftop games area were immediately popular with most of Bexhill's residents. Whilst following earlier modernist traditions, Mendelsohn introduced creamy, polished curved elements using glass and steel, which seemed to match the lightness and gaiety of a seaside resort. In building the Pavilion, however, there was a major

innovation: for the first time in Britain, welded steel was used instead of reinforced concrete, to an engineering design by Felix Samuely.

The plan of the Einstein Tower is beautiful, with a careful marriage of the rectilinear with the curving. The semicircle morphs into a tapering form, and the staircase fits into a stretched circle. The strong symmetry, around a central axis, supports the circle centres and radii, forming window reveals. It is both mechanical and organic at the same time.

One of the other architects to introduce curves to the

Figures 118 and **119**. Conversion of a Victorian interior, 1 Kensington Palace Gardens, London. Wells Coates, 1931. Which interior is the more interesting?

fabric of his buildings was Alvar Aalto.[28] We have seen, in the past, reactions against excessive decoration that have used form and materials reduced to their simplest state. Aalto followed the organic route and cleverly combined rectilinear geometry with curvilinear form. He was a member of the Congrès Internationaux d'Architecture Moderne (CIAM), attending the second congress in Frankfurt in 1929 and the fourth congress in Athens in 1933, where he established a close friendship with László Moholy-Nagy and Sigfried Giedion. It was during this time that he closely followed the work of the main driving force behind the new modernism, Le Corbusier.

Aalto described his intentions regarding the design of the Finnish Pavilion as follows:

> *Therefore in this pavilion I have attempted to provide the densest possible concentration of display, a space filled with wares, next to and above and beneath each other, agricultural and industrial products often just a few inches apart. It was no easy work – composing the individual elements into one symphony.*

We need to return to Frank Lloyd Wright, for his Guggenheim Museum in New York opened in 1959. It incorporated a spiral ramp as the main viewing platform for seeing the displayed artwork. This was a hugely creative act, not only in display terms but as an expression of function in the built form.

We now come to perhaps the leading figure of

Figure 120. *Above.* The Finnish Pavilion, New York World's Fair, 1939. Alvar Aalto. Courtesy of Esto.

Figure 121. Baker House, MIT campus, Boston, Massachusetts. Alvar Aalto, 1947–8. Photos courtesy of Philip Greenspun.

Figure 122.
Left. Solomon R. Guggenheim Museum, New York. Frank Lloyd Wright, 1959. Interior. Photo by author.

Figure 123.
Right. Solomon R. Guggenheim Museum, New York, exterior. Getty Images.

modernism, otherwise known as the International Style – Le Corbusier. His seminal work, *Towards a new Architecture*,[29] was one of the most influential books on architectural theory to be published in the 20th century. The following two illustrations are of his chapel in Ronchamp, France, built in 1955. In his words:

> *The shell has been put on walls which are absurdly but practically thick. Inside them however are reinforced concrete columns. The shell will rest on these columns but it will not touch the wall. A horizontal crack of light 10 cm wide will amaze.*

This building became a sculptural tour de force, and architecture could now break free from the rectilinear constraints of the past. The building is reminiscent of so many derivatives, yet culminates in a totally new kind of architectural form. The roof is almost like the underside of the hull of a boat. The sloping walls with window slots remind us of Ancient Egyptian architecture such as the Temple of Philae. The stone tower, reminiscent of clay moulding, has a primitive quality.

In the quotation overleaf, Salingaros explains how architecture before Modernism used fractal scales, which were devices for controlled relatedness. Modernism broke free of such laws.

Figures 124 and **125**. Chapel of Nôtre Dame du Haut, Ronchamp, France. Le Corbusier, 1955. Exterior and interior views. Photos: Simon Glynn.

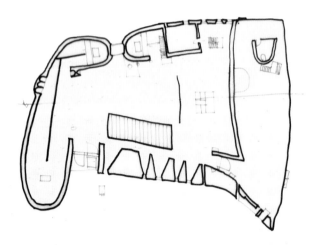

Figure 126. Diagrammatic plan of the Chapel of Nôtre Dame du Haut, Ronchamp, France. Compared with the symmetry of Mendelsohn's Einstein Tower, this building is totally asymmetrical – it is almost drawn as a doodle, in a playful way. Drawing by author.

Great buildings of the past, and the vernacular (folk) architectures from all around the world, have essential mathematical similarities. One of them is a fractal structure: there is some observable structure at every level of magnification, and the different levels of scale are very tightly linked by the design. In contradistinction, modernist buildings have no fractal qualities; i.e., not only are there very few scales, but different scales are not linked in any way. Indeed, one can see an unwritten design rule in the avoidance of organised fractal scales.

Nikos A. Salingaros, *Fractals in the New Architecture*, 2001 (see also Chapter 7, p.124)

THE LATE 20TH CENTURY

During this period, great innovations in building took place because of technological developments in engineering and materials. This was matched by a new, transparent and reflective architecture. Norman Foster's[30] Willis Faber Dumas office building in Ipswich demonstrated this new gymnastic capability. After examining various concepts, ranging from a tower block to low rise rectangular blocks on a restrictive site, Foster decided to maximise the given area by designing a curved exterior skin that hugged the perimeter of the site. This then reduced the height

Figure 127. Willis Faber Dumas office headquarters building, Ipswich, Suffolk. Foster + Partners, 1975. View at night. Photo: Nigel Young.

Figure 128. The Willis Faber Dumas building in daytime. Photo: Ken Kirkwood.

of the building if designed on more traditional tower block lines. This skin was reflective glass, which met the pavement edge without any intervening plinth (see Figure 128). So, during the day it secured the privacy of its interior workings by reflecting the buildings around it, and by night the illuminated interiors were exposed for all to see (see Figure 127). The exterior is clad in a dark, smoked-glass curtain wall. The central escalator well leads up to a rooftop restaurant for the staff, surrounded by a rooftop garden. This kind of architecture was called high-tech. Richard Rogers and Nick Grimshaw are two other architects whose ingenious engineering solutions fit this label.

Herman Hertzberger's[31] Central Beheer project was innovative in creating interior spaces that were not divided by partitions, but rather shared open volumes of stepped spaces which overlapped each other, allowing for greater and unexpected social interaction. Many recent buildings have been designed to explore this dynamic interactive conception. Richard Rogers'[32] most notable contribution to the high-tech era was the Lloyds of London underwriters' office building in the City of London.

The machine-like exterior of Rogers's building is reminiscent of Japanese Metabolist[33] architecture. Exposed services, elevators and spiral escape staircases finished in polished stainless steel give the building the appearance of a polished product. This placing of services outside the perimeter of the working floor was first proposed by the American architect Louis Kahn.[34] It prepared a clear, open floor within which the office's facilities could be planned.

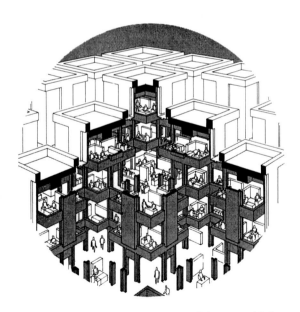

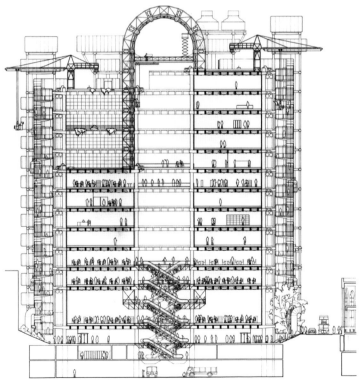

Figure 129. *Above.* Cutaway perspective of the Central Beheer Offices in Appeldorn, Netherlands. Herman Hertzberger, Architectuurstudio HH, 1972.

Figure 130. *Right, top.* Lloyds of London office building. Richard Rogers, 1984. Wikimedia Commons. Photo: Andrew Dunn.

Figure 131. *Right.* Section through the Lloyds of London building. Courtesy of Rogers, Stirk, Harbour + Partners.

To see the difference between a 1950s-style office block and an open-plan modern office building, look at the following diagram:

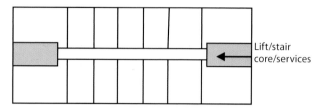

Cellular 1950s office building with central corridor

Lift/stair core/services

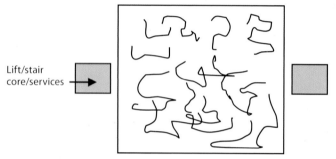

Lift/stair core/services

Deep span open planned office space

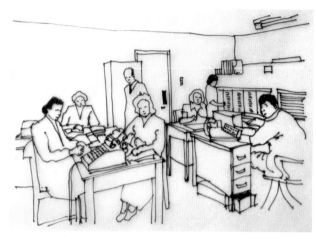

Figure 132. Typical office interior, 1943. Drawn by the author.

Figure 133. Herman Miller's 'Action Office, Series 2', currently being marketed. Courtesy of Herman Miller Inc.

OFFICE INTERIORS

Open-plan offices were developed in the 1950s by the German 'Quickborner' design team, who began the office landscape movement, or *Bürolandschaft*.[35] This coincided with the development of deep-span buildings with few – if any – columns, thus releasing a free open space within which to plan the office spaces. Walls could therefore disappear and lightweight screens appeared in order to help define areas of work and break up the space. This allowed companies to plan for the flexible use of a space and respond to changing needs in a more dynamic way.

Initially, such offices would just be filled with the same old furniture they had always had, and the open views of such spaces were a mess. It was not until Herman Miller's[36] furniture came on to the scene that a properly planned and visually coordinated workspace came into being. This company already had a pedigree in design from its use of the services of designers such as George Nelson and Charles Eames. Herman Miller's 'Action Office' furniture system, introduced in 1964, designed by Robert Propst, was the first successfully coordinated system of desking, shelving, storage and screens that had ever been produced.

As can be seen from the 1940s interior, it was a drab environment with bare walls, surface-mounted fluorescent lighting and not much space to move around in. The latest offering from Herman Miller cries efficiency, flexibility, comfort and lightness of mood. Originally designed in 1964 on a modular, adjustable system, Miller's 'Action Office' could incorporate wiring for power and light supply if so desired. The basic principle that the system offered was that worktops, shelving and storage units were cantilevered from adjustable-height uprights off freestanding screens, supported by the mobility of pedestals and chairs.

As global business enterprises expanded in line with manufacturing output, so there was a huge need to build administrative centres to support this and cope with more sophisticated communications technology. Over the years the 'open office' concept was combined with variations of enclosure, from the traditional private cellular office to screens and storage systems. The plenum space above the ceiling housed the supply of services such as air-conditioning and general illumination. The environment was designed with acoustically absorbent materials on the floor, screens and ceilings. Full-height partitions that were completely demountable could also be supplied, offering even more flexibility of use.

But there was one setback to this environmental progress: many office workers began to report that they felt unwell, suffering from what was later described as 'sick building syndrome'. This was a direct result of working in an unhealthy environment that lacked fresh air, as well as being a psychologically depressing space because it was so quiet that people began to whisper to each other! To counteract this, 'white noise' was introduced into the ceiling's plenum space to provide artificial background noise, as a comfort gesture to employees.

Figure 134. Guggenheim Museum, Bilbao. Frank Gehry, 1997. Wikimedia Commons. Source: Ardfern.

THE CURRENT SCENARIO

Bernard Tschumi[37] has written about how, until the 20th century, architecture was based upon the notion of *familiarity*. He says in his book, *Architecture and Disjunction*:

> *If the prevalent ideology was one of familiarity – familiarity with known images, derived from 1920s modernism or eighteenth-century classicism – maybe one's role was to defamiliarise. If the new, mediated world echoed and reinforced our dismantled reality, maybe, just maybe, one should take advantage of such dismantling, celebrate fragmentation by celebrating the culture of differences by accelerating and intensifying the loss of certainty, of centre, of history.*

Tschumi is asssociated with the Deconstructivist movement, which is a development of postmodern architecture that began in the late 1980s and challenged previous norms of structure through the work of such architects as Daniel Libeskind,[38] Peter Eisenman[39] and Rem Koolhaas.[40] The work illustrated in Figure 134 is part of this movement. Deconstructivism is anarchistic in spirit and destabilising in its effect. It is designed to shock and surprise, which is what the punk movement in design and music set out to achieve in the mid-1970s. Whilst I can admire the creative energy behind

Figure 135. National Museum of 21st-Century Arts, Rome, Italy. Zaha Hadid and Patrik Schumacher, 2010. Courtesy of Zaha Hadid Architects. Photo: Iwan Baan.

such work, I feel that it is encouraging a direction that reminds one of the worst times in life (see Chapter 8, p.168–169).

The following is a beautifully written extract of the rationale behind Zaha Hadid's project for the National Museum of 21st-Century Arts in Rome (organic rather than Deconstructive). Language is such an important and necessary accompaniment to the design that the meaning of specific descriptive terms is explained below the text.

Space vs. Object
Our proposal offers a quasi-urban field, a world to dive into rather than a building as <u>signature object</u>. The Campus is organised and navigated on the basis of <u>directional drifts</u> and the distribution of densities rather than key points. This is indicative of the character of the Centre as a whole: <u>porous, immersive, a field space</u>. An <u>inferred mass</u> is subverted by <u>vectors of circulation</u>. The external as well as internal circulation follows the overall drift of the geometry. Vertical and oblique circulation elements are located at areas of <u>confluence, interference and turbulence</u>. The move from object to field is critical in understanding the relationship the architecture will have to the content of the artwork it will house. Whilst this is further expounded by the contributions of our Gallery and Exhibitions Experts below, it is important here to state that the premise of the architectural design promotes a <u>disinheriting of the 'object'-orientated gallery space</u>. Instead, the notion of a 'drift' takes on an <u>embodied form</u>. The drifting emerges, therefore, as both architectural motif, and also as a way to <u>navigate experientially</u> through the museum. It is an argument that, for art practice is well understood, but in <u>architectural hegemony</u> has remained alien. We take this opportunity, in the <u>adventure of designing</u> such a forward-looking institution, to confront the material and <u>conceptual dissonance</u> evoked by art practice since the late 1960s. The path led away from the 'object' and its correlative sanctifying, towards <u>fields of multiple associations that are anticipative of the necessity to change</u>.

GLOSSARY OF TERMS USED ABOVE

Signature object: Personalised solution identified with the designer.

Directional drifts: Emphasising flowing connections rather than separate entities.

Porous, immersive, a field space: Again, explaining an interactive quality rather than separateness.

Inferred mass: The building's form is gently perceived.

Vectors of circulation: Human beings are guided organically through the spaces.

Confluence, interference and turbulence: Describing how variable the circulation experience can be, depending upon the function of that particular area.

Disinheriting of the 'object'-orientated gallery space: Not acceding to object prominence but rather witnessing an integrated spatial solution.

Embodied form: Emphasising the 'wholeness' of the design.

Navigate experientially: Visitors will gain comfort from not being confused or lost.

Architectural hegemony: Being critical of 'what architecture should be'.

Adventure of designing: This is what designing should be all about – it is wonderful to see it written.

Conceptual dissonance: The multifarious movements and ideologies expressed in art.

Fields of multiple associations that are anticipative of the necessity to change: Summing up the final design as consisting of various interlinked entities that will be capable of being adapted and flexible to the demands of change without destroying the original harmonic concept.

ADVANCES IN SOFTWARE

Great progress with computer software programs such as Autocad and Revit has enabled designers and architects to manipulate 3D form and realise their dreams in a way that was not possible before. Frank Gehry[41] and Zaha Hadid[42] are two leaders in this field. With these sophisticated tools, presentations can be made in 3D with animation, almost equating to a photograph of the finished project. So we have computer systems that can provide measured solutions to our sketched ideas, and can produce drawings and specifications by organising information in a way that is efficient and allows clarity and completeness.

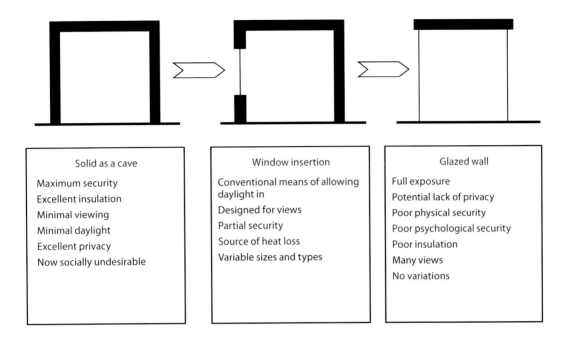

Solid as a cave	Window insertion	Glazed wall
Maximum security	Conventional means of allowing daylight in	Full exposure
Excellent insulation	Designed for views	Potential lack of privacy
Minimal viewing	Partial security	Poor physical security
Minimal daylight	Source of heat loss	Poor psychological security
Excellent privacy	Variable sizes and types	Poor insulation
Now socially undesirable		Many views
		No variations

GLASS: A WORD OF WARNING

Juhani Pallasmaa sounds a word of warning on high-tech glass architecture in his book *The Eyes of the Skin*[43]:

> *As buildings lose their plasticity, and their connection with the language and wisdom of the body, they become isolated in the cool and distant realm of vision. With the loss of tactility, measures and details crafted for the human body – and particularly for the hand – architectural structures become repulsively flat, sharp-edged, immaterial and unreal. The detachment of construction from the realities of matter and craft further turns architecture into stage sets for the eye, into a scenography devoid of the authenticity of matter and construction … The increasing use of reflective glass in architecture reinforces the dreamlike sense of unreality and alienation.*

Let us examine the three stages of the design of the external skin, or the enclosure of a building, from solid to a state of transparency (see diagram above).

What is the motivation or reasoning for building a glass box? Once the technology became possible and the economics made it an attractive proposition compared with the construction of a traditional skin, the world became full of jewelled diamonds of glass. Consideration of the natural human desires for protection, security and privacy have gone out of the window. Excuse the pun! I do admit that reflective glass aids privacy to a certain extent, but Pallasmaa's comment is still a worthy criticism. Look at the vulnerability exposed by the terrorist attacks on the Twin Towers in New York, and other city-centre bomb explosions. In Japan, they design buildings that have to withstand the threat of earthquakes, and therefore they do not go for a total glass skin but tend to include a proportion of solid framework.

Another comment, from John Outram's website (www.johnoutram.com) states:

> *Young architects continuously manipulate this notion of 'surface' through the computerised, prosthetic digitalia of their absent hands, hands that no longer even feel the agony of their amputation, or the pens and pencils they once (very recently) held. Phosphorescent surfaces slide and wave and billow, sliced, meshed and rotated, inverted and translated to and from until no one knows any more what is surface and what is surfaced, what is past, present or future. The aimless computer surges with a hopeless, lifeless unintentionality, like a giant sponge with no millennial hope, or ambition, towards a vertebrate cortex.*

DESIGN CAPABILITY PROGRESSION

The following five sequential stages express the process of making and building through history:

1. Design according to the *availability, strength and handling* of materials such as stone, wood, clay and concrete (non-structural). (From primitive man onwards.)
2. Design according to an *increase in hand skills*, using stone, wood, clay and concrete (non-structural). (Until the late 18th century.)
3. Design according to the invention of *factory processes* – iron, steel and reinforced concrete. (From the late 18th century.)
4. Design according to an increase in *structural engineering* skills – iron, steel, concrete, glass, cables and membranes (tensile structures). (From the late 19th century.)
5. Design according to invention of *computer-aided design* – iron, steel, concrete, glass, cables and membranes plus the invention of lightweight cladding materials. (Developed in industry in the 1960s, but did not become common in architecture until late 1970s.)

When we examine the progress of technology, we see that the original, primitive excursions into tools and craftwork are threatened not only by sophisticated means of production, but by cost. Unfortunately, the mass-produced item is cheaper to make and sell. The question I want to ask is whether old craft skills can ever contribute to the progress of design, or whether they have they had their day. Are they consigned to the museum or merely tourist attractions?

WHAT IS THE DESIGNER EXPRESSING?

This chapter deals with expression and meaning by giving examples of past styles as well as examining how the use of materials in making and building become expressive elements. In addition to this, below are five important categories that a designer draws from when expressing his or her work:

■ **The client's needs and activities** – identity, image, space requirements, facilities, staffing and users. It is very important to know your user.

■ **The designer's intent** – philosophy and ideology, the making of a statement.

■ **An acknowledgement of site and context** – the character, history and condition of the building, and the constraints imposed by orientation, structure, aspect and climate.

■ **Cultural references** – socio-economic factors, arts, politics, trends and market forces.

■ **Technology** – materials, construction, services in the face of 'green issues'. Mass-produced items/craft items, prefabricated/*in situ*.

Having established a full descriptive content and aims for a project from the above list, the designer will be conscious of further more emotive and expressive characteristics that have been passed on through history and are a reflection of cultural and social needs. Before examining these characteristics, we should first explore what is meant by the identity of a building.

Although a commissioned building may fall into one of the categories listed under 'What sectors does interior design cover?' in Chapter 1, as far as the designer is concerned there should not be any preconditioned formula that suggests what form or character a building will take. The Metric Handbook provides useful design data under a designation of building types, but in no way should that data dictate a building's formal solution. History has provided us with visually recognisable buildings (see Figure 136) that reveal their purpose and function – the station, the airport, the cinema, the office block, the department store and so on. From the 1960s, when the International Style became a global phenomenon, buildings were designed within cost constraints on one hand, and with a liberating technology on the other.

For example, a client's brief may not ask for a 'cinema building' as such, but instead ask for a certain amount of space for a certain number of people, performing certain activities such as watching films, for a certain amount of money. It is up to the designer to interpret this data into a building. The end result is that a building's function and identity is now not so easily identifiable as before, and we are faced with many buildings that do not shout out their identity, and which can make the entrance very difficult to find! The British Film Institute's IMAX cinema building in Figure 137 is reminiscent of a gas storage cylinder or water tank, rather than communicating anything to do with the watching of films.

Figure 136. Electric Pavilion Cinema, Brixton Oval. Horner Lewis, 1911. Now called the Ritzy Picturehouse, this was one of England's earliest purpose-built cinemas, seating over 750 in the single auditorium. Photo courtesy of Lambeth Archives.

Figure 137. *Right, top.* BFI IMAX cinema, Waterloo, London. Avery Associates Architects, 1999. Photo courtesy of BFI IMAX.

CATEGORIES OF DESIGN EXPRESSION

FORTIFIED BUILDINGS

The need to defend one's home has existed for centuries. The real threat of invasion, however, has diminished with time and the style has been diluted into an expression of the status of the resident, meeting the requirement for security against burglars and maintaining privacy. Up until Georgian times, the exterior still tried to maintain the look of fortification, with the quoins reminiscent of the crenellations of old castles, as seen on Caerphilly Castle (see Figure 138). The amount and quality of security applied to today's buildings tends to be directly proportional to the wealth of the owner.

Figure 138. *Right, centre.* Caerphilly Castle, Wales. Built in the 13th century. Getty Images.

Figure 139. *Right.* Château de Chambord, Chambord, Loir-et-Cher, France. Built in the 16th century. Shutterstock. Photo: Andlit.

Figure 140. Perpendicular Gothic: King's College Chapel, Cambridge University, England. Built 1515. Photo: Reginald Ely. Courtesy of Cambridge2000.com.

Figure 141. View of the sea from a restaurant in Greece – uplifting, peaceful and restful in a natural setting. Photo by author.

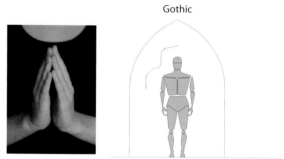

SPIRITUAL BUILDINGS

Religious worship has inspired some of the most enduring buildings in the world, especially those built from ancient to medieval times. They inspire awe in worshippers and non-worshippers alike. This suggests that a strong belief begets a strong solution. The Greek island shown top right similarly induces feelings of contentment and peace.

The Gothic period must embody one of the most astoundingly powerful design languages ever created: vertical structures reaching to the heavens; repetition of form and pattern that provides reassurance; the Gothic arch that greets a person more humanistically than the common rectangular doorway we are all too familiar with. This characteristically pointed arch was applied to windows, arches, flying buttresses and rib vaults throughout the building's design. The transitional arch (see Figure 141a), as seen in the south transept of Canterbury Cathedral, shows that by overlapping the Norman arch above it, the Gothic arch is produced.

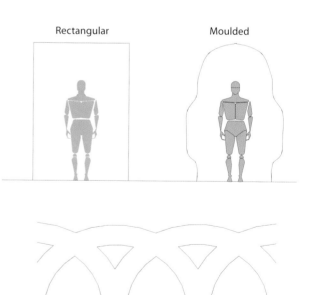

Figure 141a. Photo by author.

In the diagram on the left, the Gothic doorway and the moulded opening follow the shape of the human form more sympathetically than the rectangular solution. It is quite easy to appreciate that the popularity of the rectangular solution is due to economic necessity in the building process. The moulded solution, which is more ergonomically suitable, and reminiscent of a carved-out opening such as a cave, hardly exists. It is also interesting to note how the Gothic opening seems to echo hands clasped in prayer – a beautiful, meaningful connection to the purpose of the building, according to my own analysis. But it would appear that the main reason for the appearance of the pointed feature was a structural one – it suited the use of stone. The walls of Gothic buildings could be thinner because the weight of the roof was supported by the arches rather than the walls. The Romanesque Durham Cathedral revealed the following:

> *The new vault, groined, ribbed, and domed, was in a class by itself, apart from anything that had gone before. Particularly did it differ from the Roman vault in that, while the latter had a level crown, obtained by using semicircular lateral and transverse arches and elliptical groin arches (naturally formed by the intersection of two semicircular barrel vaults of equal radius), the 'Lombard' vault was constructed with semicircular diagonals, the result being that domical form which was always retained by the Gothic builders of France because of its intrinsic beauty. Finally, the new diagonals suggested new vertical supports in the angles of the pier, and so we obtain the fully developed compound pier, which later, at the hands of the English, was to be carried to such extremes of beauty, and to form a potent factor in the development of the Gothic structural system.*

Catholic Encyclopaedia – New Advent

NATURAL/FIGURATIVE BUILDINGS

See Figures 142 and 143. There has always been a desire to reflect our natural environment through visual imagery or by using natural materials. The designers of the Boston restaurant, Banq, have been inspired by the organic growth of natural forms and they have uniquely merged the design of the column and ceiling into one.

BUILDINGS TO REFLECT WEALTH AND STATUS

See Figures 144 and 145. Palaces are home to a nation's rulers and it was usually the richest people in a country who could afford to build on a huge scale, using the best

Figure 142. The Peacock Room by James McNeill Whistler, 1876–77. Courtesy of Freer Gallery of Art and Arthur M. Sackler Gallery, Smithsonian, Washington, DC.

Figure 143. Banq restaurant, Boston, USA. Office dA, 2009. Photo: John Horner.

artists and craftspeople in the world. The interiors were designed to accommodate many guests for ceremonial and celebratory functions, so the design of a palace reflected the aspirations of a nation rather than the owner.

Today, the beach house is perhaps a common sign of personal economic achievement, providing all the luxuries of modern-day living as well as views and access to the sea. Richard Meier's design, seen overleaf, is made up of separate units of form that are connected and help to frame shared spaces.

Figure 144. The Hall of Mirrors, Palace of Versailles (restored 2007), built by Louis XIV, 1668. Photo courtesy of RMN (Château de Versailles)/Michel Urtado.

Figure 146. Guildhall, Lavenham, Suffolk. Tudor, early 16th century. Photo by author.

Figure 145. Beach house, southern California, USA. Richard Meier and Michael Palladino. 2009. Photo courtesy of Esto.

Figure 147. Haddon Hall, Derbyshire. Dates from the 12th century. Reproduced with the kind permission of Lord Edward Manners.

BUILDINGS THAT PROVIDE COMFORT AND SECURITY

See Figures 146 and 147. Wood is warmer than stone. It also scores heavily for being more abundant, easier to extract from the earth than other materials, and renewable. It therefore came into its own during the Tudor period in Europe. (It had always been a natural resource for building in Scandinavia, the Far East and America.) Tudor buildings consisted of close-framed timber walls, which were expressed inside and outside the building. Their stepped, overhanging upper floors and roof added to feelings of security. Wall panelling,

as illustrated in the photo of Haddon Hall, created great warmth, not only visually, but in contrast to cold stone or rendered surfaces.

HIGH-TECH BUILDINGS

The work of Rogers, Foster and Hadid previously shown will suffice as illustrations of the high-tech expression of structure whilst stretching engineering skills to the limits. This includes the exploration of new materials and the provision of facilities in combinations that demonstrate new ways of using a building and servicing it.

EXPRESSION OF ACTIONS

It is time to examine detailed operations of use, the hand movements of which are explained in Chapter 7 under 'Mechanics of Operation' (see p.138). Such operational devices have often been ignored by designers as worthless items because they are usually small in scale and have consequentially been marginalised in favour of the larger, symbolic and more decorative interior elements. Of course this current scenario is largely due to advances in technology, but sometimes we need to pause and reflect as to how effects are made and whether we need to go down the route of miniaturisation and concealment. We need to recognise opportunities for expression and match the design solution with these generative possibilities. The following proposals may initially be challenged as not making economic sense. This is where philosophy, values and meaning in our lives can influence the way forward. The Globe Theatre in London, built in 1997, is an example of architects negating modern theatre building and technology by designing a new theatre that resembled the original 17th century construction in which many of Shakespeare's plays were produced. The purpose being that the audience would experience Shakespeare's works as they were originally performed.

POWER SWITCH

It is possible to flick a tiny light switch, held between thumb and forefinger, to power hundreds of light fittings in a multi-storey building. This tiny action, of minimal effort, does not match the powerful result of illuminating an entire building. Really, what is required is a huge lever that would match the end result, as is the case in power generating a building.

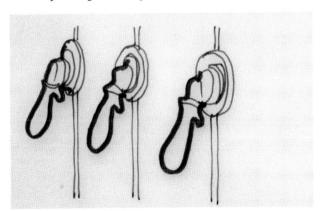

Figure 148. A more expressive light switch? Drawn by author.

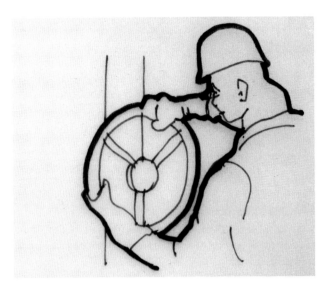

Figure 149. Sound control? Drawn by author.

SOUND CONTROLS

The operation of sound volume is usually done with a small rotating knob or a sliding fader – again by thumb and fingertip control. The sound produced can fill huge auditoriums, so why can't the operational device match the powerful end result? The illustration above shows a huge wheel that matches the effect of the sound.

LARGE VERSUS SMALL

Of course the general reaction to suggestions such as those above is that the miniaturisation of what used to be much larger devices has brought about a more economic and space-saving solution. This also sums up the direction that mobile phone technology and other miniature electronic products have gone in, additionally offering ease of portability and transportation. Yet this in itself produces a climate of fear in people, who worry either that they will lose the item or have it stolen, simply because it is easy to do just that. Small is risky; big is safer. The other mind-numbing effect upon our senses is the knowledge that these devices can now contain masses of information with huge communicative powers; many years ago, this would have meant large parcel deliveries over a period of days if not weeks! Now this kind of information can be sent in seconds. If someone loses their device, this is potentially devastating, adversely affecting their human relationships or job security.

This reductivist approach is not necessarily one that lightens the soul. How often do we relish an oversized object because it displays to us a generosity of material and possibly comfort? The location of power switches and sockets in interiors has been woefully ignored as an integrated design element (with some exceptions), and they are mostly carelessly placed on an architrave or wall without any other reference to the overall design. The more sophisticated computerised controls offer better-looking products, but they are still a separate entity (to be concealed) rather than positioned with a celebrated flourish, as with light fittings. In the conversion of Glendower House chapel (see Appendix), the light switch can be seen to be integrated into the joinery. Commercial and multi-occupational interiors have exercised more control over services, with trunking that offers control and flexibility of use.

REVIEW

At this stage in the book, the reader should now understand the theoretical basis upon which a designer has to work in order to fulfil his or her professional obligations. All work produced by anyone is ultimately an expression of that person, that time, that age, and the materials used within the social, political and financial constraints of the day. It is the embellishment of ritual, of performance, of an event that is to be seen, used, participated in and enjoyed by the recipients of the project.

Everything that is made and built has levels of soul-lifting effects, from the one that makes the heart miss a beat to the one that produces boredom and possibly revulsion. Examples of this range of emotional responses can vary from the most basic of buildings, such as a crofter's cottage in Scotland, to the grandest palace such as the Palace of Versailles, seen earlier in this chapter. Yet these buildings may not necessarily equate with the emotional range described. Many people may find the crofter's cottage heartwarming and welcoming, and the palace overwhelming, overbearing and revolting. It is a question of the building's relevance in and relatedness to our time. Therefore it is vitally important that designers are fully cognisant of the scope of their work, and are in possession of all material that feeds into the design process in order to allow these emotional connections to make an input. It takes courage, great effort and vision to realise a dream, to realise a passion whilst at the same time working within the constraints of modern society. The writer Edna O'Brien said in 1981:

We live in an age where feelings are in short currency. You have to be sensitive to feel them; but you have to be tough and hard to show them, and to write about them. To risk being naked; to risk being ridiculed.

PART FOUR
DESIGN PROCESS

7: THE THEORETICAL BASIS THAT ALLOWS THE DESIGN PROCESS TO WORK

ABOUT THIS CHAPTER

The purpose of this chapter is to peel away many of the platitudes that are commonly expressed in interior design circles, in order to expose the very real core of designing. It should be read in conjunction with the job sequence diagram in Chapter 1 (see p.25). We begin by examining design methodologies and the way that 3D form and colour are generated in terms of the growth of an idea. Ideas have to be structured in relation to the hierarchical distribution of interior spaces. The drawing and thinking processes of manipulating form are described and related to the skill of planning. The act of planning relies on getting different spaces to cohabit successfully in order to realise the overall design. We will examine various space types that are common to many interiors, adding some observations about a lack of care in the way that some situations have been handled.

THE DESIGN PROCESS

The full design process is a sequence of working that helps the designer organise and collate information, formulate design procedures and exercise control over the progress of a contract to the satisfaction of the client. It involves problem-solving and calls upon you to implement a design methodology.

All designers, from whatever discipline, work through various problem-solving sequences and the following headings summarise three of these sequences – instinctive, methodological and professional – which converge to form one controlling method.

Instinctive

Motivation ⇨ inspiration ⇨ idea ⇨ action ⇨ resolution

This is working at an emotional level, allowing one's own feelings to dominate any thought processes that may germinate. It is governed by excitement and risk-taking endeavours, fuelled by a determination to succeed. This is where design concepts (see Chapter 2, p.55) are born.

Methodological

Research ⇨ analysis ⇨ synthesis ⇨ evaluation ⇨ solution

This is a more disciplined procedure, concentrating on the efficient, problem-solving process that confirms the emotional procedure of the instinctive approach.

Professional

Briefing ⇨ programming ⇨ research ⇨ market comparisons ⇨ prototype ⇨ technological feedback ⇨ presentation of optional solutions ⇨ revision of designs ⇨ acceptance of final solution ⇨ making/site supervision ⇨ product completion

This sequence ties in with both the instinctive and the methodological approach in response to the professional demands of running a contract.

There follows a collection of some of the most influential methodologies to be published, albeit from an engineering background; but first, the best definition of design that I have come across, from Bruce Archer[1]:

> *Design is that area of human experience, skill and knowledge that reflects man's concern with the appreciation and adaptation of his surroundings in the light of his material and spiritual needs. In particular it relates with configuration, composition, meaning, value and purpose in man-made phenomena.*

He highlights the fact that the designer's work is about *adapting* the environment, as discussed in Chapter 2. An important quality of a designer's work is *meaning*. A designer should be able to explain *why* he has done what he has done. We respond to human need by producing solutions that should mean something and that are expressive.

Essentially, the problem-solving part of the design process usually involves the following stages:

1. *Analysis:* The problem is identified, researched, dissected and analysed; this means breaking down the problem into identifiable parts.
2. *Synthesis:* Selected parts of the problem are pulled together to form a way forward.
3. *Evaluation:* All the factors are checked in order to arrive at a final solution.

Hans Gugelot,[2] designer of Braun products and lecturer at the Hochschule in Ulm, Germany in the early 1960s, worked to the following system:

1. Information stage – company, clients, product comparison.
2. Research stage – user requirements, context of use, possible production methods, function.
3. Design stage – new formal possibilities, consider needs of the makers.
4. Decision stage – response from sales, marketing and production management.
5. Calculation – design adjustment relies upon good communication and understanding.
6. Prototype made.

Morris Asimow[3] (*Introduction to Design*, Prentice Hall, 1962), from the field of systems engineering, used the following problem-solving techniques:

■ **Identify the problem** – Develop a list of problems; select problems to tackle.

■ **Analyse the problem** – Gather information, focus attention, find possible causes.

■ **Solve the problem** – Develop solutions, provide alternative solutions, evaluate all solutions, pick the best solutions, develop follow-up plans, decide and implement solutions.

■ **Monitor the outcomes** – Communicate and record the data, compare the collected data against expectations, adjust the process.

■ **Document the results**.

Bruce Archer was Professor of Design Research at the Royal College of Art at the same time that I was a student there, and in 1965 the Council for Industrial Design published his famous paper entitled 'Systematic Method for Designers', which became highly influential. His preferred design method (1963) proposed feedback loops, which had never been propounded before. This was not a simple sequential process, but one that looped back on itself and provided feedback. The following chart explains:

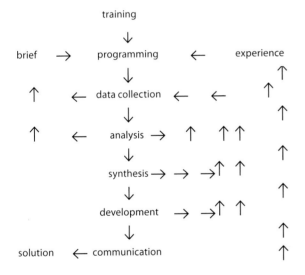

Christopher Jones[4], in his 1970 book, *Design Methods*, defined design method as follows:

> *The method is primarily a means of resolving a conflict that exists between logical analysis and creative thought. The difficulty is that the imagination does not work well unless it is free to alternate between all aspects of the problem, in any order, and at any time, whereas logical analysis breaks down if there is the least departure from a systematic step-by-step sequence. It follows that any design method must permit both kinds of thought to proceed together if any progress*

> *is to be made. Existing methods depend largely on keeping logic and imagination, problem and solution, apart only by an effort of will, and their failures can largely be ascribed to the difficulty of keeping both these processes going separately in the mind of one person. So systematic design is primarily a means of keeping logic and imagination separate by external rather than internal means.*

He concluded that the key parts of the process of designing were:

■ **Analysis** – Design requirements to performance specifications.

■ **Synthesis** – Solutions for each performance spec directed towards a single solution.

■ **Evaluation** – Alternative designs tested against performance specs.

Clive Edwards, in his book *Interior Design – A Critical Introduction* (2011), presents a linear design process which he states is in reality a complex, interwoven, reflexive and unpredictable process.

1. Formulation – inception and feasibility.
2. Programming – research and scoping.
3. Outline proposals – scheme, detail and product information.
4. Representation.
5. Presentation.
6. Movement and implementation.
7. Project supervision – site, completion.
8. Evaluation – reflection, feedback, POE (post-occupancy evaluation).

GENERATING 3D FORM AND COLOUR

USING SPACE, FORM, COLOUR AND TEXTURE

Having established a methodology for approaching design problems, it is now necessary to understand how form and colour is generated in our conceptual thinking. Geoffrey Broadbent[5] lists four ways that humankind has developed design systems. We have inherited each one of these methods, improving, modifying and tailoring them to suit current agendas.

■ Pragmatic method

Primeval man learned how to do things by a process of trial and error, finally arriving at the optimum solution for that moment in time.

■ Iconic method

As tribes and communities began to form, skills developed and the resultant way of life expressed was iconic in design. This would be in the form of self-adornment, decorating their habitat and any events of spiritual significance.

■ Analogic method

The beginnings of a system of design dependent on premeditation and drawing, based upon the adaptation of inherited methods of building.

■ Canonic method

The application of a geometric system over a grid whilst imposing order and authority and thus establishing feats of high intellectual endeavour.

In Chapter 4, we examined the growth of form from a dot to the first prime solid, the tetrahedron. The dot can exist in a design in the form of a decorative element or as the exposure of fixing devices such as screws, dowels and bolt heads; in the same way, lines can be expressed as joint lines between panels, tiles etc. Whatever shape is finally chosen, there is a conceptual understanding of the relative growth of 3D form in rectilinear mode: four members make a frame, a line of members make a plane, and a line of planes make a mass.

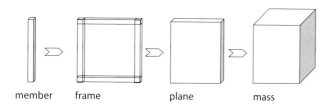

member   frame   plane   mass

In essence, we design structures that are perceived as being made up of these units of form, but with endless geometric variations and combinations. A member could be part of a skeletal structure made from wood, plastic or metal. A frame is made up for use in furniture or the construction of a partition. A plane can be a panel or the skin part of a structure, and mass represents a volumetric shape of sufficient depth such as a storage unit, plinth or building structure.

Here is the same series, but within a simple curve mode. The cubic mass form becomes a cylinder.

Here is another viewpoint, which is endorsing traditions established over centuries but with stronger reference to the organic nature of 'fractal' relationships of form:

> *All the folk architecture built by people around the world tends to have fractal properties. I believe that our mind is 'hard-wired' to construct things in a certain way, so inevitably we build fractal structures. Most great creations of humankind go far beyond strictly necessary structure; we feel a need to generate certain types of forms and geometrical interrelationships. Only when influenced by some style do we depart from what comes naturally to us.*
>
> Nikos A. Salingaros, *Fractals in the New Architecture*

The diagram below illustrates how a mathematical fractal is generated (from Salingaros). It emphasises the growth of form and how the parts organically relate to the whole (gestalt).

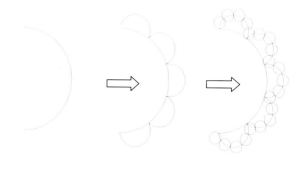

COLOUR

Colour exists in the materials used, as well as in light effects (see Chapter 2, p.35). This book is not intended to dwell long on the subject of colour, as many references are available elsewhere, but I would like to outline how the *concept* of colour should be approached. Colour is one of the eight concepts listed in Chapter 2 (see p.55), that need to be formulated for a total interior design scheme to be implemented. The following guide details those topics which influence decisions on colour choice and specification.

- A single colour can play a *dominant* role.

- Colour may appear as a *blend* with other colours.

- The *location* of a colour has to be determined.

- You must estimate the *proportion* (quantity) of a colour in relation to other colour sources.

- You must decide on the *shape* that the colour will occupy.

- You must decide on the choice of material, to satisfy colour choice.

- You must decide on the degree of reflectivity (if relevant) – matt or gloss.

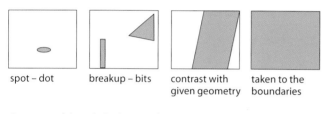

spot – dot   breakup – bits   contrast with   taken to the
                                            given geometry   boundaries

Sequence of thought in the *growth* or apportionment of colour

The above considerations are not always adhered to in current practice. For example, the choice of material can override a colour choice because the designer has a penchant for a particular material. The designer therefore avoids the task of democratic decision-making by making the selection of material an easier route to the design.

AXES AND FORCES

The axis is a line of direction leading to an end.

Le Corbusier

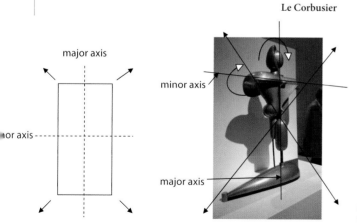

major axis

minor axis

or axis

major axis

Figure 150. Oskar Schlemmer, *Abstract Figure*, 1923. Sculpture in the round. Getty Images.

An analysis of Oskar Schlemmer's sculpture reveals forces that sum up human posture and movement. *Abstract Figure* was based upon his studies of dance when he taught at the Bauhaus. The major axis is the predominant one, upon which everything else hangs. When designing anything in 3D, the structural rationale will consist of an axis and directional forces, as a way of exercising control over the form. We have learned from nature about the structure of form, and the axes and forces inherent within it. Whatever shape a structure takes, the axes will follow that shape.

Figure 151 a,b,c,d. Growth of form. The tree is perceived as a complete structure, from trunk to branch, twig and leaf. Photos by author.

When undertaking the planning and designing of interiors, it is essential that this organic sense of 'wholeness' and structure permeates the design process. In adopting this approach there is no predictive influence over the outcome in terms of style, character or fashion. It is merely an aid to the design process in terms of democratic control, not dictatorship.

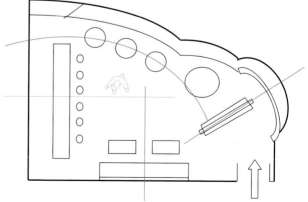

Café plan showing four main axes (in red; usually centre lines), for working out a planning concept. They are the centre lines of major geometric components. This plan will contain many more factors that give it shape and form: see the remaining seven design concepts listed in Chapter 2 (see p.55).

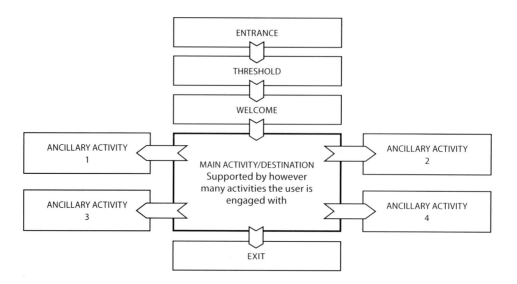

INTERIOR SPATIAL SEQUENCE

The simplified diagram above can be applied to any building but could expand to allow for more complex space-use areas. It shows the interior spatial sequence that people encounter when they enter a building, plus circulation links.

If it was the basis for an office then the visitor would move from the entrance to the welcome/reception area, to the main activity/conference room, to areas for ancillary activities such as refreshment, and to toilets or offices. The hierarchical sequence here does not equate to the size of each space but is merely ranked in terms of priority usage. Hence the main activity is shown to be of primary importance by the larger size box. The exit could be the same as the entrance. Upon entering a space, decisions have to be made as to one's direction, distance of travel and orientation.

It is worth remembering that while designers are working in 2D drawing mode, they are always *thinking* in 3D. Throughout the duration of the design process, they are always mentally visualising the spaces they are designing in various stages of development, from the original given building (emptiness), to the gradual filling up with contents.

DRAWING MECHANICS

All design work is formulated into communicative drawings that describe the project, to be presented to a client so that he or she can see how the interior will look when finished. There are also more technical drawings produced for the building contractor, which describe and specify how the interior is to be built. The mechanics of producing these drawings is described in simple terms as a means of clarification.

THE PLAN

The plan is not a view of an interior: it is a floor, a 2D image of a 3D space, a cross-section usually at around 1400 mm (55 in.) from floor level. As Corbusier said, 'The plan is the generator'. It is usually the starting point in any design project. For a client assessing the appropriateness of a building, it is the plan that quantifies the usage and cost per square metre, not the elevations or any calculations of volume.

Our experience of a building is always based on the many 3D views we collect by walking around it. We never see it in plan form, so why don't we design in 3D straightaway? The answer is that our 3D views inform us of the overall size and impact of a space, but we cannot easily distinguish distances or measurement between the objects and other components of the structure. We need the plan because it is a *measured* record of the building to a *scale* that enables decisions to be made on the placement of objects and components *relative to each other*.

THE ELEVATION

It is interesting to note that in so many cases, the project plan communicates the basic energy and spirit of a design, whereas the elevations fall flat by comparison. Why is this, when we cannot visually see the plan of a completed project physically in the space? Why are elevations not as interesting on a set of drawings when they are the main focus of our attention by being face to face when we enter an interior? It is because the drawings delineate the elevations with a border (floor, adjacent walls and ceiling) and subsequently flatten the reality of their being. When we enter a space we do not read walls as 'elevations' because we are consumed by the 3D experience. We do not walk into an interior and comment 'what lovely elevations'. The term 'elevation' is mainly consigned to drawing terminology.

These drawn elevations are 2D representations of 2D surfaces, with some element of 3D-ness in terms of possible relief work or built-in fixtures. Walls appear in the planning (in terms of thickness), as does furniture. Walls are also seen in elevation drawings (in terms of surface), but loose furniture is not, because it is not fixed to the wall (except on sections through a space, whereby the furniture is shown *in front of* the wall). We are so used to walls being designed as vertical elements, from their plan position, that they do not have the substance or leading generative power that a plan wall has. This is because the act of planning involves the placement of walls as a cutaway section (a plan is a horizontal slice through vertical structures). Elevations are not planned in the same way. Perhaps this is why they often shout out for some decorative treatment to relieve the boredom. The recent advance of more organic curved solutions, through the might of computer-aided design, will help to give more substance to the elevation because of the holistic and integrated 3D nature of the design. (See Zaha Hadid's rationale in Chapter 6, p.112.)

THE 3D VIEWS

The perspective view is the final result that designers are aiming for, because this view represents how the user experiences the interior. Clients are able to 'read' and understand these drawings more so than plans, sections and elevations, and therefore these drawings ultimately sell the scheme. The axonometric view is favoured by designers because of the speed with which it can be drawn up with the given information of plans and elevations. The hand-drawn perspective requires a lengthy setting-up process; CAD animation can provide a 'walk-through' of the 3D views and assists greatly in communication.

The next step in the process is to establish a grid on which to work and plan out the above drawings of the design.

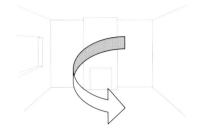

3D view – perspective
What we see and interact with but cannot measure

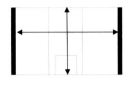

Elevation
What we measure and apply as being static

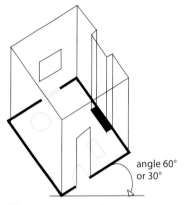

angle 60° or 30°

3D view – axonometric
Combination of measured plan and elevations together

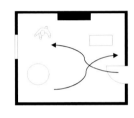

Plan
What we measure and position to allow for movement

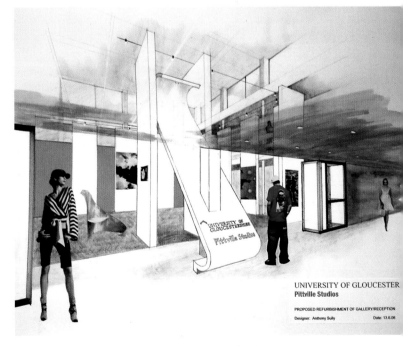

UNIVERSITY OF GLOUCESTER
Pittville Studios

PROPOSED REFURBISHMENT OF GALLERY/RECEPTION
Designer: Anthony Sully   Date: 13.6.08

Figure 152. Hand-drawn perspective. Drawing by the author.

GRIDS

THE EARTH'S GRID

Geometers and builders of ancient civilisations laid out measured grids to help work out sizes and divide areas of land for development. The world's latitude and longitude system, developed by the Portuguese navigational explorers in the 16th century, is an example of a grid system applied to a near-spherical Earth. Maps are produced with longitude and latitude references that enable places to be located. My research reveals several people who seem to be responsible for discovering this mapping system: Hipparchus (190–120 BC) the Greek astronomer, who devised a method of locating geographical positions by means of latitudes and longitudes, the Roman scholar Claudius Ptolemaeus (AD 90–170), and the Indian Aryabhata (around AD 500), who presented a mathematical system that took the Earth to spin on its axis, which was through the North and South Poles. This set the basis for the development of longitudinal circles or meridians, 111 km (69 miles) apart at the Equator, that pass repeatedly through these poles. The 0° line of latitude is defined by the Earth's Equator, a characteristic definable by astronomical observation and midway between the poles.

It is fascinating to know that if you start your journey from a point on the Equator, the maximum length of travel going north (the same applies to going south) is only a quadrant of the longitude meridian (if you keep going past the North Pole, you then continue going south), whereas from the same point going east or west, you travel endlessly east or endlessly west. From naval charts to the points on a compass, north, south, east and west became common directional references. They have been described as 'the four corners of the Earth'. Why, when the Earth is spherical? Even the Flat Earth Society never dictated that the Earth was square. We accept that the four corners refer to the compass directions, rather than actually pointing to a corner.

One of the rare indications of compass points in the landscape is provided by the weathervane, also known as a weathercock. The design of the weathervane is a figure mounted on an upright rod atop an arrow. The arrow and the figure are set above the fixed direction indicators for north, south, east and west. As the wind blows, the figure is free to spin around the rod and point in the direction of the wind's path. Weathervanes have existed for thousands of years and were once very important to farmers in particular. The need for

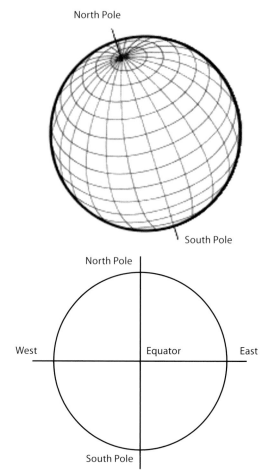

LONGITUDE
- Each circle (meridian) is usually measured at 5º or 10º from the Earth's centre (east–west axis), but the maximum could be 360º.
- Each meridian passes through two points (poles).
- Each meridian is the same diameter.
- On any meridian, the maximum length of travel north or south is always for only half the diameter of the Earth.
- Lines of longitude are described as vertical lines – why? Surely it depends on which way you view the Earth.

LATITUDE
- Each circle is usually measured at 5º or 10º from the Earth's centre (north–south axis), but the maximum could be 181º.
- All circles are concentric and equally spaced, with diminishing radii as they reach each pole.
- On any circle, if you set off east or west from a given point, you can travel for the complete diameter of that circle continuously.
- There is no east or west point or pole.

GRID
- Lines of longitude and latitude cross to create a series of diminishing trapeziums (more or less) from the Equator, as can be seen in the above illustration of the globe.

Figure 153. Weathervane at Lord's Cricket Ground, London, 1926. Reproduced with the kind permission of Marylebone Cricket Club.

Grid on squared base

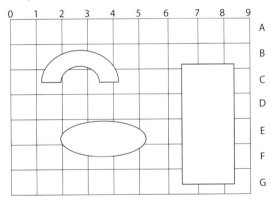

Other grid examples

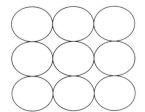 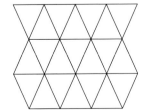

weathervanes has been superseded by the advanced weather forecasts that are now broadcast in the media.

ARCHITECTURAL GRID

An architectural grid is a set of coordinates spaced apart on a modular basis to suit building components, such as a grid of 500 mm or 600 mm in both directions. As with mapping, a grid enables the location of objects to be planned in relation to each other by referring to the coordinates. As seen in Albarn's work in Chapter 5 (see p.95), the designer uses the grid to try out many planning variations before the optimum solution is found. A grid can vary from being drawn on a squared base to any other geometric pattern that suits the particular project in hand.

DESIGN CONCEPT DEVELOPMENT

We will only examine three of the eight minor design concepts, as listed in Chapter 2 (see p.55), as the remaining ones are covered under 'Design Elements' (see earlier in the same chapter) in terms of defining what they are. Those discussed here are: planning, circulation and construction.

PLANNING CONCEPT

Planning is the act of producing a 2D drawing of a 3D space. This can be supported by 3D sketches and a working model. To have full control over the complete 3D design solution, the designer should imagine the viewpoint from every possible position a person can stand in within an interior. These viewpoints should be based on a 360° x 360° rotation, so that the final design can be a confirmation of every possible view.

The illustration overleaf shows the number of rotating viewpoints that would be manageable. In practice, designs can be based on just a few views that are considered the main selling points to the client, or they are the most popular views to be had. How many times has the experience of a much-praised interior been damaged by a neglected minor view? This type of final solution will not, therefore, realise its full potential.

There are several stages in the planning process, which relate to the possession of certain information and data, as well as the recognition that not all decisions can

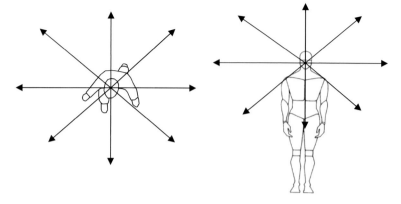

be made at once. The nine essential ingredients of the planning mix are as follows:

■ **Areas**: Apportionment of the right amount of space for the proposed activity to take place.

■ **Human circulation**: Working flow patterns of the directional movement of people.

■ **Enclosing structures 1**: Responding to the given building form and openings – primary structure. These are usually immovable load-bearing structures.

■ **Enclosing structures 2**: Manipulating and shaping secondary structures. These are usually not load-bearing and a wide variety of lighter-weight materials are used.

■ **Interconnecting spaces**: These are mainly circulatory.

■ **Positioning of support/storage/display elements**: Manipulating and shaping these.

■ **Allowance for mobile furniture elements**: Optional positioning.

■ **Lighting**: Location of electrical operational outlets and light source.

■ **Building services**: Location of cabling and trunking and outlet placement.

All of the above will be carried out to the satisfaction of the client and according to the image and concept to be aimed for, encompassing expression, meaning and the identity of the client. It will be controlled by a geometric order using proportion, a methodology of approach, and with reference to the intended technological concept of construction and materials.

In working from a client's brief, the first action is usually planning (see Chapter 1, p.19, 'What does an interior designer do?'). The brief will list all the major activities that take place that define a particular space, the number of people performing detailed activities,

and the requirements of these activities. In sketching early planning ideas, an activity is represented by a circle (bubble). Together with the other activities that are adjacent to each other, a series of bubble diagrams are drawn up simply to establish the spatial relationships of these activities. This is done in isolation from the building's plans first of all, before testing how they fit into the building. For example, stage one is as follows:

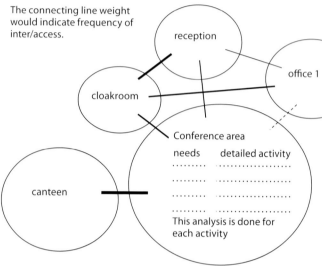

Having analysed the needs and requirements of each activity and established approximate spatial relationships, the next task is to ensure that they coexist with each other so that the design ingredients of space, form, colour, texture, materials and lighting are harmoniously connected. Stage two is as follows:

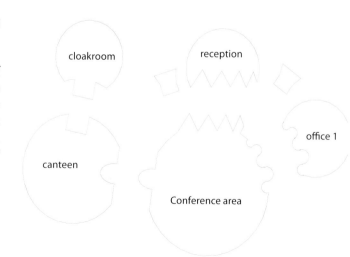

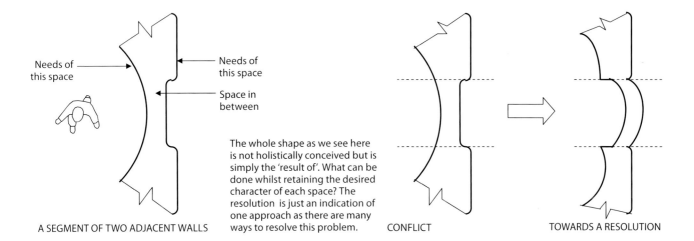

Needs of this space

Needs of this space

Space in between

The whole shape as we see here is not holistically conceived but is simply the 'result of'. What can be done whilst retaining the desired character of each space? The resolution is just an indication of one approach as there are many ways to resolve this problem.

A SEGMENT OF TWO ADJACENT WALLS

CONFLICT

TOWARDS A RESOLUTION

The third stage will be the fitting of all this into the building form and making concessional alterations along the way. The diagram opposite is designed to illustrate this conceptually, so that each space takes on a shape and character that reflects the activity and character of that space. (Remember that planning is one of eight concepts that have to be established before the total design becomes an entity.) They should then each fit into their respective adjacent spaces to demonstrate compatibility and design linkages, rather than each space being designed separately as a disassociated element. If there is a loose connection between one space and another (which damages the original concept of the design), then that part of the design demands modification as illustrated in the sketches above.

Through a progression of readjustment and concentrated unification, a series of profiles can be arrived at. Bringing in other factors such as construction, which contribute to the overall design concept, will assist with resolving problems. The process of designing sometimes involves compromise if there are two opposing forces at work (see diagram above). Also see *Designing Interiors*.[6] Such issues of resolution between two major parts of a design come under the heading of 'duality'. We are confronted by duality problems throughout the design field, examples being tabletop/leg supports, window frame/glass, light/shade, and so on.

CIRCULATION CONCEPT

The thread that links all spaces together is human circulation. When a person begins the journey around a building, various decisions have to be made such as whether to go left, right, up, down or straight ahead. The design of the space must help the person make these decisions. These decisions recur at every point of exit/entry in each space.

Horizontal circulation

There are three means whereby people move around a building from space to space, sometimes via narrow spaces called corridors (these spaces must be adjusted to respond to numbers of people):

1. A prescribed route within a space.
2. An undefined route through a space.
3. A corridor with access to minor spaces off it.

People walk to a destination with purposeful strides, or they walk at a leisurely pace whilst viewing a display of some kind, or they walk whilst performing a job-related

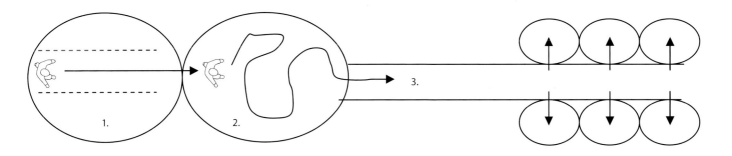

Figure 154. Multi-directional circulation. Photo by author.

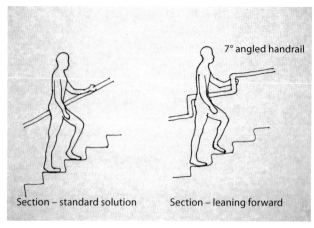

Section – standard solution   Section – leaning forward

Figure 155. Ascending a staircase.

Figure 156. Descending a staircase. Sketches by the author.

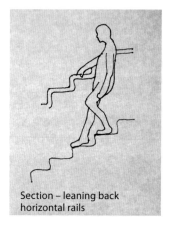

Section – leaning back horizontal rails

task. The recommended circulation width is 800 mm (31½ in.) for one person or 1,200 mm (47¼ in.) for two people.

There are also general circulation areas on concourses and transport-associated buildings where the direction of travel is multifarious.

Vertical circulation

The current means at our disposal for vertical circulation are fixed stairs, moving stairs and elevators. Let us consider them in turn.

Fixed stairs

When climbing a staircase, the human body is leaning forward and uses the handrail for additional assistance to pull the body up the stairs – great effort is required. When descending a staircase, the body does not assume the same posture but instead is either upright or leans slightly backwards to safeguard against falling forwards. Less effort is required, but it is a rather more dangerous situation nevertheless: many people fall down stairs. As the ergonomic posture, energy expended and the feelings of the person are very different in both cases, it does suggest that perhaps there ought to be either two staircases (one for going up, the other for going down) or that a single stair should be divided into two halves to cater for these two conditions.

The sketch on the left of Figure 155 shows the standard staircase plus a handrail. The sketch on the right shows a proposed adaptation. Figure 156 is intended to address the earlier observations. There doesn't need to be any difference with regard to the treads and risers, as they suit both conditions. For the sake of this exercise, we have concentrated on the handrail. A handrail of some kind is necessary, not only to satisfy regulations, but to provide support. Handrails can differ in design depending upon the structural surround and balustrading, if any. We shall look at a tubular rail as an example.

Ascending: To secure good leverage, a suggestion is an angled upright almost parallel to the climber for the hand grip, connected by sloping rails. These are calculated to occur every other tread, because the climber releases the hand at the moment the next upright appears.

Descending: The present angled handrail, as shown in the first sketch, is ergonomically uncomfortable because the hand and wrist are bent too far forwards. Hence the suggestion of a horizontal grip in Figure 156, or this could be angled upwards even more (if it suited the designer's aims), as it would be easier to hold than the standard arrangement. The grips are connected by vertical tubes and these are designed to occur at every tread, because a more regular hold may be required.

The next stage in this process (not done here) is to compare both suggestions and see what common rationale can be applied to make the design more economically viable and visually acceptable.

These ideas would present themselves to a designer because of his or her own observations of usage. This therefore illustrates how a designer should work by making observations, then trying and testing any solutions that emerge.

Moving stairs

Escalators and passenger conveyors take the standard stair profile and handrail, and provide exactly the same design for ascending as well as descending, the difference being that one side moves up whilst the other moves down. The operators can also reverse the motion depending upon need, or have them both moving in the same direction. The stairs can also be locked in a stationary mode if circumstances require it. There does not seem to be a maximum length of travel, but a handling capacity of 1,600 people in 30 minutes per 600 mm of step width is stated in the *AJ Metric Handbook*.

Elevators

The design of elevators has, over the years, gone from being a hidden sliding box that was not expressed in the building form, to transparent capsules achieving futuristic status. The hidden box, which is still specified today, does make people feel uncomfortable when they are thrust together with people they do not know, especially in a small, confined space. Many people prefer to use fixed stairs because of this. The old department stores and hotels had lift operators who stayed in the lift for the duration of their working hours, making conversation and announcements, and generally making the passengers feel at ease. As a boy, I was intrigued by their dominant stance, as though they were the captain of a ship, and you felt safe in their hands. They would use some complicated wheel and lever to control the lift, and they also opened the doors manually to allow people on and off.

Modern transparent capsules, despite looking more dangerous, are less claustrophobic, no matter what size they are, as well as being visually entertaining to both the travellers and spectators. The only drawback is that some travellers suffer from vertigo and will not travel on them.

CONSTRUCTION CONCEPT

We are assuming that the structure of the building either exists or is being designed by others, so that we can carry out the design and planning of the interior according to the type of installation required (see Chapter 2, 'Environment', p.30). In my teaching experience, students always assume that construction is worked out *after* the whole design has been completed, and that working drawings are something to be done *at the end of a project*. Let me correct this impression by asserting that the act of designing is first *thinking* about all aspects of the interior from plan forms to 3D forms, to materials, colours, furnishings and so on. The next stage is to put those thoughts into some sort of *drawing*, which will begin the process of change, amendment and articulation. The way that these concepts come to fruition is dependent upon how the interior is to be built and put together. The details of walls, partitions, ceilings, doors, built-in joinery and other purpose-made artefacts need to be related to each other in a binding, *constructional* way. Also, the emotional charge put into the planning by the designer is very strongly linked with construction and materials. If you look at the work of Frank Lloyd Wright and Arne Jacobsen,[7] the spirit of their buildings and internal spaces is echoed in the details. They both designed everything, right down to the cutlery.

The procedure of forming this concept is by the following:

- Determine the structural means necessary – columns, frame, panels.

- Determine the form and shape of structures.

- Determine heat and acoustic properties.

- Determine degrees of transparency, if relevant.

- Choose appropriate material – timber, metal, plastics, concrete etc. Choice of material is governed by the limitations of that material, also by the type of connections/fixings/installation method.

- Ensure that the final choice conforms to the intended visual qualities of the interior.

The process is not linear, as the designer will always loop back to modify an earlier decision.

The forms we design are fixed to walls, or wedged between ceiling and floor, or floorstanding, or suspended from the ceiling. The following analysis focuses on the creation of the forms alone.

HOW DO THINGS COME TOGETHER?

This book is not intended to go into any depth about fastenings and fixings, as that is a whole subject in itself, but it is important to put forward the conceptual thinking necessary to establish the desired principle of connection, one that would conform in spirit to the grand concept and scheme of the whole interior, and satisfy the goals of expression. It uses the example of the junctions of members (which make up frames) and panels.

It is important to note that the examples below are suggested as the first basic thoughts of a construction principle, which then becomes more complex when considering variety of shape and the constraints of certain materials.

MEMBER TO MEMBER

END TO END	END TO END
meeting	gap meeting
END TO END	FACE TO FACE
overlap	crossover

PANEL TO PANEL

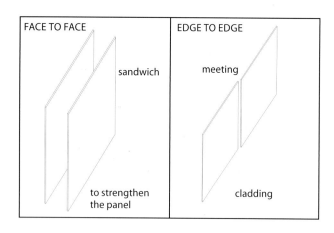

FACE TO FACE — sandwich — to strengthen the panel

EDGE TO EDGE — meeting — cladding

PANEL TO PANEL

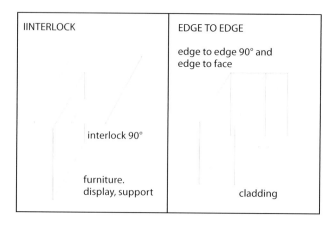

IINTERLOCK — interlock 90° — furniture. display, support

EDGE TO EDGE — edge to edge 90° and edge to face — cladding

PANEL TO MEMBER

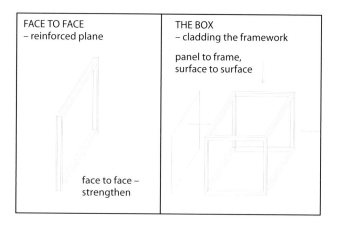

FACE TO FACE – reinforced plane — face to face – strengthen

THE BOX – cladding the framework — panel to frame, surface to surface

SOME EXAMPLES FROM INDUSTRY

METAL FRAMING: MEMBER TO MEMBER

The steel tubing system has a variety of connectors such as elbow fittings for joining two tubes at 90°, as well as other angles. Also, the system has plates for fixing the tubing to the building structure.

TIMBER FRAMING: MEMBER TO MEMBER WITH PLANE CLADDING

The softwood framework in the conversion of Glendower Chapel (Figures 159 and 160) was designed to receive veneered MDF board cladding (seen in Figure 160). Complex angled sections met in the corner. Note the curved framing for receiving the curved cladding.

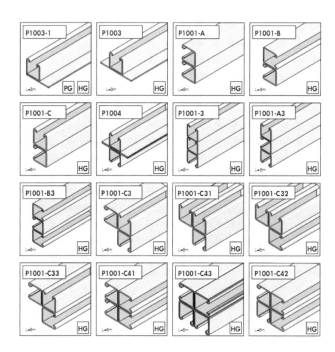

Figure 157. *Above.* Unistrut – a popular, strong, multi-use steel channel section that is used for all kinds of fixings of building services, lighting and machinery. The firm also makes slotted angle and telescopic tubing.

Figure 158. *Right.* Kee Klamp fittings. Popular steel tube framework for multipurpose use. Courtesy of Kee Safety International, 2011.

Figure 158a. *Below.* Kee Klamp used as overhead structure in a bar. Courtesy of Kee Safety International, 2011.

Figures 159 and 160. *Below.* Glendower House – chapel conversion, 2002. Designer: Anthony Sully. Architect: Graham Frecknall. Photos by author.

Contractor's temporary floor (removed later)

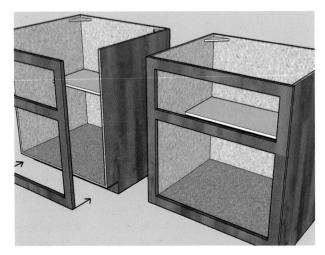

Figure 161. Cupboard carcass using chipboard panels. Courtesy of www.Home-style-choices.com.

TIMBER PANEL CONSTRUCTION: PLANE TO PLANE

Figure 161 shows a cupboard carcass made entirely of panels. The face panels have had large sections removed so as to create a 'framed' element.

GLOSSARY OF DESCRIPTIVE TERMS

As a designer, it is so important to have a good command of vocabulary in order to describe what you are doing, as well as to describe the qualities of the finished solution. The following list is indicative but by no means exhaustive.

Adjacency: Spaces or objects near to one another.

Balance: Described to ensure evenness in the design.

Corner: Usually defined by walls at 90° to each other.

Directional: The forces mentioned earlier as well as under 'Element 9: Information' in Chapter 2 (see p.53).

Emphasis: Used to describe a dominant feature or leading planning strategy.

Flowing: Used to describe the organic liquid quality of a design.

Harmony: Describes peaceful coexistence of ingredients.

Hierarchy: Explaining the order of things.

Holistic: Being of one whole.

Integral: Part of the design.

Labyrinth: Complex series of spaces.

Layers: Finishes in one layer, furnishing in another, followed by lighting, etc.

Overlap: By spaces, activities or functions.

Perimeter: The edge or contour of a plan.

Rhythm: The heartbeat of a design; what bounces off the eye.

Scale: The size of elements in relationship to each other.

Sequence: The journey through a building is a series of sequential experiences.

Symmetry: Evident in nature and classical architecture, but asymmetry (the opposite) also has its place.

Wedge: An area or form between two other areas or forms.

Unity: A unified design – complete.

Here is an extract from John Outram's website (www.johnoutram.com) which is beautifully descriptive:

> *In JOA's buildings, classical ideas are reinterpreted in a completely new way. The logs of the raft are often expressed above the capitals. They are still dripping wet, the swirls reminding us of the chaotic waters of the flood. Above the logs is placed a green deck or table upon which the ark rides, and where people can actually 'live'. As the waters of the flood receded, it eroded the mountain on which the ark had come to rest into the river valley, revealing in the process the orderly hypostyle of columns. This erosion is evident in the geological striations expressed on the columns.*

BUILDING ANALYSIS

Apart from carrying out a survey of the building that houses the interior to be designed, an analysis should be made of its geometry, condition and character before any application of design ideas take place. This includes relevant external landscaping elements.

In the Glendower House conversion, note that the main axis of the chapel runs through the entrance door to where the altar used to be. My design, as shown in the Appendix (see p.200), follows the 45° axis as a strong determinant, as well as the radiating circles from the columns, to form niches. The plan of Glendower House[8] shows the main geometric forces that are suggested by the building's structural layout. These forces are suggested by walls, window and door openings, as well as the seven cast-iron columns. The columns are circular in section and therefore suggest waves of concentric circles emanating from their centres. The same analysis must be done in section and elevation in order to have a comprehensive understanding of the building.

The building's history and *context*, and the way that it has been used, all add up to the spirit of the place – important sensitive data that feeds into the design process. The drawing of repeated horizontal, vertical and diagonal lines in combination with the concentric circles helps to provide a built-in grid that reflects the spirit of the building and which can help with making positional design decisions with regard to the new structural insertions. These do not have to dictate what follows, as the designer can introduce other influences and inspiration to contradict this data; if that is done, it is done *relative* to, and as a *reaction* to, given circumstances.

Figure 162. *Right.* Computational Engineering Faculty, Martell Hall of Duncan Hall, Rice University, Houston, Texas. Architect: John Outram, 1997.

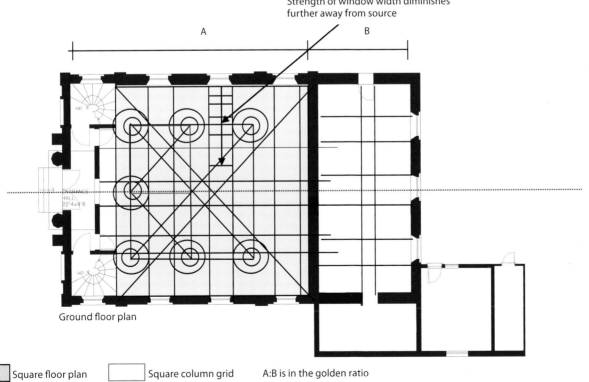

Strength of window width diminishes further away from source

A   B

Ground floor plan

Square floor plan   Square column grid   A:B is in the golden ratio

Figure 163. Plan for Glendower House, chapel conversion, 2002. Designer: Anthony Sully. Architect: Graham Frecknall.

MECHANICS OF OPERATION

Before we examine the detailed design factors of space usage (see p.142), we need to understand the possible actions that allow us to achieve mobility, flexibility and adjustability. Buildings are designed as static structures but there are many component parts and operational devices that are moveable for a variety of reasons, and we need to analyse these movements ergonomically.

The formation of the hand varies with each action. The horizontal pull could also be a push, and in some instances a doubling-up of actions can be applied. For example, the turning of a door handle as a first action will also result in the door being pushed with the same grip for the second action, even though the handle was primarily designed for the hand to turn it, not push it. The slide can demand a variety of hand postures, depending upon the construction of the doors. This illustration shows sliding and folding doors. The following terms are commonly in use:

■ **Push**: Door plate, mobile furniture, screen.

■ **Pull (horizontal)**: Door handle, mobile furniture, screen.

■ **Press**: Bell, lift controls, electronic devices.

■ **Lift**: Horizontal shutters, hinged flap/door to furniture.

■ **Twist**: Shower/tap control, electronic knobs, furniture mechanisms, locks.

■ **Pull (vertical)**: Cord, cable, chain to operate a variety of functions.

■ **Turn**: Lever handle to doors, plumbing device, electric power.

■ **Slide**: Doors to walls, doors to furniture, furniture, partitions.

PROPORTIONAL CONSIDERATIONS

A judgement has to be made, which follows the overall design concept, about the sizes and shapes of all those interior elements that coexist – enclosure, floor level, storage/display, and support. It is about height versus width, which involves scale. We begin by looking at the space occupied by people sitting and standing in order to establish dimensional space occupation.

Figure 164. Mechanics of operation. Photos: author.

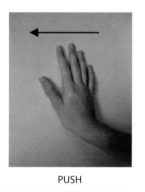

PUSH

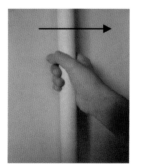

PULL horizontal

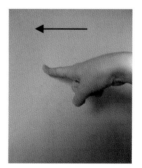

PRESS

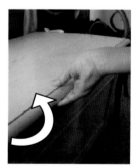

LIFT

TWIST

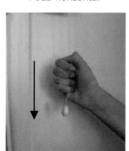

PULL – vertical

TURN

SLIDE

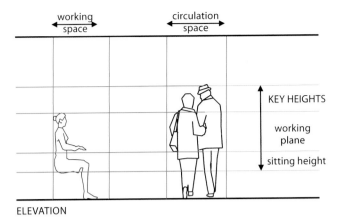

ELEVATION

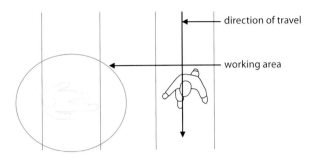

PLAN

In terms of the 3D view of the interior, what are the directional options available to us? The circle and square are fairly static and do not have a prioritised directional emphasis. The rectangle will either emphasise the horizontal or the vertical:

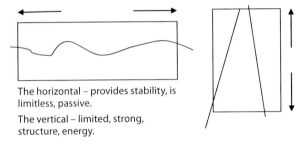

The horizontal – provides stability, is limitless, passive.

The vertical – limited, strong, structure, energy.

Whilst accepting varied shapes relating to whatever the design contains, the horizontal or vertical can still be emphasised. The perspective view (see diagram below) can enable a designer to realise that the above elevational effects can combine to produce something else. All surfaces have two directional qualities bound by their edges. Space has a flowing quality. When you see all these forces at play, the realisation is that the proportional considerations of each surface become interrelated, together with the flow of space, to produce a well-balanced scheme.

WHAT GOVERNS THE CREATION OF A LINE IN THE DESIGN?

A design consists of a combination of 3D forms and surfaces. These are delineated by lines when drawing, but what is actually being drawn in linear terms?

- The edge of a 3D object such as a wall/screen division or furniture.

- Break-up of a surface within own material or change of material/structure (doors, windows).

- Applied markings.

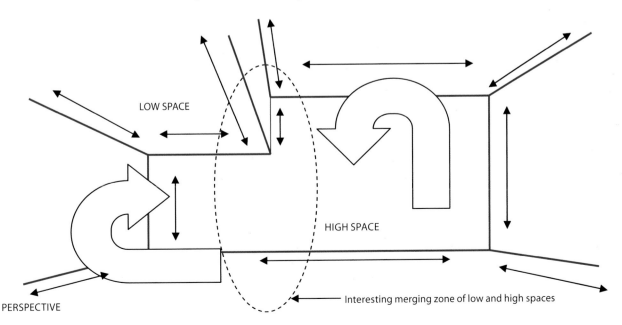

PERSPECTIVE

HOW DOES FORM GROW FROM THE GROUND PLANE?

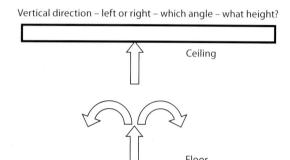

Vertical direction – left or right – which angle – what height?

Ceiling

Floor

Designers should think of form growing as something akin to planting a seed in the ground. As explained earlier in this chapter, in the section 'Generating 3D form and colour', every thought and action has a beginning. Every line starts as a dot before it is extended into a line. The earth's gravitational pull dictates all matter. It begins on a ground plane and we build upwards. So a designer's thought processes should have such a beginning in preparation of the numerous imported forms and products such as proprietary wall systems and furniture, which can stifle the possibility of any creative solution being realised.

ENTRANCES AND EXITS

HOW DO WE MOVE THROUGH WALLS?

Walls surround our interior spaces. Doorways and openings provide a means of access from one space to another. Not enough thought is given by designers to these points of transition. Let us now examine the opening, the access facility, and the doorway territory.

> *How concrete everything becomes in the world of the spirit when an object, a mere door, can give images of hesitation, temptation, desire, security, welcome and respect. If one were to give an account of all the doors one has closed and opened, of all the doors one would like to re-open, one would have to tell the story of one's entire life.*[9]
>
> Gaston Bachelard

DESIGN CONSIDERATIONS

Here is a list of basic considerations that a designer should attend to. There will be further issues to resolve depending upon specific uses.

■ **Opening**: Decide on the width, height, shape in elevation – proportional considerations.

■ **Depth**: Determined by surrounding structure on plan.

■ **Facility for opening/closing**: What sort of mechanism and action? Hinged, sliding, revolving, folding.

■ **Purpose of opening**: What are the functions of the spaces either side?

■ **Density of division**: What degree of separation of sound and vision?

■ **Door**: Is it designed as part of the wall or as a separately expressed element?

■ **Moving walls**: A whole wall can move to create the desired opening.

THE OPENING

A deeper thickness to the wall makes it become a corridor-type space.

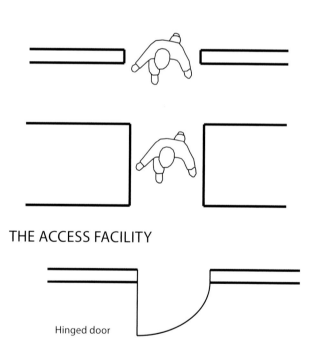

THE ACCESS FACILITY

Hinged door

Pocket door

Sliding door on the outside
Concealed (pocket door in thickness of wall)

The hinged door is the most common type of door action that we are used to. This door is, however, an annoying and unwanted appendage when opened, as it disturbs the space by being intrusive. It is only at rest when it is in the closed position. The sliding door is an attempt to reduce spatial disturbance by achieving a flat presence parallel with the wall. The pocket door goes one better by concealing the door altogether, offering no clues as to its existence.

Because of this comparison and a desire to rectify the intrusion of a normal hinged door, a possible design approach, which warrants some study, could be to offer the hinged door a swing of 180º so that it fits into a recess, against the wall, that is framed in the same manner as the door is framed.

Figure 165. Large steel gate to shopping centre, semi-concealed against the wall. Photo by author.

The illustration below shows a basic idea of how a hinged door can be opened into a recess, by changing from a flapped hinge to a pivot mechanism allowing a full 180º rotation into the same line as original position. The wall has radiussed vertical pilasters forming a modular panelled appearance. Thus when the door is open and housed into the recess it becomes lost within the wall elevation. The elevation is designed as a repeated module of this door solution.

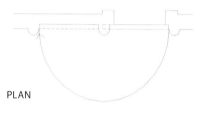

PLAN

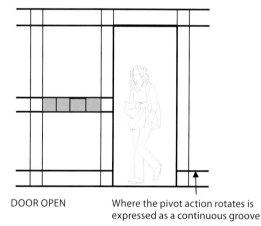

DOOR OPEN   Where the pivot action rotates is
                    expressed as a continuous groove

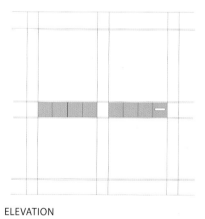

ELEVATION

Door handle is shown on a metal plate
which is continued in repeat as a frieze.

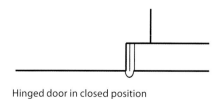

Hinged door in closed position

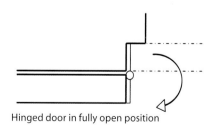

Hinged door in fully open position

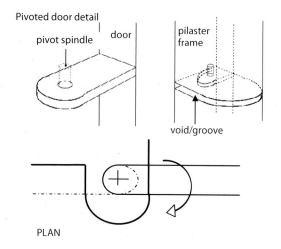

Pivoted door detail

pivot spindle   door

pilaster frame

void/groove

PLAN

Pivoted door detail

There would be three pivot plates per door, and they would rotate on the pivot spindle in the void within the pilaster frame.

DOORWAY TERRITORY

If we examine a door in a partition wall leading into a destination area, the territory space is divided into two parts and defined as the outside zone and the inside zone:

In the solution (below) a neutral zone is created, which is territory shared equally by both sides of the

Outside zone – approachable from 180° direction. Visitor has perhaps travelled further than inside person. High expectation of destination activity. Leaving person has mission accomplished. Closing the door on leaving – freedom.

Inside zone – Greater area of territory. Accessibility reduced by doorswing intrusion. A greeting awaits – welcome. Closing the door on entering – confinement. Visitor has less distance to travel.

How can we improve on this imbalance if a hinged door is the preferred choice?

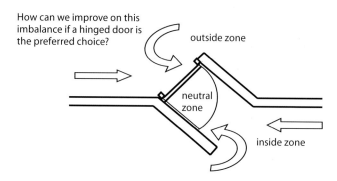

outside zone

neutral zone

inside zone

partition. The door does not impinge on the space as it opens into the neutral zone. The sacrifice of some space in the outside zone is made, but this can be accepted as an expression of the door location more positively, also relieving the monotony of a straight wall. Upon entering the inside zone, the neutral zone acts as a gentle introduction into the space.

GENERIC SPACE-USE TYPES

There are five main types of space as defined by human posture, not the type of interior, as follows:

■ **Circulatory space:** Covers walking (see 'Design concepts', p.55).

■ **Standing space:** Motionless stance.

■ **Seating space:** Restful repose.

■ **Workspace:** Can be any of the above plus the performing of a particular task.

■ **Lying-down area:** Rest or relaxation.

Designers need to consider the postural demands of the human form as part of the assessment of needs for making design decisions.

STANDING SPACES

As mentioned in Chapter 2 (see p.37), the ground plane, upon which people stand and walk, is always level and there can be many levels within a building. The ceiling plane, however, has no constraints imposed upon it except that it should be of sufficient height from floor level for the appropriate human activity to take place. It therefore has more free scope in its form than walls and floors do.

Standing is a passive activity (apart from performing a task) that can involve:

■ **Waiting** – to meet someone, for a train, for delivery of something, or for a toilet to become vacant.

■ **Queuing** – for refreshment, for tickets, for transport or for service.

■ **Viewing** – an exhibition, a gallery, a concert, a sporting or leisure event, or a retail display.

Figure 166. Shopping arcade: viewing. Photo by author.

Figure 167. Queuing at an airport. Photo by author.

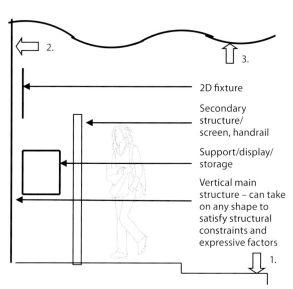

2.

3.

— 2D fixture

Secondary structure/ screen, handrail

Support/display/ storage

Vertical main structure – can take on any shape to satisfy structural constraints and expressive factors

1.

LEVELS OF USAGE – WEAR
1. Floor plane would receive wear from human traffic to objects and appliance usage
2. Walls receive the next heaviest usage in terms of fixings of fixtures and fittings and a high level of human interaction
3. Ceilings receive minimal physical contact

Figure 168. This diagram contains all the components that could surround a standing person.

Audience has three objects of attention – the speaker, the interior, and the accompanying display

Free space left in centre as a combination of respectful distance from speaker, and shyness

Social distance varies according to relationship with adjacent person

Figure 169. Audience standing in a gallery space (Glendower House) listening to a speaker. The audience had a free choice about where to stand. Glendower House designed by Anthony Sully, architect Graham Frecknall, 2002. Photo: Media Services LCSF, University of Glamorgan.

SEATING SPACES

People sit on a variety of items of support, commonly called furniture. These will vary in design depending upon the type of activity taking place. They can be designed to support more than one person, should the occasion demand it. The types of seating spaces are as follows:

Refreshment areas (Figure 170)

This covers spaces for eating and drinking, domestic or public (in varied groups). Restaurants and cafés are popular places for sustenance, rest and meeting people. Unfortunately, refreshment areas in stations often fall short on comfort, as well as displaying a lack of storage provision for luggage.

Historically, we began by eating whilst sitting on the floor, as is still customary in some countries. So which came first: the chair or the table? Sitting on rocks and logs possibly created the desire to eat off a surface that was higher off the floor. Adjacency to other people in terms of levels of conversation and the hierarchical importance of each person can influence seating arrangements.

Commercial spaces (Figure 171)

This covers office, educational or other working environments, used by people singly or in groups. Office environments vary according to how much investment the client puts into them, and what type of business is being run. Offices consist of actual working areas as well as peripheral areas such as display, meeting, reception and refreshment spaces. Seating is needed either for working at a desk, meeting around a table, or waiting in reception. Mobility of seating is an important factor.

Waiting areas (Figure 172)

Like standing spaces, waiting areas such as the reception for a workplace, hospital or clinic cater for groups. Comfort and visual calmness are essential, because people may be in a state of anxiety while awaiting an unknown outcome. The provision of enough seating to cater for visitors is an important factor, as is the provision of visual stimuli, such as murals.

Viewing areas (Figure 173)

Viewing areas, for large-scale performances in the arts, sport, leisure and education, have to cater for many people. Auditorium seating can be very difficult to achieve satisfactorily, because there are so many factors for the designer to consider: a desired level of comfort, but not so much that causes the audience to fall asleep; maximum

Figure 170. Café in a London railway station. Photo by author.

Figure 171. IBM Forum Centre, London. Tilney Shane Design, 2003.

Figure 172. IBM showroom, London. Austin Smith Lord Architects. Designer: Anthony Sully, 1971.

seating, but not at the expense of ease of access; the layout of raked seating must ensure good sightlines of the stage, as well as satisfy safety considerations.

Relaxation areas (Figure 174)

Lounge seating, whether for domestic use or a leisure facility, provides support for relaxation, reading, watching TV and conversation. In Figure 174, the area is a large space, but still maintains an intimate designated area. Comfort is the predominant factor.

Seating for travel (Figure 175)

Trains, boats, aeroplanes and buses all require seating for passengers. It is interesting to note, in Figure 175, how similar trains and aircraft are becoming. In fact, apart from the windows (which are a giveaway), the profile of this interior is very close to that of an aircraft. Fixtures that tolerate a high level of wear are essential, as these public spaces are open to abuse.

WORKSPACES

A workspace may be anything from the interior of a corporate office to a teaching space, a workshop/lab, a retail establishment, a hospital, the preparation area in a restaurant, café or pub, or a specialist space such as a ticket office, dental surgery or operating theatre. Various activities are carried out, so requirements for standing, sitting or walking may apply.

Corporate open-plan office

Planning for this type of office is discussed in Chapter 6 (see p.110). Figure 176 shows a more relaxed layout, on a

Figure 173. The art deco interior of the Apollo Victoria Theatre, London, designed by Ernest Wamsley Lewis and W. E. Trent in 1929. Photo by author. Courtesy of the Apollo Victoria.

Figure 174. Lounge, Glendower House. Designer: Anthony Sully, 2002. Photo: Media Services LCSF University of Glamorgan.

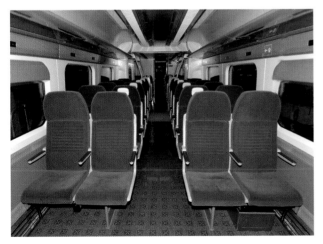

Figure 175. Interior of Southeastern Trains' Class 395 Javelin units, UK.

Figure 176. BBC Worldwide, London. DEGW London, 2010.

rectangular grid, with a relaxation area.

Factory (Figure 177)

Factory environments take a lot of punishment, with the amount of machinery and storage requirements they have to cope with. It is therefore paramount that working conditions are made as pleasant as possible for the workers.

Medical (Figure 178)

Hospital interiors are dominated by medical requirements and health and safety regulations. However, these are normal constraints for designers and it should be possible to come up with something better than an unfriendly, clinical environment. However, this is a situation where hospital authorities lay down the rules, and it will take a brave designer to challenge them.

Teaching (Figure 179)

Teaching spaces have improved greatly over the past few years in terms of the use of communications technology. But the increasing dominance of computers in study/studio areas has posed a problem for designers: how do you reduce the production line effect whilst providing the opportunity for individual expression? The enclosing elements need to help support the learning experience as well as the concentration required for computer work.

Catering (Figure 180)

Commercial kitchens are run with machine-like efficiency and therefore need to be designed to fit that ethos. It is an intensive and sometimes frenetic environment to work in, so the design needs to address those conditions.

Retail (Figure 181)

Retail design is a very popular field to work in because it provides designers with scope for expression – of the client and of the products for display. Display is a particular branch of interior design and provides the opportunity for dramatic, staged and interpretive designs.

LYING-DOWN AREAS

The most common posture adopted must be that for sleeping, considering the time we spend doing this during our life. However, our lives have become so

Figure 177. Scharffen Berger, chocolate-maker, Berkeley, California, 2008. Photo: Andreas Praefcke.

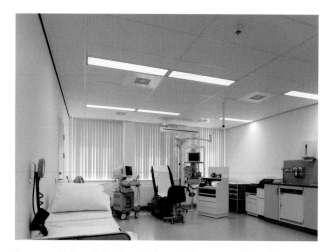

Figure 178. Specialist hospital ward. Courtesy of Ecophon.

Figure 179. Computer lab, Hereford Sixth Form College, 2010.

Figure 180. Commercial kitchen by Garners' Food Service Equipment, UK.

Figure 181. The Kurt Geiger shop, Regent Street, London. Found Associates, 2006. Photo: Hufton and Crow.

complex and sophisticated that in normal residential accommodation we hardly ever provide a space that is just for sleeping in. Spaces for sleep alone continue to exist in prisons (confined spaces, albeit designed for minimal living), dormitories, youth hostels and similar places.

Institutional (Figures 182 and 183)

Bunk beds started being used in Victorian workhouses, military establishments and on board ships, where floor space was limited. These double up the numbers of people who can be accommodated in a space, a beneficial alternative to single beds in hostels and schools.

Residential/commercial

Bedrooms in our homes have increasingly become used for many purposes other than sleeping. To many young people, a bedroom is a bedsitting room with a desk, TV and sofa, where they may entertain their friends. Adults' bedrooms can also be adapted for other uses, indicating that all spaces in the home call for a radical rethink towards becoming multipurpose spaces.

The hotel room illustrated in Figure 184, overleaf, is trying to create an upmarket domestic feel with a table lamp, pictures on the wall and luxurious bedding. Why doesn't the hotel industry review their accommodation and provide something less formulaic, incorporating some real design ideas? The design of the floor-to-ceiling glass window, whilst representing the height of fashionable coolness and daring, increases feelings of insecurity especially on higher floors. More sensitivity is required with regard to human need.

Figure 182. Dormitory at Beaminster and Netherbury Grammar School, 1950s. Photo courtesy Lesley Rundle.

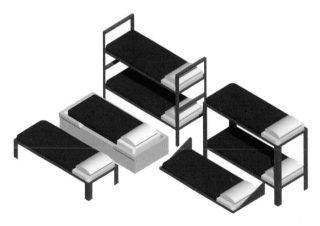

Figure 183. Bunks for a correctional institution. Courtesy of Architechnology.

Figure 184. Bedroom in St David's Hotel and Spa, Cardiff. Architect: Patrick Davies, 1999.

Figure 185. *Right.* Solar Umbrella master bedroom and bathroom, Venice, California. Brooks + Scarpa Architects, 2005. Photo: Marvin Rand.

The modern domestic bedroom in Figure 185, plus integrated bathing area, fits together architecturally with modular storage units and varying floor levels.

Furniture

As well as the existence of rooms for sleeping and relaxing in, certain items of furniture fall into this category too. In Ancient Rome and Greece, people used to recline on sofas and couches to eat, as was the tradition in the Far East; they would also be used for entertaining and conversation. Furniture in this category, with a straight base, is still made today for people to recline on. In the 1920s, the LC4 chaise longue was one of the first items of furniture to be designed that was neither a chair nor a sofa, and was the first piece of furniture to be ergonomically designed to fit the human form in a reclining position. Of course, flat couches allowed the sitter to adopt a variety of postures with the aid of moveable cushions and rolls, whilst the LC4 only permitted one posture – a hint, perhaps, of the dictatorial aspects of early modernism.

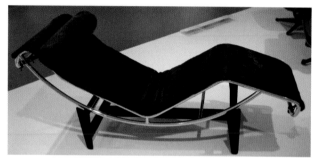

Figure 186. The LC4 chaise longue was designed by Le Corbusier, Pierre Jeanneret and Charlotte Perriand in 1928, and dubbed 'the ultimate relaxing machine'. Wikimedia Commons. Author: Sailko.

Figure 187. A *triclinium* – an ancient Roman dining room with couches. Wikimedia Commons. Author: Mattes.

READY TO DESIGN

So far in this book, you have learnt about the sort of preparation a designer must make in order to be ready to design, from the client briefing and research, to the building and context, planning for the human form, and shaping and moulding space and structure according to strong theoretical reasoning. The next chapter will explore new dimensions, which it is hoped will provide some inspiration. Meanwhile, we have reached the conclusion that in this current social climate, two factors are apparent: anything is possible, and there is a need to combine functions to provide integrated solutions.

1. ANYTHING IS POSSIBLE
Freedom

Putting regulatory procedures to one side for the moment, and assuming that cultural and expressive freedom exists, the brief is wide open to interpretation, and there are no rules or expected methods of designing. There are also no stylistic formats to acknowledge and no other dictatorial source of instruction. This freedom is found in all the arts whereby innovation and experimentation are the themes.

Constraints
- **Budget**
- **Political climate**
- **Technological limitations**

Pressures
- **Fashion** – current trends
- **From peers** – the design fraternity can be influential
- **Breaking with tradition and public familiarity**

2. THE NEED TO COMBINE FUNCTIONS

There is still much conformity when dealing with the interior components of an interior. These components need to be thought of in a more interconnected way to liberate the organisational process of a design and release manufacturing potential. In other words, by overlapping or merging two components, the result can be the creation of a new component. It is stereotypical to rely on and use the terminology for present standard components. Existing products that lead the way in this field are bathroom furniture 'suites' that combine washbasin with storage, and mirror with storage. Here are some examples that explore other possibilities:

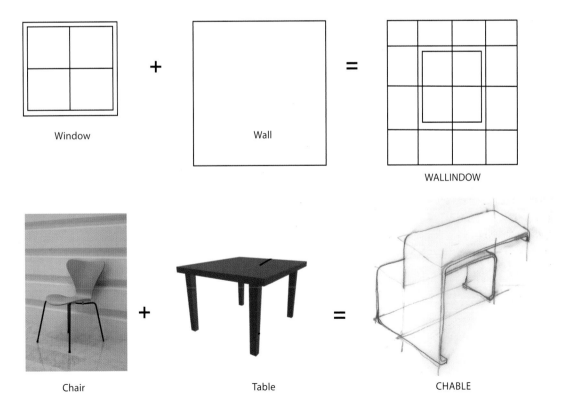

Window + Wall = WALLINDOW

Chair + Table = CHABLE

EXISTING EXAMPLES OF COMBINED FUNCTIONS

Figure 188. Concrete picnic unit – seat and table. Dominion Precast.

Figure 189. *Kencot Writing Tablet Chair*, Race Furniture. A lecture room chair/writing surface.

Figure 190. *Overhead Hanging Bench*, Word of Design, UK. Courtesy of Lion Steel. A changing room unit comprising seat, storage and hanging space.

Sloping desk lid – ergonomically correct for writing

Groove for pens and pencils

Storage for books

Inkwell for dip pens

Lift up seat was required because pupils stood up when teacher entered the room

This piece of furniture was durable, functional and convenient to move around. It offers a much better solution to the modern school furniture that is made today. They could also be made for two people.

Figure 191. Victorian English school desk. A superb example of combined functions. Courtesy of Trainspotters.

George Nelson[10]

George Nelson designed a storage wall, called the Omni System/Comprehensive Storage System (CSS), in the 1950s. The system combined a wall/divider with storage. He used extruded aluminium uprights, which could be wedged in between the floor and ceiling by spring-release mechanisms. The storage units themselves covered a whole range of options, from shelving to enclosed containers, with varied specific requirements to suit the functions of the interior. The whole thing was revolutionary and afforded the client a great degree of flexibility in layout and provision.

Nelson then combined his efforts with Robert Propst of Herman Miller in the USA, to produce the Action

Figure 192. The storage wall by George Nelson. Courtesy of Furniture Fashion.

Figure 193. A Herman Miller Action Office, 1969. Courtesy of Herman Miller Inc.

Office range in 1965. Propst went on to refine the design for serious marketing in 1969, and this became the world's first flexible modular range of furniture, which incorporated screens upon which were hung storage units, shelving and worktops. This system could respond organically to any fluctuations in the size of a company's workforce. It also corresponded with the *Bürolandschaft* system of open-plan offices, as mentioned in Chapter 6 (see p.110).

Industrial

Sliding, folding partitions offer the opportunity for the full partition of a space; or the partition may be folded back to create one space from two. Also, segments can be folded out to allow door access.

Figure 194. *Movawall Type 200*, Chessington, UK.

Multipurpose

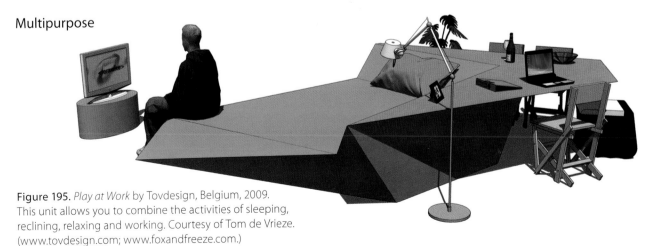

Figure 195. *Play at Work* by Tovdesign, Belgium, 2009. This unit allows you to combine the activities of sleeping, reclining, relaxing and working. Courtesy of Tom de Vrieze. (www.tovdesign.com; www.foxandfreeze.com.)

METAMORPHIC FURNITURE

Having examined the possibility of combining traditional functions in order to create newer solutions, metamorphic furniture comes close to this particular category. The word 'metamorphic' (which comes from a Greek word meaning an object that *changes* in composition or structure) applies to furniture that changes its form in order to perform two functions. Modern examples exist, such as the sofa bed, high chair, and tables that change their form to adapt to a different function. There have been examples historically since the 17th century, such as a richly inlaid chest of drawers that combines a bookcase and writing desk. The chair illustrated above was made for a library that had shelves beyond the reach of a standing person, so the chair was designed to convert into steps, thus enabling the higher shelves to be reached. In no way did the performance of either action adversely affect both usages.

Another practical convertible form was the settle or bench/table combination from the late 18th and early 19th centuries. When its high back was in a vertical position, it contained and reflected the heat from the fireplace and provided shelter from draughts. Swung down to the horizontal position, the hinged back became a table.

REVIEW

This critical chapter sets out to explain how a designer works sequentially from concept development and analysis through to the realisation of a scheme. Concepts prepare the way forward through drafting. An understanding of the growth of form and colour coexists with the realisation of materials and construction. Axial planning is necessary to give structure and shape to a plan. The handling of dualities of different components of form and space requires democratic judgement. Doors, openings, doorways, staircases and corridors that deal with people in circulation all require greater attention than is currently given. There is a vast opportunity for design here.

8: SEARCHING FOR CODES

How could the modern language of architecture be widely spoken without a code?[1]

Bruno Zevi

ABOUT THIS CHAPTER

This chapter is in two parts. Part 1 investigates the origins of classicism before examining how and why styles were established, using key designers and the distinguishing features of their work as examples. These designers have been selected because they produced work of an original identity and style, which influenced the future of interior design. This leads to Part 2, which begins with the question 'where are we now?' because it sometimes seems that design has lost its way and is constrained by too many commercial and socio-political pressures. Computer-aided design (CAD) has opened up a whole new world, which is fuelling even more schemes that lack integrity and sense. Part 2 continues by challenging existing trends and proposing a new investigation into how interiors can be unitised and gridded as never before. It is hoped that this might reinvigorate the discipline and make a valid contribution to the continuance of this profession.

The dictionary definition of a code is: 'established principles or standards, a system of rules and regulations'. Why search for codes? What are they, and do we need them? This chapter hopes to explain, with some historical references, how certain codes (the word 'style' is more commonly used, but has connotations) were established as a means of expressing structure, first of all, followed by decoration, which identified people with their world, as demonstrated in primitive cave paintings or the hieroglyphic art of the Ancient Egyptians. Gradually, these codes laid down the standards of status and function of a particular space. Throughout history, global trade exchanges have produced a desire to express these newly established sources, and people who have acquired wealth want to reflect this: as a result, interiors became more complex to handle.

Major historical events, inventions, discoveries and people of significance influenced artists and designers and consequently had some bearing on the style of the day. Hence, the codes of practice and terminology used have essentially been the same since the Middle Ages – until the eruption of modernism and the sweeping away of tradition. Whilst the scope of design has been opened up, there are many observations in this book that sound warnings about a detachment from our cultural history. Perhaps it is time for a re-evaluation of the world of design?

PART 1, THE PAST: THE ORIGINS OF CLASSICISM

In a survey of past design styles from the 16th century onwards, there are certain designers who stand out because of the originality of their work and the contribution they have made. This chapter will now proceed to examine their work and to provide a summary of its design content (code). They all inherited the strong classical traditions from Egyptian, Assyrian, Greek and Roman times but applied their own reinterpretations, establishing new codes of design.

From around 4000 BC, the Egyptian civilisation developed an architecture of column and lintel construction, which used motifs taken from the lotus flower, lotus bud, feathers, palm leaves and reeds (see Chapter 2, 'Element 8: Decoration', p.49). The origins of the Greek and Roman classical orders have been discussed by Quinlan Terry[2] as being the result of people using natural materials such as a palm tree cut off and driven into the ground to act as a post, which then sprouted leaves. This reference would then be formalised into the capital of a column. The use of rope, timber, rams' horns and other materials soon enabled further development of what we now know as the Doric, Ionic and Corinthian orders. One of the earliest known formations of a column and beam design exists in the tomb of King Darius in Iran, although it only resembles that form of construction, as it is a rock carving.

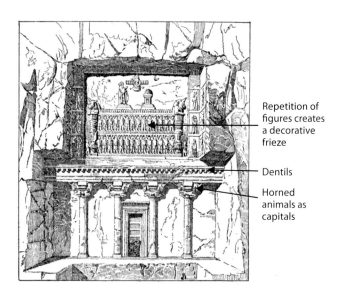

Repetition of figures creates a decorative frieze

Dentils

Horned animals as capitals

Figure 198. Rock-cut tomb of Darius I (521–486 BC). Near Persepolis, Persia.

The diagram below is intended to illustrate the basic ethos behind the construction methods of the classical orders: the interpretation of forces in action, the expression of man's capability to challenge nature's own structures, and a demonstration of man's power. The verticality of columns matches the vertical human form.

SKELETAL STRUCTURAL BASIS OF CLASSICAL DESIGN

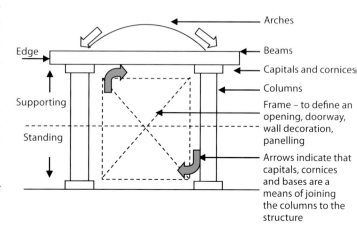

Arches

Beams

Capitals and cornices

Columns

Frame – to define an opening, doorway, wall decoration, panelling

Arrows indicate that capitals, cornices and bases are a means of joining the columns to the structure

Edge

Supporting

Standing

WERE THE VISUAL CHARACTERISTICS OF THE HUMAN HEAD AN INSPIRED SOURCE FOR THE CLASSICAL ORDERS?

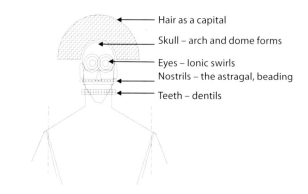

Hair as a capital

Skull – arch and dome forms

Eyes – Ionic swirls

Nostrils – the astragal, beading

Teeth – dentils

In the long process of transformation over a period of time, man's creative powers of invention produced a stylised interpretation of this classical form of structure. It is as well to quote Ernst Mach[3] here, from a lecture he gave at the University of Vienna in October 1895, 'On the Part Played by Accident in Invention and Discovery':

The majority of the inventions made in the early stages of civilisation, including language, writing, money, and the rest, could not have been the product of deliberate

methodical reflexion for the simple reason that no idea of their value and significance could have been had except from their practical use ... But granting that the most important inventions are brought to man's notice accidentally and in ways that are beyond his foresight, yet it does not follow that accident alone is sufficient to produce an invention ... He must distinguish the new feature, impress it upon his memory, unite and interweave it with the rest of his thought; in short, he must possess the capacity to profit by experience.

A code is defined here as a form of discipline that provides a framework of form and decoration that is recognisable as a style. Some of the designers who have influenced change since the Renaissance, and who have developed their own codes in interior design in a way that was more directed towards a domestic scale, are as follows: Robert Adam, Sir John Soane, William Morris, Charles Rennie Mackintosh, Josef Hoffmann, Frank Lloyd Wright, Gerrit Rietveld, Charles and Rae Eames, Carlo Scarpa, Eva Jiřičná, Tadao Ando and Enric Miralles.

ROBERT ADAM[4]

Robert Adam's book, *The Works of Architecture* (1773), attempted to relate his inventive drawing style (which had a simple geometric basis) to the picturesque style of the past which used natural sources almost directly. This had dominated the preceding 20 years of his practice. He transformed the prevailing Palladian style in architecture by adopting elegant variations on classical themes. He developed the concept of an integrated interior with walls, ceiling, floor, ironmongery and furniture all designed as a single scheme. His rules – we shall call them codes – were all explained in *The Works*, which consisted of detailed drawings of structure and decoration that served as a guide to all of the buildings he worked on. As with classical decoration of the past he used animals, shells, the spider's web, wings, flowers, laurel and acanthus leaves, papyrus, the lotus flower and honeysuckle (anthemion) in his designs. Mouldings and other motifs were designed using the triglyph, dentil, egg and dart, torus, scotia, vitruvian scroll, rose, leaf and dart, antefix, griffin, fret, rope and feather, bead, and bead and reel. The draped swag, ribbon or laurel leaves with urns and pots was a constant feature. Doorways, windows, mirrors and fireplaces became a focus of attention.

Figure 199. Entrance hall, Syon House, Brentford, Middlesex. Robert Adam, 1762. Note that the floor pattern echoes the ceiling pattern. Getty Images.

Figure 200. Syon House, detail of decoration. Getty Images.

Figure 201. Details from Derby House in Grosvenor Square, London. Robert Adam, 1777. Wikipedia.

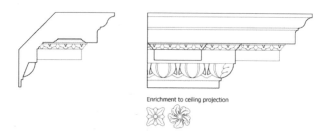

Figure 202. Ceiling cornice in entrance hall, Hatchlands Park, East Clandon, Guildford. Robert Adam, 1750s.

Figure 203. Details of Derby House, Grosvenor Square, London.

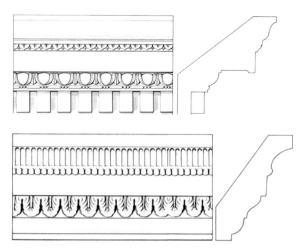

Figure 204. Other examples of Adam's cornice designs. Mouldings courtesy of Stevenson's of Norwich.

REPETITION OF A MOTIF ADDS RICHNESS

Adam's use of geometry was varied but ordered. Apart from repeating motifs in the normal way, he would also reduce a shape in series, as the Romans did, for the decoration of semicircular domes such as the one in the entrance hall of Syon House. It must be remembered that the column orders in classical architecture were so predominant as a force simply because they were an important structural feature and not merely decorative. They became non-structural, in the form of pilasters, as relief decoration as well as being used on furniture. They have been used as a common architectural language in the world ever since their inception. Below are some of the 2D shapes that Adam used as a basis for dividing up surface areas; these would then be given ornate borders and an infill. The designs were about *framing* and *joining* one plane to another:

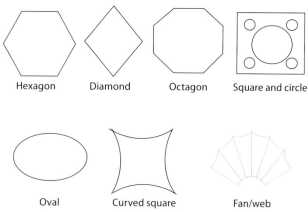

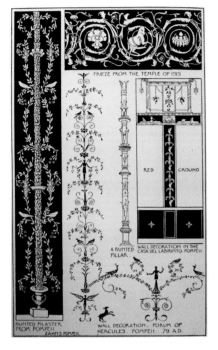

Figure 205. *Left.* From *A Manual of Historic Ornament* by Richard Glazier (London: Batsford, 1899), p.8, Pompeii.

Figure 206. *Above.* From *A Manual of Historic Ornament* by Richard Glazier (London: Batsford, 1899), p.28.

The two illustrations above show Roman decoration, which was a key source for Adam.

You can see from Glazier's illustration of the ornamentation of Pompeii[5] that Roman style was the source for Adam's swag and leaf motifs. The inset wall elevation shows the quality of proportional spaciousness and elegance that Adam strived for as well as the 'framing' technique and dado-height border.

As we have seen up to now, the development of a design style begins with a method of building and making, which by a process of refinement over time becomes architecture, which can then be defined in terms of a style by the comparison of one era to another.

SIR JOHN SOANE[6]

Soane was one of the most original designers the UK has produced. What he designed at 13 Lincoln's Inn Fields (now Sir John Soane's Museum) was an entirely new experience for people. His inventiveness in the use of space, light and reflective space was astonishing. The use of joinery elements, integrated with the structure and decoration of the building, created a totally harmonious environment. His work is distinguished by clean lines, the massing of simple forms, decisive detailing, careful proportions and the skilful use of light sources. The use of a rich Pompeian red in the dining room at Lincoln's Inn Fields is an archaeological reference many of his

clients would have recognised and been impressed by.

The picture room is a good example of Soane's striking and original design work. Built in 1824, this room contains hinged panels on three of the walls, which open out into the room to reveal a further display of paintings. This innovative design feature allows the small space of 4.1 x 3.75 m (13 ft 8in. x 12 ft 4 in.) to be capable of containing as many pictures as a gallery more than twice the size. Mirrors of varying proportions and shapes (flat and convex) also play a vital role in Soane's manipulation of space by adding other dimensions to the possibilities of virtual space.

Figure 208. The dining room, from the library. Courtesy of the Trustees of Sir John Soane's Museum.

Figure 207. The breakfast room, Sir John Soane's Museum, London. Sir John Soane, 1812. Courtesy of the Trustees of Sir John Soane's Museum.

Below. Diagram of the sail dome.

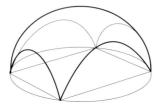

Mostly to be found throughout the first floor, these mirrors create double or multiple dimensions within the rooms, while allowing additional outside spaces to enter the room one is standing in. For example, in the dining room, mirrored surfaces are used near the windows to reflect a view of Monument Court, and in the library they are used in the alcoves to produce an illusion of space extending beyond the physicality of the walls. These mirrors often enable the objects on display to be viewed from a multitude of angles, as well as helping to diffuse and direct light throughout the building. The use of stained glass and coloured glass panes creates vibrant colours that help to evoke certain atmospheres. For example, the yellow glass in the small

lean-to and the triangular skylights covering the dome passages cast a warm, romantic light over otherwise colourless marble and casts, contrasting starkly with the dimly lit sepulchral basement.

The square plan of the breakfast room is capped by a sail dome without the usual circular base ring of a normal dome. But then the circle is made evident above the segmental arches and at the apex, with radiating lines from the central octagonal lantern light.

In the dining room, there is an innovative division of space achieved by using two thin, panelled canopies, curved in an almost arabesque fashion, springing from piers but connected to joinery plinths by ornate metal rods. Behind these is a strip of mirror that gives the illusion of a recess.

WILLIAM MORRIS[7] AND THE ARTS AND CRAFTS MOVEMENT

William Morris is mentioned here not because he created a 'Morris style' in interiors, but because he helped to instigate a large movement promoting the production of arts and crafts in a genuine way that was true to the skills of workmanship, from the design of buildings right through to the design of furniture and artefacts. (However, his wallpaper designs did create a 'Morris' look when in use.) The cosy 'cottage' style soon grew to be popular amongst designers such as Voysey in Britain, and Greene and Greene in the USA. Other proponents of this movement – the Arts and Crafts Movement – were Mackmurdo, H. Fuller Clark, William Lethaby, E. W. Godwin, Edward Prior, Guy Dawber, Charles Holden, C. H. Townsend and Leonard Stokes.

The Black Friar Pub was converted from the ground floor of a mid-Victorian office building in 1905. There was a Dominican monastery on the site until the mid-16th century, then a theatre, which burnt down in the Great Fire of London of 1666. The pub is crammed full of works of art and craft such as bronze friezes by Henry Poole, multicoloured marble wall finishes and bar counters, mosaics, bronze reliefs of jolly-looking monks, and decorative touches such as the elaborate fire basket with goblin ends. There is a frieze, above door height, of mottos of wisdom such as 'Finery is foolery', 'Don't advertise, tell a gossip', 'Haste is slow' and 'Industry is all'.

Figure 209. The Black Friar Pub, Queen Victoria Street, London. H. Fuller Clark, 1905. Photo: Dr Jaqueline Banerjee. Source: www.victorianweb.org/art/architecture/pubs.

Some of the distinguishing features of this period, using wood as a predominant material, are: tapered architraves, arches (also in brick and stone), frames – panelling and beams, wide board panelling, and variously proportioned windows. These were used in common with picture rails and dados. Arches would exist over doorways, fireplaces, windows or divisions of space. The Arts and Craft Movement overlapped with the truly organic art nouveau movement.

ART NOUVEAU MOVEMENT

One of the most famous works of the Belgian designer Victor Horta (1861–1947) was the Tassel House (1892-93) (see Figure 102, Chapter 6). Horta was a founder member of the art nouveau movement and enjoyed many other commissions, but as the years went by, and due to post-First World War austerity measures, he simplified the style. This movement was full of symbolic mysticism and epitomised Romantic ideals. As Mario Amaya[8] states in his book on art nouveau:

> *Often the term has referred to a decorative object made about the turn of the century, of free-flowing or organic form, based on some floral abstraction, linear, swirling, flatly patterned, with a skipping or undulating rhythmic design that often obscures the entire surface or structure of the thing it decorates. Its restless, moving agitated line takes on a nervous, expressive quality, either dictating the shape of the object or else complementing it in some unusual or unpredictable way.*

Upon closer examination, the ceiling borders and cornices, wall framing and panelling, arches and doorways, as well as furniture, all follow previous traditions but are joined together by organic, swirling curves that sometimes break through individual boundaries and overlap. Horta's sources of inspiration included plants, animals, swirling water, smoke and human hair.

Figure 210. The study in Jerome Doucet's house, Clamart, France, 1902. Drawing by the author.

Figure 211. William Blake (1757–1827), *Christ as the Redeemer of Man*. Inspired by John Milton's epic poem, Paradise Lost. Courtesy China Toperfect Co. Ltd.

Figure 212. El Greco, *Laocoön*, 1610. Wikimedia Commons. El Greco (1541–1614) was a Spanish painter of Greek origin.

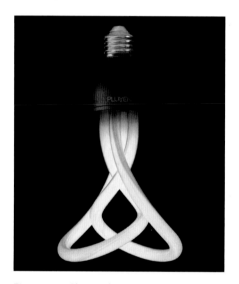

Figure 213. Plumen low-energy light bulb by Nicolas Roope (b. 1972) and design company Hulger. Photo: Andrew Penketh.

Figure 214. Tree roots. Photo: Jonathan Sloman.

There is little doubt that one of the many influences for this movement was tree roots. As with Frank Lloyd Wright, designers formalise natural sources into a geometry that can be built. Earlier visionaries, such as the English painter and poet William Blake, anticipated the art nouveau movement by using a similar extended flowing movement and singularly gliding rhythms, as well as asymmetry and a closed graphic form. When William Blake was aged 20, it was about 160 years after the death of El Greco, who also expressed some of the features of art nouveau in his elongated human forms and swirling elements, as seen in Figure 212.

The modern light bulb in Figure 213 is an example of the stretching of technology beyond normal acceptance, and by so doing it achieves the visual qualities associated with art nouveau.

For more on the art nouveau movement, see p.100.

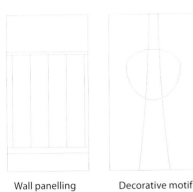

Wall panelling

Decorative motif

Used in doors, windows, furniture

Wood, furniture

Figure 215. *Right.* Armoire from Katharina Biach's room. Josef Hoffmann, 1902–03. Made of pine painted white, blue and black, maple veneer with inlays of black-stained wood, and white metal. Private collection. Courtesy of Neue Galerie, New York.

CHARLES RENNIE MACKINTOSH[9] AND JOSEF HOFFMANN

We shall single out these designers because of their distinctive styles and the powerful influence and praise that was bestowed upon them for their skill and originality. Charles Rennie Mackintosh (1868–1928) designed buildings, interiors and furniture (see examples in Chapter 6, p.101). Josef Hoffmann (1870–1956) had an architectural background, but was drawn into the community of artists. As a result he be came more widely known for his interiors, furniture and glass products. They each created their own style from a blend of the styles of the Arts and Crafts Movement and art nouveau. The main characteristics of their combined work are wall panelling, decorative motifs on doors, windows and furniture, and exploiting the craftsmanship of wood. Mackintosh's wall panelling consisted of wide panels with a picture rail that was thinner than the skirting. Curved patterns were more restricted than other art nouveau designs, and were contained within frames or controlled repeats.

Hoffmann's designs for furniture, products and interiors contributed to the modernist movement in their combination of sleekness, the repetition of the square motif, and captured decorative motifs that were contained and controlled. The integration of furniture with enclosing walls was restrained in comparison with past styles. Edges and frames were minimal items of expression compared with surfaces. The Kubus sofa used the repeat-square design, as did his metalwork.

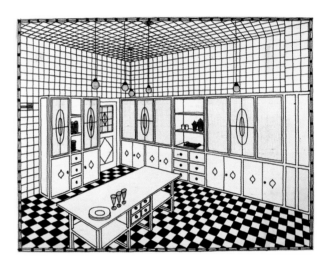

Figure 216. Draft for the kitchen in the Stoclet Palace in Brussels. Blueprint from the atelier Josef Hoffmann, 1905–1910. Getty Images.

Figure 217. Kubus Sofa. Josef Hoffmann, 1910. Copy of original. Courtesy Blue Suntree.

FRANK LLOYD WRIGHT[10]

THE BEGINNINGS OF THE MODERNIST MOVEMENT

Wright was inspired by the 19th-century writings such as *Grammar of Ornament* by Owen Jones[11] (1856), *The Discourses on architecture* by Eugène Emmanuel Viollet-le-Duc[12] (1875), and *Principles of Decorative Designs* by Christopher Dresser[13] (1873). The organic qualities of Wright's architecture embraced a superb geometric interpretation of natural form, as his famous hollyhock plant motif reveals.

In the interior of the Unity Temple shown below, the space and walls interact and overflow into each other, thus demonstrating a new-found freedom in planning

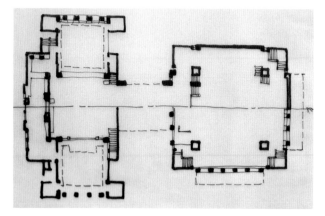

Figure 218. Diagrammatic plan of Unity Temple. Drawn by the author.

Figure 219. Unity Temple, Oak Park, Illinois. Frank Lloyd Wright, 1906. Getty Images.

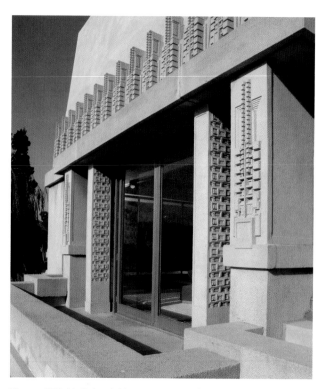

Figure 220. Hollyhock House, Los Angeles, California, USA. Frank Lloyd Wright, 1919–21. Photo: Larry Underhill.

and space use. Wright is still keen to ensure continuity of surface, with framing and line definition, evoking the sinuous connectivity of the art nouveau style. His prairie-style house designs expanded space, harmonised with the external environment, and emphasised the horizontal with overlapping planes.

The characteristic square shapes in the hollyhock pattern are vaguely related to the Unity Temple plan, where squares are repeated in corners, between windows and on internal columns. Both forms have a central axis and symmetry.

SUMMARY OF CHARACTERISTICS

This sums up the integrated relatedness of Wright's work

GERRIT RIETVELD[14]

Rietveld was a leading member of the Dutch De Stijl group, together with Theo van Doesburg (see Chapter 6, p.102). They had purist ideals and were single-minded about their philosophy on design.

Rietveld's design for the Schröder House has a conventional ground floor, but is radical on the top floor, lacking fixed walls but instead relying on sliding walls to create and change living spaces. The design is like a 3D realisation of a Mondrian painting: Rietveld expresses linear elements combined with primary colours linked by black connecting devices. The Red and Blue Chair was a striking design and it contrasted with anything that had been produced up to that time. It powerfully expresses a design philosophy that is still admired to this day. The intersecting frame members are influenced by Japanese construction. The comment has to be made that it is most uncomfortable to sit in! But this is true of so many design icons, and they should be accepted for their makers' contribution to design thinking.

The original version of the sideboard shown in Figure 223 was designed by the architect E. W. Godwin in 1867, for himself. It epitomises the influence of Japanese art and design on British decorative art in the 1860s and 1870s. It also goes very well with the Rietveld chair, even though there are 50 years between them.

Figure 221. Schröder House, Utrecht. Gerrit Rietveld, 1924. Wikimedia Commons. Photo: Hay Kranen.

SUMMARY OF CHARACTERISTICS

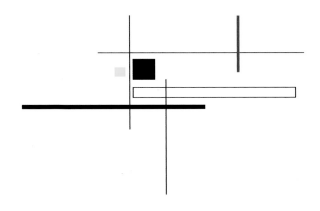

Figure 222. Red and Blue Chair. Gerrit Rietveld, 1917. Wikimedia Commons. Photo: Elly Waterman.

Figure 223. *Far right*. Sideboard by E. W. Godwin, 1867. Courtesy of the Victoria & Albert Museum, London.

CHARLES AND RAE EAMES[15]

In furniture design, Charles Eames experimented with moulded plywood work, as well as fibreglass and plastic resin (for chairs) and metal (to make the wire mesh chairs designed for Herman Miller).

The Eames House, which the Eameses designed for themselves, is a steel structure with sliding walls and windows. Designed for cheap, speedy construction, it took five men 16 hours to raise the steel shell and one man three days to build the roof deck. Spacious, light and versatile, the vividly coloured house was described by the design historian Pat Kirkham as looking like 'a Mondrian-style composition in a Los Angeles meadow'. This style follows on from the work of Mies van der Rohe mentioned in Chapter 6 (see p.104) – the style known as 'Miesian' was very rectangular and square-gridded, and used structural steel and glass.

The design of the Eameses' Plastic Armchair was first presented in 1948 for the Museum of Modern Art's competition, 'Low-Cost Furniture Design', in New York. It was the first mass-produced chair made of fibreglass-reinforced plastic, and was manufactured by Herman Miller and Vitra until 1989.

Figure 224. The Eames House, Los Angeles, USA. Charles and Rae Eames, 1949. Courtesy Eric Wittman.

Figure 225. Plastic Armchair. Charles and Rae Eames, 1948. Courtesy Vitra.

SUMMARY OF CHARACTERISTICS

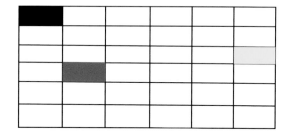

CARLO SCARPA[16]

Carlo Scarpa is recognised as one of the most important architects of the 20th century. His formative experiences as an artist took place above all in Venice, where he was part of a circle of artists and intellectuals associated with the Venice Biennale and the Fine Arts Academy (Accademia di Belle Arti), from which he was awarded a diploma as Professor of Architectural Drawing in 1926.

The work of Scarpa remains highly influential today for its originality in using varied textures of concrete, marble, metal and other natural materials. His concepts of layering, stepped forms, cantilevered structures, and recesses combined with a pure and uncluttered geometry, seem to relate to the classical traditions of Italian architecture. The staircase illustrated above may catch a first-time viewer by surprise, but the design only acknowledges the way that we climb stairs. The church of Sant'Agostino in Figure 228 shows some of the influences that medieval Italian architecture had upon Scarpa. The detail and character of this building is echoed in Scarpa's work.

Figure 226. *Above.* Staircase at Museo di Castelvecchio, Verona, Italy, 1956 – 1964. Courtesy Seier and Seier

Figure 227. *Right.* Wall light in Museo di Castelvecchio, Verona, Italy, 1956 – 1964 Courtesy Seier and Seier

Figure 228. Church of Sant'Agostino, Rome. Giacomo di Pietrasanta, 1483. The photo shows steps, recesses, linear framing and smooth surfaces. Wikimedia Commons. Author: Lalupa.

SUMMARY OF CHARACTERISTICS

EVA JIŘIČNÁ[17]

Eva Jiřičná is probably most famous for her work on shop interiors, as well as nightclubs. Jiřičná's hallmark is to transform ordinary shop units into elegant displays for luxury goods and clothes in the high-tech[18] architectural style. She was one of the pioneers of the use of glass as a structural material, partly because it improved transparency and daylight in the shops, but she also exploited its potential to surprise and delight. Shoppers found themselves ascending staircases with transparent treads, supported by filigree-like stainless steel wires whose reflectivity made them almost invisible.

Figure 229. The William and Judith Bollinger Jewellery Gallery, London. Eva Jiřičná, 2009. Courtesy of the Victoria & Albert Museum, London.

SUMMARY OF CHARACTERISTICS

TADAO ANDO[19]

Ando's work followed on from the Brutalist movement in architecture, which began in the 1950s with the work of Le Corbusier and the English architects Alison and Peter Smithson. Its philosophy was the use of exposed raw concrete and other structural materials as finishes in their own right, without any applied cladding or material. Ando perfects beautifully smooth finishes in buildings that are often characterised by complex 3D circulation paths. These paths weave between interior and exterior spaces forming inside large-scale geometric shapes and in the spaces between them. He is masterly with the interplay of light and shade, solid and void, and open and closed.

Figure 230. Galleria Akka, Osaka, Japan. Tadao Ando, 1988. Courtesy Thomas A. Kronig.

SUMMARY OF CHARACTERISTICS

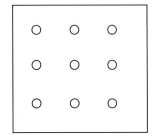

ENRIC MIRALLES[20]

Enric Miralles' design for the Scottish Parliament expresses the strength and elegance of steel. The building seems to have a mosaic of fractured layers of cladding defining openings and access points. His interpretation of the Scottish traditions and history are realised in a very personal and poetic art. As with Frank Lloyd Wright and Arne Jacobsen, Miralles would always design a building right down to the details of the interior furnishings. There exists a very strong visual relationship between the interior and exterior simply because the dynamics of the form and structure are shared.

Figure 231. The debating chamber, Scottish Parliament Building, Holyrood, Edinburgh. Enric Miralles, 1999–2004. Getty Images.

SUMMARY OF CHARACTERISTICS

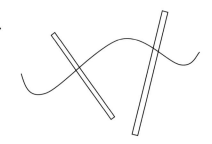

PART 2: WHERE ARE WE NOW?

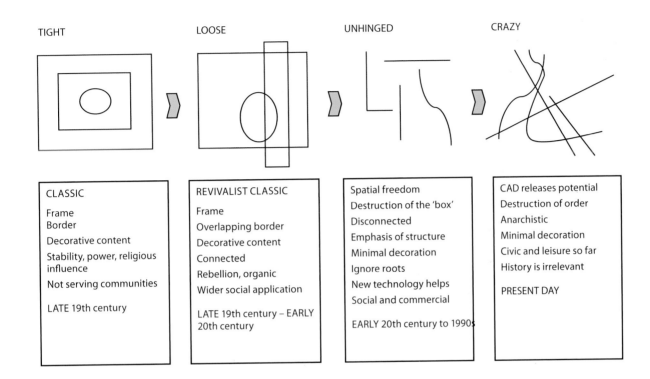

TIGHT	LOOSE	UNHINGED	CRAZY
CLASSIC Frame Border Decorative content Stability, power, religious influence Not serving communities LATE 19th century	**REVIVALIST CLASSIC** Frame Overlapping border Decorative content Connected Rebellion, organic Wider social application LATE 19th century – EARLY 20th century	Spatial freedom Destruction of the 'box' Disconnected Emphasis of structure Minimal decoration Ignore roots New technology helps Social and commercial EARLY 20th century to 1990s	CAD releases potential Destruction of order Anarchistic Minimal decoration Civic and leisure so far History is irrelevant PRESENT DAY

Let us review the progression of the basic codes of design through time, as they appear through analysis simply on a conceptual basis. There have been four stages in this process: classical, classical revivalism, spatial freedom, through to the present-day stage of post-CAD (see the section entitled 'Crazy', below). This does not allow for variations in decorative content that have been inspired by nature, living creatures and human beings, as well as pure geometric pattern.

CRAZY

This term 'crazy' is meant as a warning that we could be heading for some unpleasant situations if insufficient attention is paid to the effects that the new world is having – and this does not mean green issues. This may sound overly traditionalist, but it is of the utmost importance that designers today take heed of their environment in all the design work that they do, and learn from the past.

We now have a climate of freedom in design and building that has never existed before. As is provocatively suggested in the diagram above, 'history is irrelevant'. So whilst we are confronted with exciting new possibilities, we are also entering a period of fragility and vulnerability, that is open to abuse and mistaken causes. This is exemplified by town planning that has not solved traffic problems; many examples of 1950s and 60s housing estates that have been demolished for being social disasters; and the horrific sterility of new towns in the UK such as Milton Keynes in Buckinghamshire. A familiarity with what was considered to be beautiful architecture and design is being eroded by a new world order that is changing those perceptions. The concept of beauty usually has associations with the visions, objects, places and sensations that arouse pleasure in people. The concept of ugliness is associated with those aspects of civilisation that remind us of catastrophes, disasters and horrors that people do not wish to be exposed to in real life. Unfortunately, the media forces us to confront such events on a daily basis. However, both of these concepts are used for *artistic* and *creative* purposes in producing work in all sectors of the arts and creative industries, and the best of these products are to be warmly received. Let us examine some not-so-good ideas.

Figure 232. War-damaged buildings. Getty Images.

Figure 233. Earthquake-damaged buildings. Getty Images.

SHAVEN HEADS AND TATTOOS

The fashion for the shaved head started in the 1960s and led to the subculture of skinheads. There is a certain amount of rebelliousness evident in this fashion and it now has associations with aggression and undesirable racist extremists. Prisoners held in Nazi war camps in the Second World War had their heads shaved as a demeaning measure. The rear view of the skull is not very appealing because of the way the vertebrae meet the skull, and it is a wonder how it has become a fashionable trend. Tattooing, which was originally an indicator of time served in the forces or prison service, has now become fashionable. Adolf Loos[21] had this to say: 'Tattooing is a sign of degeneration and is only used by criminals or degenerate aristocrats.' It is questionable whether such permanent body adornment enhances someone's appearance, as it sometimes appears to be more of a rebellious aggressive statement. The point is that some of the environmental designs currently being produced may also draw similarly unfavourable reactions.

DECONSTRUCTIVISM

The following images are the result of war or catastrophe, which seem to inspire designers today to design buildings that look as though they have collapsed or suffered from an earthquake.

Projects of our times

Whilst the technology of these CAD buildings and the creative energy necessary to calculate complex junctions is admirable, it is hard, if not impossible, to accept these examples as soul-enriching architecture for the reasons stated above. Anything that relates to instability, and

poses a threatening gesture, cannot be acceptable. Roger Scruton, who is critical of such architecture, wrote in *The Times* newspaper on 9th April 2011: 'Townscapes built from such architecture resemble landfill sites: scattered heaps of plastic junk from which the eye turns away in dejection.'

Figure 234. Dancing House, Prague. Vlado Milunić in cooperation with Frank Gehry, 1996. Shutterstock. Author: Radhoose.

Figure 235. The Ray and Maria Stata Center (Building 32, Massachusetts Institute of Technology). Frank Gehry, 2004. Wikimedia Commons.

 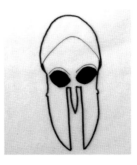

Figure 236. *Left*. Cardinal Place shopping centre, Victoria, London. EPR Architects, 2006. An aggressive and pointed architectural statement at street level. Photo by author.

Figure 237. *Above*. Threatening images: an owl and a medieval helmet. Drawn by the author.

Figure 238. Alcatraz prison: interior. Getty Images.

Figure 239. *Far right*. Mall in Grand Arcade, Cambridge. Photo by author. Courtesy of Grand Arcade.

The shopping mall on the right has clear similarities with the prison on the left!

More Deconstructivism

Figure 240. Monaco House, Melbourne, Australia. McBride Charles Ryan, 2007. Photo: John Gollings.

Figure 241. Rubbish. Photo by author.

COMPUTER-AIDED DESIGN

Computer-aided design (CAD) is a tool that allows designers to create 3D imagery so that clients can see – almost in photorealistic form – what they will be getting. The impact that CAD has had on the design profession is unlike anything that has previously influenced the way we build and communicate internationally. All through history it has been changes in *building*, the *sourcing of materials* and political, economic and social pressures that have influenced designers. CAD has enabled concepts of form to be drawn which could not be drawn by hand before. But what is leading the design concept?

Where is the connective evolutionary trail that we have seen over the past centuries?

In the past, a client's briefing has usually been made with some knowledge of the expected outcome (not detailed design or appearance) in terms of building mass, numbers of floors and so on. With the new powers of CAD, the potential arrangement of internal spaces and fluid skin/structure is limitless. The designer's role becomes much more aligned with the power of the gods, and with it comes overwhelming responsibility. But there is still much work to do for building technology to satisfy the geometric wonderland of CAD. The following quotation is a comment on the gap between geometric sourcing from inorganic structures (such as the hexagon) and the intricate and organic complexities of natural form.

> *Structural patterning in inorganic materials synthesis at this scale still falls a long way short of the organically template-directed processes that result in the complexity of form and structure in biological minerals such as bones, shells and teeth.*
>
> S. Mann and G. A. Ozin, 'Synthesis of Inorganic Materials with Complex Form', *Nature* 382 (1996): 313–18.

The process of designing, as far as shaping the built form is concerned, occurs by using a combination of past knowledge of construction (which will lay down certain parameters) with an idea that has not been built before. This new idea will then require some degree of testing to discover its viability. The following is an extract from *Engineering a New Architecture*, written in 1996 by Tony Robbin:

> *A few dozen engineers and architects share the view, currently considered revolutionary, that geometry drives architecture forward. To be ignorant of complex polyhedra, four-dimensional geometry, fractals, 3-manifold topology and the like, to have the cube and the octatruss as the only geometric options is to restrict structures with a severity that not even nature demands, its severe doctrine of optimisation notwithstanding.*

> *Moreover, there are aesthetic considerations; technobuffs may look lovingly at row after row of tetrahedra, but the public sees these as mechanical and boring, just more inhuman examples of Eiffel-Tower truss work. Why bother looking at something we just saw!*

But the complaint against mechanistic architecture, when considered honestly, is not that geometry is alien to human structures – geometry is unavoidable in structures; the complaint is that the geometry used is at least 100 years old, and was fresh in another context entirely. The computer makes this new impetus to mathematically generated form possible.

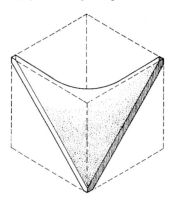

Figure 242. A saddle-shaped, curved-surface building module. US Patent 1994. Courtesy of WikiPatents.com.

Figure 243. Example of a complex curved form from Revit.

Figure 242 provides an example of how complex curved forms are being designed in modules and generated for CAD use, and Figure 243 shows a recent example of the capabilities of Revit 3D software. CAD works well in countries with prescriptive design legislation, allowing a successful idea to be adapted and repeated.

ZAHA HADID

Figure 244 shows another example of Hadid's work, which is a fine example of a CAD product. It is a wonderfully calm interior, marred only by the enforced

Figure 244. Bedroom in Hotel Puerta de America, Madrid, Spain. Zaha Hadid, 2005. The hotel commissioned many designers to design various parts of the hotel. Hadid designed similarly styled rooms that were either black or white, with one bathroom entirely in a red finish. Courtesy of Zaha Hadid Architects and Silken Hotels.

presence of the TV (which needs to be tilted forwards if viewed at such a high angle) and the telephones. In such a heavenly atmosphere, it must feel as though you are walking amongst clouds (although if you were not wearing white, you might feel very conspicuous in the space).

UNITS OF FORM IN INTERIORS

Let us now try to make some sense of our current state through an analysis of common building elements, with the intention of arriving at units of structural form (not loose objects or furniture) that are visible in many interiors. What do we mean by units of form? Up to now, if you analysed any interior through history, you would be able to identify the following twelve generic architectural components of building form:

- **Columns:** Vertical structural support.

- **Beams:** Horizontal spanning structural support.

- **Arches/vaults:** Curved spanning structural form.

- **Domes:** Hemispherical spanning structure.

- **Walls:** Vertical enclosing planes or spatial divisions.

- **Floors:** Horizontal plane – sometimes stepped or sloped.

■ **Ceilings**: Variously shaped overhead form – underside of roof or other floor, suspended or structural.

■ **Windows**: Framed and glazed plus coverings such as blinds, curtains and shutters.

■ **Doors**: Means of passing through walls, or from one space to another.

■ **Staircases**: Vertical means of circulation from one level to another.

■ **Fireplaces**: Strong source of heating – focus of room, with iconic status (mainly domestic). Now considered an optional extra, depending on heating requirements.

■ **Built-in furniture**: Storage/display component fixed to structure.

These components of form have become established as the norm for two main reasons:

1. Structural development has led to a formalisation process, which has become a familiar global vocabulary for use in building.
2. Period styles have further maintained the continued use of these components.

At this stage, it is important to remind ourselves how the interior of a building has been formulated – it is either:

■ Through the building structure, without any further adornment, as explained in Chapter 2 (see p.31) and as epitomised by the work of early Modernists: 'Form follows function'. Thus the interior effect is mainly achieved through the strength and permanence of the building's structure (which has limitations of choice compared with the next category). We shall call this '**nuda veritas**'.

■ Through a series of insertions and interventions, in varying degrees, which override the building structure – hence the interior 'scenery' and cladding systems can hide, or partially hide, the building's architectural character and impose their own identity. The interior effect is achieved by a greater palette of available products and materials than is offered by nuda veritas, simply because the conditions of use are lightweight compared with a building's structure. We shall call this '**masque**'. (This would include the Responsive and Autonomous categories outlined in Chapter 2, p.31).

Initially in this analysis, we shall not distinguish between these two processes until it is necessary. There are more ways of breaking up the interior of a building into identifiable and usable units (instead of components) of form, which are not based on past methods of building. The purpose of this exercise is to modularise a building form in a way that advances the concept of building beyond traditional techniques, and enlarges the scope for design opportunity. It is simply another way of ordering structure. We will expand the existing vocabulary of form in a way that can help the designer formulate more controlled concepts. This will also feed into the expansive possibilities that CAD has opened up. We will begin by examining a simple square room (architectural solutions would emanate from this study) and breaking this down into identifiable units. The following studies are initially based on a rectilinear mode. Let us look first at plan units.

PLAN UNITS

The standard plan units of form of this simple square room, from existing building methods, would be:

4 x walls, 1 x door, 1 x window, 1 x chimney breast.

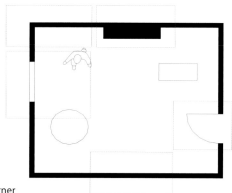

1. Corner
2. Chimney breast
3. Window frame
4. Door frame
5. Wall section

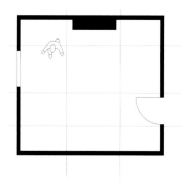

The next action to take is to impose a grid which creates total unitisation of this box room including floor and ceiling parts. There will remain two central floor/ceiling units which are not attached to perimeter wal components and will therefore remain as separate plane units.

If we now imagine the same room as a 3D box cut up into units, as indicated by the purple squares, we have five types of unit in total, which includes the ceiling and floor planes. In terms of quantities of each type in this plan, there are:

4 x unit 1, 1 x unit 2, 1 x unit 3, 1 x unit 4, 3 x unit 5.

This exercise does of course require the sizing of each unit in a modular way, which could, in the case of very long walls, break them down into more than just one number.

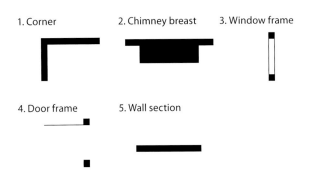

1. Corner   2. Chimney breast   3. Window frame

4. Door frame   5. Wall section

PLAN OF EACH STANDARD UNIT

We will now examine a fuller range of units on a simple geometric basis that seems to account for a variety of popular structural situations, which are not intended to be exhaustive but serve to illustrate the direction we are taking. First we will look at *elevational* unit forms, which are not necessarily of the plan units because these generate different conditions. This will be followed by an analysis of *plan* unit forms (not of any specific interior), because planning generates the first ideas in tandem with 3D visions. These 3D visions show the beginning of the 90° angled unit as a new concept of interior form. It must be appreciated that many geometric variations can be applied to this system.

Elevational studies

These are composed of wall, opening and frame – the dimensions and shape of which are based on considerations of proportion and the concept.

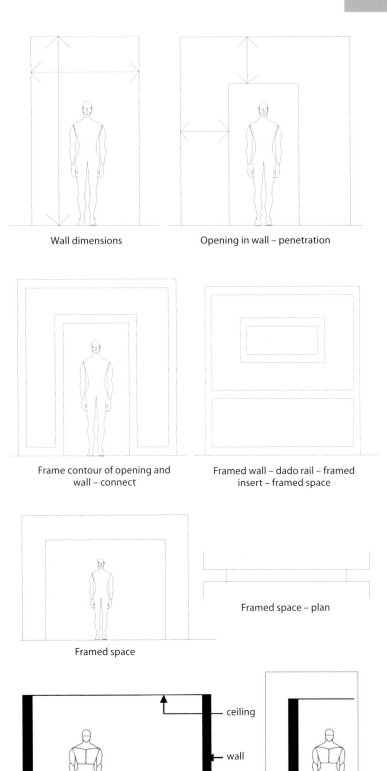

Wall dimensions

Opening in wall – penetration

Frame contour of opening and wall – connect

Framed wall – dado rail – framed insert – framed space

Framed space

Framed space – plan

Section through box room planes

ceiling

wall

floor

Unit composed of wall and part floor and ceiling

Plan view of perimeter planar unit types

This shows the main forces plus 3D views including floor and ceiling planes.

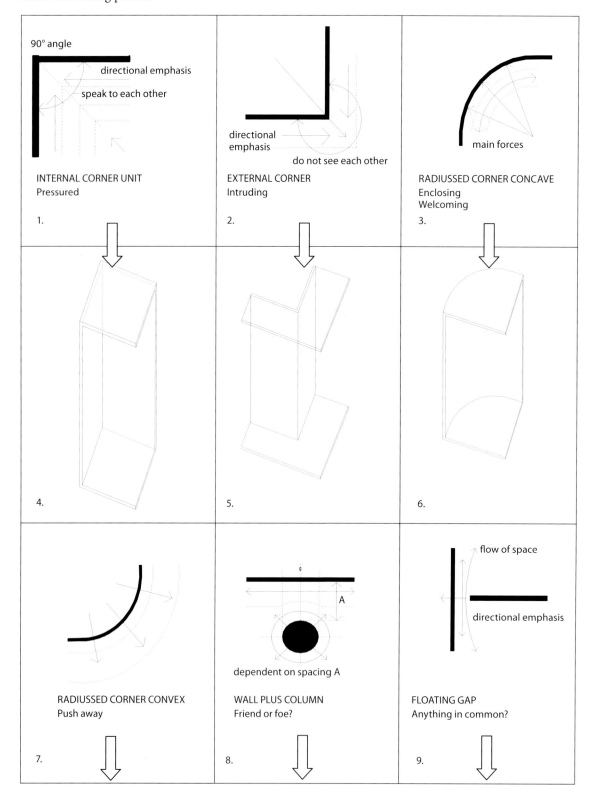

90° angle
directional emphasis
speak to each other

INTERNAL CORNER UNIT
Pressured

1.

directional emphasis
do not see each other

EXTERNAL CORNER
Intruding

2.

main forces

RADIUSSED CORNER CONCAVE
Enclosing
Welcoming

3.

4.

5.

6.

RADIUSSED CORNER CONVEX
Push away

A

dependent on spacing A

WALL PLUS COLUMN
Friend or foe?

flow of space

directional emphasis

FLOATING GAP
Anything in common?

7.

8.

9.

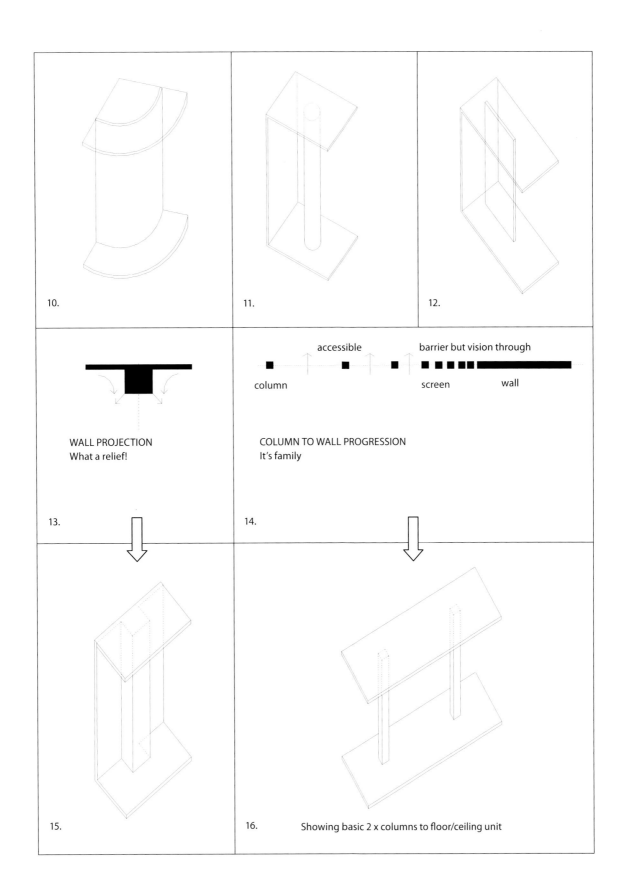

10.

11.

12.

WALL PROJECTION
What a relief!

13.

accessible   barrier but vision through

column   screen   wall

COLUMN TO WALL PROGRESSION
It's family

14.

15.

16.   Showing basic 2 x columns to floor/ceiling unit

From these studies...

We now have a sample range of newly defined plan units namely, internal corner, external corner, radiussed corner concave, radiussed corner convex, wall plus column, floating gap, wall projection and column series, which encompasses part of the ceiling and part of the floor. This requires a 90° angled prefabricated section at both ceiling and floor level.

WHY CONNECT WALLS AND COLUMNS TO PART-FLOOR AND PART-CEILING PLANES?

■ To escape from the conditioning of the 'box' – remove the corners.

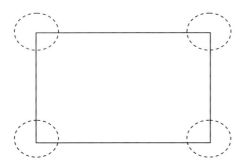

Corners create four joining lines of 'box'. I propose creating eight joining lines of new units - see below.

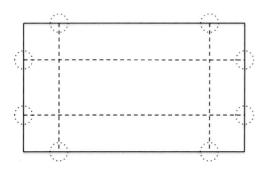

■ Because they connect with a dynamic relationship – 90° as opposed to 180° flatness.

■ Because ceiling/wall units have a greater free-form opportunity to connect above head height.

■ Because the floor and walls have commonality in terms of usage.

■ To break the monotony of the horizontal and vertical dictates.

■ Unit joining lines provide a means of breaking up the surface.

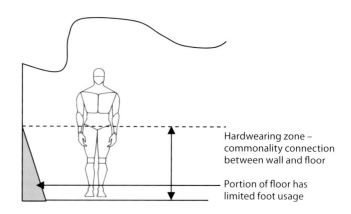

Hardwearing zone – commonality connection between wall and floor

Portion of floor has limited foot usage

Section showing horizontal break-up into three units (below)

This shows the radical departure of proposing that a 90° angled unit (can be of any profile) should be a basis for design. This implies that all units previously illustrated could be conceived in the following breakdown:

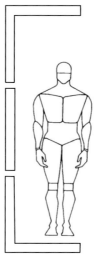

Apart from applying the 90° angle to planar unit forms it is important to emphasise that it can also be applied to framework design. The 90° form can now be made from many materials for it to be a viable building component under *nuda veritas* conditions, and much more easily with *masque* conditions.

Dimensional flexibility

Each component would be offered in varied dimensions to suit an application. Actual dimensions will vary, depending upon design requirements. All units can be of varied section following design requirements.

HOW IS THIS TO BE STRUCTURALLY VIABLE?

There two ways of approaching structural viability:

1. Building structure – designing a building system that integrates this unitisation.

2. Interior cladding system – designing a cladding system that will fix to any structure.

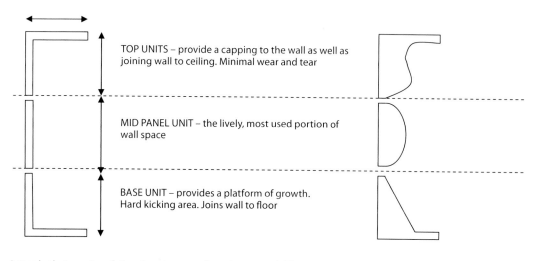

TOP UNITS – provide a capping to the wall as well as joining wall to ceiling. Minimal wear and tear

MID PANEL UNIT – the lively, most used portion of wall space

BASE UNIT – provides a platform of growth. Hard kicking area. Joins wall to floor

Let us look at a series of elevations to see various sizes at work. The joints between the units provide opportunity for installing power connections, track fixing for a variety of uses including cantilevered shelving and other furniture items.

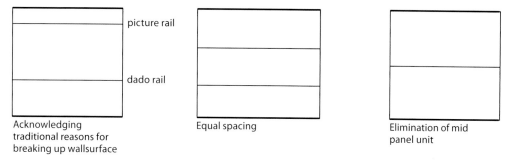

picture rail

dado rail

Acknowledging traditional reasons for breaking up wallsurface

Equal spacing

Elimination of mid panel unit

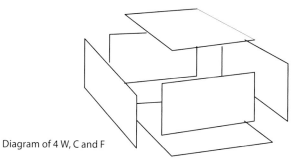

Diagram of 4 W, C and F

What has to be overcome is the dictate of the box structure of four walls (4W), a ceiling (C) and a floor (F).

The shop interior (right) is made of sections moulded from glass-reinforced plastic (GRP). The retail sector seems to produce many more modular solutions to satisfy the demands of display functions than other sectors.

Figure 245. Shop for the Italian knitwear brand, Stefanel, Hamburg. Sybarite, 2009. Photo: Marco Zanta. This shows modular units.

PERSPECTIVE OF SOME SIMPLE PLANAR UNITS

This drawing shows a modularised series of perimeter units with the ceiling and floor horizontal planes making two-directional units. The remaining wall sections in the centre form one corner unit and one flat unit.

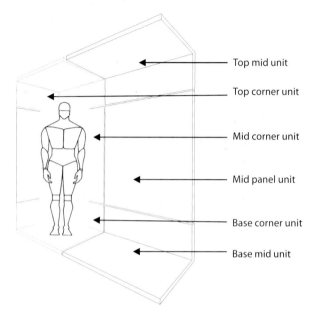

Top mid unit

Top corner unit

Mid corner unit

Mid panel unit

Base corner unit

Base mid unit

The idea of making two-directional units contravenes all known building methods or rationale. This is because my idea of designing these does not follow a traditional 'making' technique. If this approach creates new scope for expression and design, and helps solve existing problems then it deserves to be tested for validity in terms of costing and making.

Plan showing varied modular units on a grid indicating possible arrangements of perimeter units as well as flat mid units of floor and ceiling.

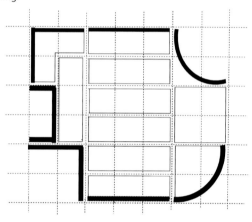

PLAN OF NON-FUNCTIONAL SPACE

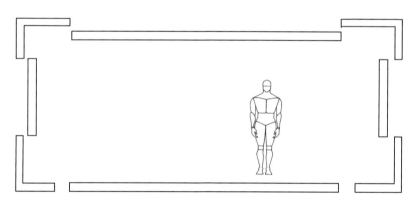

Section showing possible adjustment of these smaller units and perspective below showing modularised format with surfaces flush to each other.

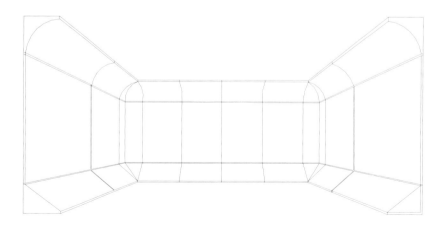

MORE CHALLENGES OF THE BOX

We have seen how the early Modernists set out to successfully destroy the concept of the box. The Deconstructivists have also destroyed the box, but replaced it with rather threatening forms that represent the worst and most destabilising aspects of humanity. A traditional economic constraint, still imposed upon buildings, might be termed 'straight wall syndrome'. Many building plans simply repeat the '4W, C and F' method rather than being based on a unitised, interlocking way of designing, as demonstrated by Moshe Safdie's housing scheme for Habitat '67, which was part of the Expo '67 in Montreal.

Another modularised scheme based on similar lines is Herman Hertzberger's Central Beheer office project, illustrated in Chapter 6 (Figure 129, p.109). The advantages of modular interlinking become more engaging and potentially fruitful when there are actual connecting devices. Let us examine the children's jigsaw puzzle.[22]

The familiar jigsaw pattern on the left, which is manufactured with many variations of printed image on the surface, has about nine variations in its pieces (excluding edge and corner pieces), and has provided endless hours of pleasure to people of all ages. A puzzle made using the plain grid on the right (toddlers' puzzles can come into this category) would not offer the same degree of excitement, as there are no connecting devices. It is the act of interlocking the pieces to make them fit, stabilising any movement, that provides the joy of resolution. The interlocking puzzle pieces have to be right to ensure a good fit, whereas the rectangular pieces can just butt up to each other (although this would not ensure that the picture on the surface was correct). Similarly, building structures that follow the plain grid epitomise

the dull results of economic necessity, so the following studies will show the benefit and potential of planning interior shells (and buildings) that can create a deeper sense of attachment and well-being with their spaces.

CORNERS OF THE BOX (OR CELL)

All the interior spaces of a building can be described as cells. The following proposals for interior cells can be adjusted dimensionally to suit the particular contract. This example assumes a continuous structural envelope, which could then be applied to other variable plan forms.

INTRUSIVE CORNER

This proposal is generic in nature and not specific to any of the social strata of activity. It could apply to any building and leads towards multipurpose, adaptable building types. As many buildings with different uses contain similar building forms and components, there has been a movement towards standardising the building forms so that they have a generic rather than a specific character and function. This movement led to the international conference Adaptables 2006 on adaptable building structures in Eindhoven, the Netherlands, July 2006 (see extract on next page).

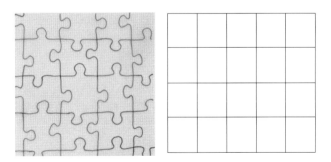

Figure 247. Typical jigsaw puzzle pattern. Drawn by the author.

Figure 248. Simple block puzzle. Drawn by the author.

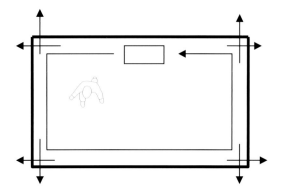

Fig A. STANDARD BOX INTERIOR

Plan showing the flexible facility of positioning of an interior component anywhere along an uninterrupted wall space. Also see how the walls' direction goes beyond the corners. Corners can be full of foreboding. Dunces used to stand in the corner in disgrace. The corner was not a place to be.

Result: economically functional BUT aesthetically dull and moribund. That is why decoration became so popular.

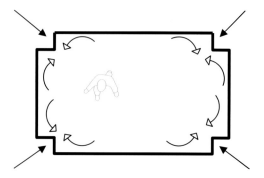

Fig B. INTRUSIVE CORNER PLAN

Plan with inverted corners generates more interest, and is more welcoming. I have created 4 external corners and 8 internal corners instead of 4, but they are not corners of the room; they are second role corners whose status is more helpful and friendly than the corner in Fig A. For example, they can receive interior components with equal access from the interior space.

Result: The corners increase intimacy and containment which reduces despair.

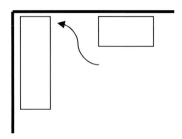

Fig C. Corner of this plan does not allow equal access to interior components

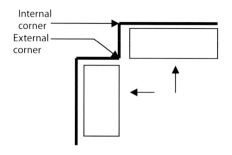

Fig D. This plan allows equal access

The paper extract below is from the 'Adaptables' conference, 2006:

This paper details an adaptable building design concept called Multispace, developed by Reid Architecture [Gregory 2005]. The intention of this study is not to develop the ultimate flexible building, but is to explore the differences between flexibility and adaptability, and to make recommendations for adaptable building design that can be fitted out, with minimal changes, to achieve a variety of uses. Our thinking is strongly aligned with that of Brand, whose seminal work on building adaptation put forward key exemplars and principles [Brand 1994]. The common features identified in the design facilitate the movement from bespoke to mass customised construction.

Co-authors: N. Davison, A. G. Gibb, S. A. Austin and C. I. Goodier, Department of Civil and Building Engineering, Loughborough University, UK, P. Warner, Reid Architecture, London.

Fig E. PROPOSED REPEATED MODULAR ARRANGEMENT OF CELLS
FOR DEFINING MULTI-USE SPACES USING INTRUSIVE CORNER PLAN

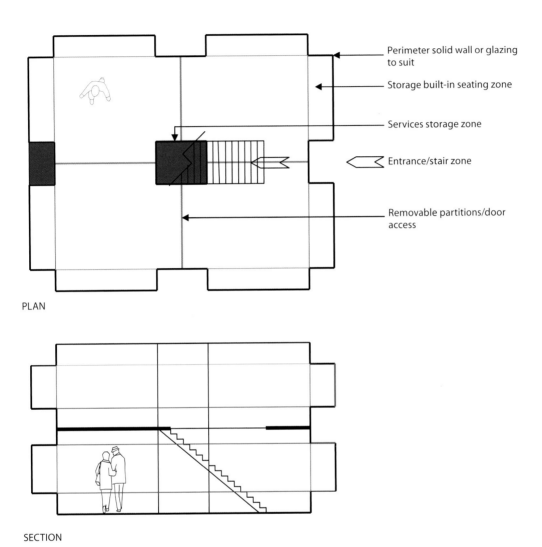

Perimeter solid wall or glazing to suit

Storage built-in seating zone

Services storage zone

Entrance/stair zone

Removable partitions/door access

PLAN

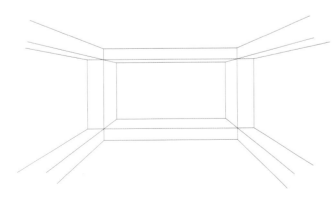

SECTION

Fig F. Perspective of one space showing how the Intrusive Corner works at all junctions of 4W, C and F.

POCKET AND CHAMFERED CORNER

All of the following examples vaporise the tension that exists in the standard 90° box and provide more expressive opportunities. Let us examine other ways of destroying the 'corner' of the box from the following plans and detail plans:

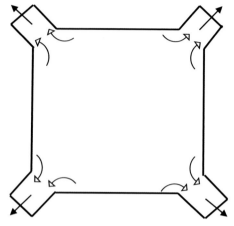

Fig G. 45° POCKET CORNER PLAN

Fig H. CHAMFERED CORNER PLAN

This solution creates a diagonal interest and creates a recessed 'pocket' with two corners in each. I have also created 8 internal angles into the arena of 225°. Four more ancillary small spaces are created for extended functions.

Result: Helps the room space expand and be liberated.

A simpler solution which reduces room area and creates an octagonal arrangement that has been done in many buildings from medieval times to the present day. Creates 8 x 135° internal angles.

Result: complete disappearance of the 90° corner

DETAILS OF CORNERS

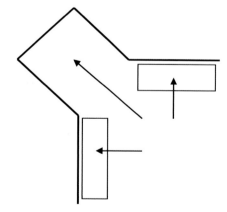

Fig J. Uninterrupted access to furniture and Pocket Corner

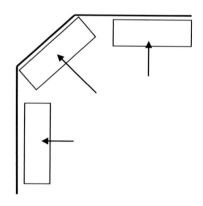

Fig K. Equalised access to all furniture

PROPOSED REPEATED MODULAR ARRANGEMENT – THIS COMBINES
BOTH POCKET AND CHAMFERED SOLUTIONS

SQUARE POCKET CORNER

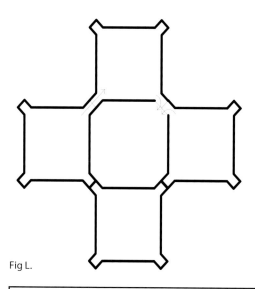

Fig L.

The choice of what is solid wall and what is glazing
is the same as in Fig E. The pocket corners connect,
providing suitable circulation links with each cell if
desired. The central area is the chamfered solution,
and could be an exterior space.

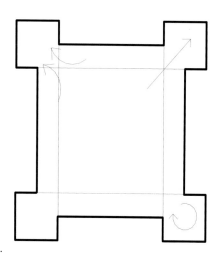

Fig N.

This plan shows a recessed square pocket which
extends the original corner and creates 12 more
internal corners and 8 external corners.

PROPOSED REPEATED MODULAR ARRANGEMENT

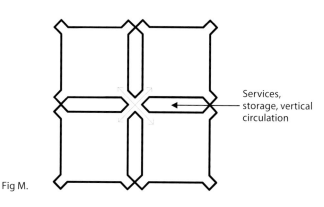

Fig M.

Services,
storage, vertical
circulation

A different cellular arrangement cancelling out
the chamfered cell. This produces cross-circulation
connections and space for potential services,
storage or vertical circulation.

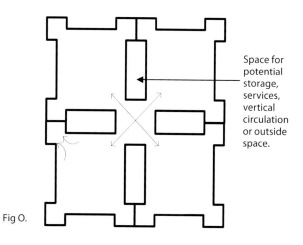

Space for
potential
storage,
services,
vertical
circulation
or outside
space.

Fig O.

The interlocking corners create potential
connections.

PROPOSED REPEATED MODULAR ARRANGEMENT

The previous ideas need to be explored further to confirm usage and application. With more variations than the standard '4W, C and F' box, the costs will increase, but the important point to make here is that the pursuit of art and the creation of a spirit in interior design should not be financially accountable at birth. Ideas must be given a chance to survive.

WALLS

Walls form part of the traditional box structure and are most commonly vertically continuous from floor to ceiling. Again this is a common building element, as we have listed, and forms part of the economic solution, common to the majority of buildings, for space division. As with the previous study of the corner of the box, the vertical wall is a rather cold and unwelcoming form. Let us examine an expansion of its functions to embrace storage and display.

An increased thickness in a wall will have a huge impact on planning and space calculations. It could be a notion that only applies to interiors that need this facility. It obviates the need to add furniture to the space, because this solution provides a built-in option for such a need.

SEARCH FOR GRID PATTERNS

Building design grids are excessively dominated by existing structural, product and material dimensional coordination. The standard modular dimension of 500mm or 600mm is governed by the availability of products that are made using these dimensions or their multiples. Also, the geometric basis of many interior designs is usually controlled by inherited architectural principles or the existing building's geometry, if the design is from nuda veritas (see p.172). At the opposite extreme, the Deconstructivist's approach is based on concealment of a regular grid and betrays no repetition in the design.

Greater relevance and harmony would be achieved if the human form served as a stronger basis for the design of interiors. Comparing architecture to interior design, one could take the view that in terms of scale, a building's exterior is more detached from the human form than the interior. The interior, as stated in the Introduction, is the second layer enclosing the human form after the clothing we wear, and therefore there is a very close connection between the human form and the interior. The following studies demonstrate a way forward. The shapes could represent enclosing/storage/display elements, but there is nothing specifically designed here as the illustrations only serve to introduce a basis for working from a new set of grids. There are many other variations to this, depending upon further observations of the human form's geometric qualities.

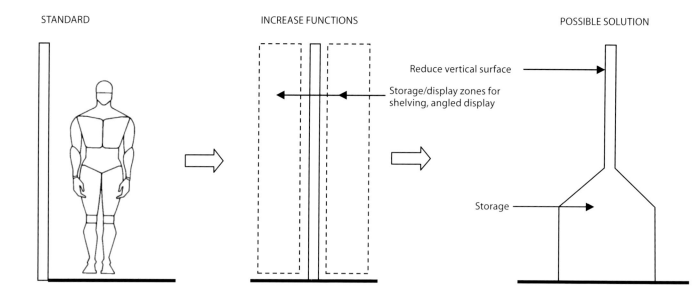

STANDARD

INCREASE FUNCTIONS

POSSIBLE SOLUTION

Reduce vertical surface ⟶

Storage/display zones for shelving, angled display

Storage ⟶

The act of designing is partially about form-making, profiling, fitting things together, and using the language of line, form, colour and texture. These studies, using the human form, are part of a way of giving reason or credence to a particular shape, to satisfy and contribute to the conceptual blend that is detailed in Chapter 2 (see p.55). There are many sources for ideas in science and nature that have inspired designers, as we have seen in other parts of this book. So it is important to stress that designers need to explain *why* they have designed something referring to points made in 'What are the main skills and qualities of an interior designer' and 'What theoretical basis does the designer work from?' (Chapter 1), p.21–22.

PLAN PROFILES TAKEN FROM HUMAN FORM GRIDS

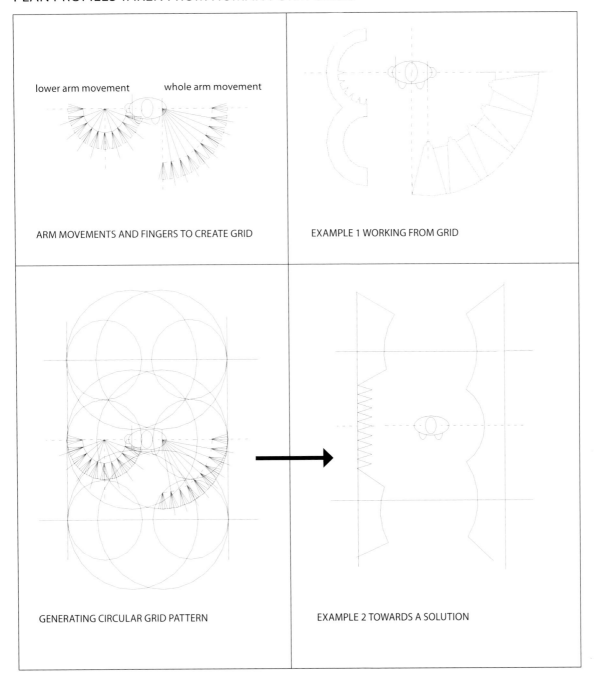

lower arm movement   whole arm movement

ARM MOVEMENTS AND FINGERS TO CREATE GRID

EXAMPLE 1 WORKING FROM GRID

GENERATING CIRCULAR GRID PATTERN

EXAMPLE 2 TOWARDS A SOLUTION

ELEVATION PROFILES TAKEN FROM HUMAN FORM GRIDS

These are simply demonstrating the potential of resultant shapes and
not the result of any specific activity.

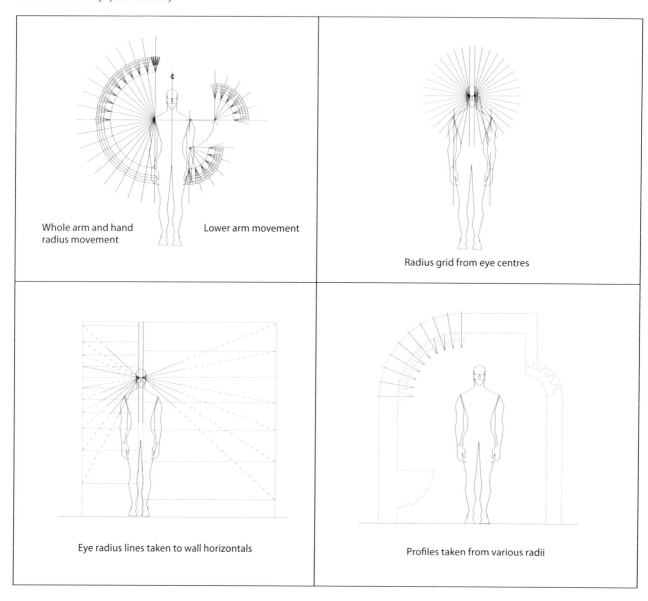

Whole arm and hand
radius movement

Lower arm movement

Radius grid from eye centres

Eye radius lines taken to wall horizontals

Profiles taken from various radii

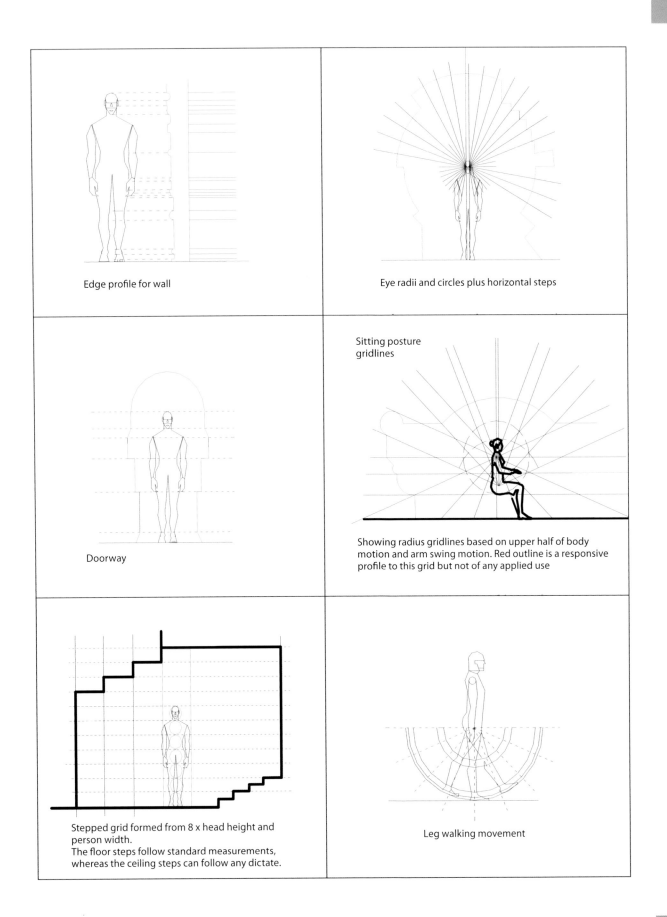

Edge profile for wall

Eye radii and circles plus horizontal steps

Doorway

Sitting posture gridlines

Showing radius gridlines based on upper half of body motion and arm swing motion. Red outline is a responsive profile to this grid but not of any applied use

Stepped grid formed from 8 x head height and person width.
The floor steps follow standard measurements, whereas the ceiling steps can follow any dictate.

Leg walking movement

TOWARDS A DESIGN APPROACH THAT INTEGRATES THE HUMAN FORM WITH THE INTERIOR

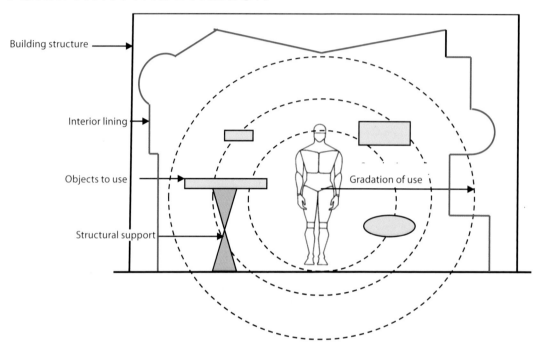

Building structure

Interior lining

Objects to use

Gradation of use

Structural support

So far in this book, we have looked at the eight concepts that need to be coordinated when producing a design solution (see Chapter 2, p.55). But there has to be a starting-off point, whereby the whole process is ignited by an idea. This idea can come from any part of the preliminary stages of the project, such as the client briefing or design research.

The planning process, which integrates and generates at the same time, is dependent upon certain known facts that help with spatial relationships and the shaping of these spaces in 3D. I would like to suggest that this process should start with the human figure's postures, activities and needs *immediately surrounding the figure*. In other words, think in terms of dressing the figure with *contact parts* (parts of the interior that the person actually touches and uses), and gradually work away from the figure to the perimeter of the particular space being designed.

The sectional diagram above illustrates the gradation of proximity to the figure of the reachable items for a defined activity. The portable items that a person needs (books, laptop or toiletries, for example) should be positioned *in space* in the desired position for access. The relationship of product to user will be classified as described in the storage section in Chapter 2 (see p.46).

The next stage in the process is to decide what structural support will be given to those objects within the defined needs of display/access requirements. Herein begins the sculptural formation of the area immediately around the figure. As this concentrated ergonomic study flows outwards from the figure, it will interact with the enclosing architectural elements of the space. The diagram above helps to spatially manage the operation.

The diagram opposite illustrates the range of possible surface positions for all activities in terms of support. Whether we are sitting or standing, we use a variety of surfaces at varying inclines, from the horizontal to the vertical.

CAN WE WEAR PARTS OF AN INTERIOR?

The above question should be given to all students at design schools, as it stretches the mind, involves the overlapping of functions and promotes exploration of the field of interior design. Much research has been done on responsive and interactive architecture,[23] which is driven by computer and sensor technology. This study could be considered within the same category; it could also be described as a somewhat mad concept!

> *Though this be madness, yet there is method in't.*
> Hamlet, Act II, Scene ii. William Shakespeare, *c*.1600

The study is based upon the notion that what the human form wears and carries has a particular relationship to the interior. Why should we want to attempt to wear something that is not clothing? This question assumes that an interior does not have any wearable items simply because nobody has designed any. Why should an interior consist of wearable parts? What would be the purpose of such a facility and what would be the benefits? This book does not intend to offer design solutions at this stage, as we are merely investigating possibilities. Let us explore further.

Figure 249 shows a fifteenth-century painting of Saint Domingo sitting on a throne. His garments are textured and patterned rather like the throne he is sitting on. The whole picture is highly decorative, integrating the figure with the background. The throne is reminiscent of a Gothic building. It is as though the Saint Domingo is wearing his surrounding environment. The suit of armour in Figure 250 was used in battle and is strongly protective. It is made up of separate rigid metal units, which are joined to allow the knight to move his limbs. Both the suit of armour and the painting have been mounted on walls for display. So, we have two examples of specialist clothing that have a strong relationship with the interior environment.

Therefore one could conclude that any interior that integrated wearable parts into its structure would provide a closer bond with the people using it.

CLOTHING/APPAREL

Today we have, on the one hand, the interior of a building with furniture, objects and so on; on the other hand, we have the human form wearing clothes and sometimes attachments. In many societies, norms about clothing reflect standards of modesty, religion, gender and social status. Clothing may also function as a form of adornment and an expression of personal taste or style in accordance with the activity at hand. For the purposes of this exercise, we shall concentrate on standard modern Western dress. The relationship of a person to the interior of a building, in terms of physical contact, is as follows:

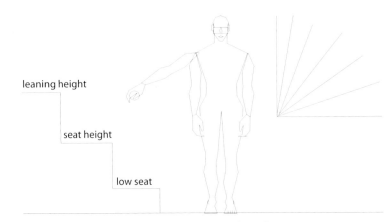

Facilities required horizontal and vertical – sitting and standing. Levels indicated as well as angled vertical surfaces down to 180 degrees.

Figure 249. *Left.* Bartolomé Bermejo, *Santo Domingo of Silos*, 1475. Prado Museum, Spain. Wikimedia Commons.

Figure 250. *Right.* Sir Henry Lee's suit of armour at the Armourers and Brasiers' Company Hall, London. Drawn by the author.

- Hands operate devices or hold on for support.

- Feet walk on floor/steps.

- Body sits/reclines on support items.

The relationship of our clothing to the interior is as follows:

■ We may wear a uniform that visually fits the interior environment and purpose.

■ Attachments such as bags and umbrellas may be taken off and placed in storage.

■ Clothing – such as hats and coats – may be taken off and hung up temporarily to keep its shape.

■ Footwear may be changed or removed according to function.

The diagram below shows an abstracted modularised figure divided into parts that wear clothing, which could influence wall parts.

The twenty-two parts of the figure, which is divided into two halves down the centre of the body, back and front (rather than down the side), could dictate twenty-two parts of outer clothing (not underwear), which are each detachable from each other as well as from the figure. This is a proposed modularised analysis of how each part of the figure could be divided up according to clothing attachments. To expand further:

■ Head (1, 2, 3, 4). Following on from medieval helmets, masks and a variety of headgear, there could be four parts.

■ Neck (5, 6). One or two collar parts.

■ Upper arm (7, 10). Two sleeve (tube) parts.

■ Lower arm (11, 14). Two sleeve (tube) parts.

■ Torso (8, 9). Two parts.

■ Buttocks (12, 13). Two parts.

■ Hands (15, 16). Two parts: glove or mitten type.

■ Upper leg (17, 18). Two parts (tubes): could be trouser type (two tubes) or skirt type (one tube).

■ Lower leg (19, 20). Two parts (tubes).

■ Feet (21, 22). Two parts: shoe type.

All items are intended to be put on and replaced individually by Velcro-type connectors for ease and speed. The standard clothing items that are currently worn (this can apply to both sexes) are as follows, with directions for dressing:

• 1 x hat. Place on head.

• 1 x jacket. Slide one arm and then the other into each sleeve and then hoist over the shoulders; button at front.

• 1 x pair of trousers. Stand on one leg and place one leg into one trouser leg. Repeat process for other leg.

• 2 x shoes. Slip a foot into each.

• 1 x pair of socks. Slip a sock over each foot.

• 1 x shirt. Same operation as jacket.

• 2 x gloves. Slip over hands.

This is a total of ten items. Additional or alternative items could be jumpers, T-shirts, ties, belt and laces.

All clothing items need to be soft and flexible (apart from shoes) for reasons of comfort, ease of replacement and cleaning. Which interior elements fall into this category? Curtain drapes, fabric wall hangings, upholstery fabric (leather and canvas), cushioned wall linings, cushioned seating, bed coverings and soft floor coverings.

So we have established that there are some common interactive possibilities, but let us look more closely at exactly where and how such a relationship can be developed. Of course we are not forgetting that clothing is personal, and therefore you might conjecture that this could only work in a private environment such as in a domestic situation; or maybe not?

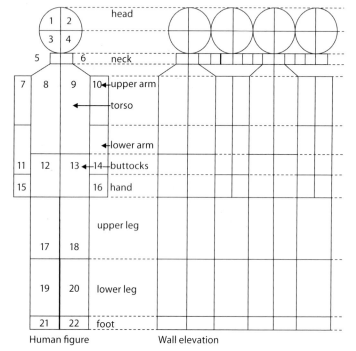

Human figure   Wall elevation

SUPPORT/DISPLAY FUNCTIONS

Let us examine further wider possibilities: the initial suggestion here was to modularise a wall into components that could be used for such an interchange. What about furniture items or indeed other forms of structure designed for such interchange?

The coat stand (see below) has obvious visual associations with the stag's head, which has also been used for hanging clothes. More importantly, the stag's head has been used as wall decoration, originally as a trophy of capture by the owner. Chalayan's item (see Figure 253) is an imaginative exploration of the relationship of the figure to furniture. Chalayan states:

> *Inhabiting this new environment has had its effect on the human body. By way of assimilation the body has been contorted into its dimensions in order to better synchronise itself with that space. As a result, it has transformed into a motif of its environment … the characters dressed in garments echoing the space cast a spell on the central figure. The central figure gets monumentalised as a marble statue further integrating itself into the environment.*

Figure 254 shows a conical lampshade that is very similar in shape to a Chinese hat. There are many hats on the market that are reminiscent of lampshades, hence it is quite logical to combine both uses of hat and shade into one. Lucie Koldava is a very talented designer who has designed a range of fitness equipment, shown in Figure 255, that fits into an interior as a wall item. The clothes butler in Figure 256, overleaf, is almost a display item and can support a jacket, trousers and accessories, as well as offering a drawer for shoes. The children's wall panel in Figure 257 is an example of soft wall units for display/storage and also includes a removable mirror.

Figure 251. Hat/coat umbrella stand, HND (UK).

Figure 252. Stag's head. Drawing by author.

Figure 253. 'After Words' fashion item. Hussein Chalayan (born 1970, British-Turkish fashion designer) Photo: Chris Moore.

Figure 254. Swan-necked mannequin lamp. Stephen Jones, Milliner, b.1957. The head and neck form of the body has been used as a lamp holder.

Figure 255. Home fitness wall product. Lucie Koldova, Czech Republic, 2009.

Figure 256. *Left.* Pine clothes butler, from Watson's-on-the-Web (www.Watsonsontheweb.co.uk).

Figure 257. *Centre.* Children's wall storage panel. 'Odds and Ends' by Haba, 2001.

Figure 258. *Right.* Coats on hooks. Photo by author.

TRADITIONAL CLOTHING ROUTE

Traditionally, clothing is stored on hangers, hooks, pegs or dummies (the last used mainly by dressmakers).

Clothing is not usually kept on display because it would take up too much space and gather dust. When visually exposed on coat hooks, coats and scarves can look extremely unsightly, and it does not flatter the garments themselves, as you can see in Figure 258. Of course the coat hook system has international acceptance as the economic and speedy way of hanging coats and hats. So we have a design problem that is not being tackled, except in the beautiful scheme illustrated in Figure 10, Chapter 2 (see p.32).

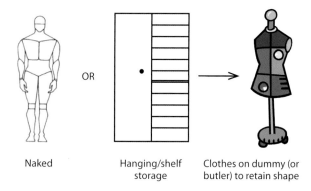

Naked   OR   Hanging/shelf   Clothes on dummy (or
                           storage   butler) to retain shape

THE HUMAN FORM'S INTIMATE CONTACT RELATIONSHIP WITH AN INTERIOR

■ **Sleeping:** Lying on a piece of furniture; wrapped in bedding; clothing changed to nightwear.

■ **Sitting:** Reclining or sitting upright on a piece of furniture; could have additional cushions and rolls; used in all states of dress.

■ **Cleansing:** Washing and bodily functions; receptacles for holding water, bathing, showering; body naked or prepared for particular function.

Attachments that the figure can wear or carry

If we are examining what a person wears we need to understand the carrying capability in order to assess the kind of connection to be made with interior components. Of course, when these attached items are not being worn or carried, they need a place within the interior to be stored or positioned.

- Jewellery
- Watch
- Wallet
- Cigarettes, lighter
- Mobile phone
- iPod
- Camera
- Binoculars
- Spectacles

- Headphones

- Walking stick

- Umbrella

- Rucksack

- Writing instrument

- Badge, name tag

Common portable objects that are placed within an interior

Whilst the items listed above are worn, or form a close bond with the figure, the following list comprises items that are carried from one space to another for a short duration. (N.B. The list of items excludes those of the kitchen, bathroom or other specialised work areas.)

- Bag, suitcase, briefcase

- Books, newspapers, magazines

- CDs, DVDs etc.

- Laptop

- Telephone handset – landline

- Audiovisual remote handset

- Files

- Laundry

- Games

- DIY tools

The bicycle is an interesting object to consider in this scenario as it is *ridden* by a person rather than being *worn*. However, it is sometimes taken into a building if space permits, or a special receiving place has been designed to accommodate it – namely, a bike rack. This is an example of the building accommodating part of a person's property, which is close to the theme of this section of the book.

What is the human form's potential carrying ability?

One example of what the human figure can carry is that of a soldier dressed for combat (see Figure 259). Whilst he needs certain bits of equipment such as ammunition, night goggles, radio equipment and so on, he needs as much mobility as possible. The soldier in Figure 260 has a rucksack with a sleeping bag, for a different type of assignment. Both examples demonstrate good carrying capability.

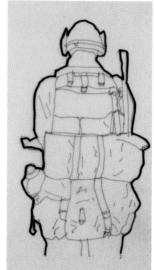

Figure 259. Soldier dressed and equipped for combat. Drawing by the author.

Figure 260. Soldier dressed and equipped for travelling some distance. Drawing by the author.

IF THERE IS A NEED TO WEAR PART OF AN INTERIOR, HOW WILL THIS BE REALISED?

We need to re-examine the list of elements from Chapter 2 (see p.29) and think of the three elements of enclosure, support, and display, storage and worksurface in a different way. We may need to add another interior element entitled 'apparel provision'. Interior walls can sometimes be lined with some form of cladding, just as the human form is clothed (which could also be described as cladding). Soft furniture forms are also clad in fabric. So what we are trying to do is to make closer connections between these three types.

In order to accept apparel provision in interiors, we have to test its validity and usefulness:

■ It has already been stated that it would make a person bond more closely with the interior.

■ A change of cladding can be made without resorting to going to another storage area.

■ The range of twenty-two items (see p.190) provides great choice for which part to detach. This will add interest as each person will make different choices.

■ Items are seen as part of the interior until removed and worn.

■ The designer is given an excuse for breaking up the interior for a *purpose* and not just for decoration's sake.

WALL GRID OF APPAREL UNITS

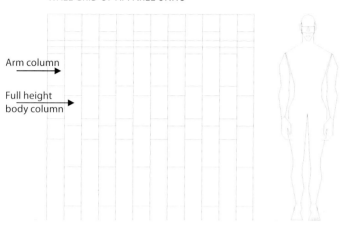

Arm column

Full height
body column

Figure 261. A white apartment for a musician, Romania. Parasite Studio, 2008. The image shows a varied arrangement of wall cupboards.

The elevation above is a rationalised version of the one on p.190 taken from the human figure. The vertical columns alternate; it does not indicate the full height of the wall; and the wall is gridded into the maximum number of panels available, which delineate potential accessible apparel. The location of these panels, and whether or not all of them would be available, would be determined by the particular function of the interior and should be included as a requirement along with all other requirements of the project. The dimensions would be adjusted to suit.

SOME QUESTIONS AT THIS STAGE

Q: How is the apparel fitted to the wall?

A: By Velcro-type fasteners – either as peelable layers or hidden behind panel doors.

Q: The grid appears to dictate a rectangular modular format – is that correct?

A: As with any design idea, this concept needs to be developed in order to test how many variations are possible with regard to provision and shape.

Q: Can people choose a particular style, colour or material?

A: This is dependent upon the type of interior activity, which will dictate such properties. People have already made a choice by entering the interior and becoming part of it.

Q: What are the circumstances for someone to change or add to their clothing? Normally we discard certain items of clothing because of varying weather conditions, or we

change for a sporting activity. In this scenario, people would change or swap some or all of their clothing in order to identify themselves with the interior.

A: This idea challenges existing custom and habits and therefore requires exhaustive research and test applications to try it out. It would be fascinating to see designers take the idea on board as it would no doubt widen our understanding of, and attachment to, the interiors of our buildings.

Figure 261, whilst not dealing with 'wearable units', does show an example of a wall divided up into storage units of varied shapes and colours.

It is not the task of this book to entertain any specific solutions to this idea of apparel provision. This exercise serves to demonstrate an imaginative stretching of the normal boundaries of interior design, which it is hoped that the reader will find inspiring.

REVIEW

In design, there is no end of searching and exploration. But as far as this present mission is concerned, this chapter should help to advance ideas that stimulate fresh directions. Some readers may feel that imposing some sort of code on a way of working is restrictive and could impose limitations. It is a question of control and being systematic. Through the historical examples given here, readers will understand that a system provides a means of doing. Without a system that acknowledges inherited methods, designers lack that element of connectivity to our roots which gives credence to new ideas.

9: CONCLUSION

When I started writing this book, I had a rough idea of content and message. But as an inexperienced writer, I had no idea how creative an occupation it would prove to be. Instead of everything being preordained, the content of what I wanted to say expanded as I wrote. The core of the book was initially designed around my lecture notes on design theory. It soon became apparent that so many more issues needed to be addressed. Also, I was aware that much of what I have written about was never delivered in my classes simply because there was no time in the curriculum to deliver this additional material at an undergraduate level. This may indicate that postgraduate study would create such an opportunity, and perhaps some of the content of this book could be suitable for such study.

I stated in the Preface that I had no intention of repeating what can be found elsewhere, except where relevant. I actually found this posture rather difficult to maintain, because in attempting to contain an argument or issue, and illustrate where necessary, I have probably repeated myself. So I hope readers will forgive me, and find that the points I make are illuminating and helpful.

I hope that students of this discipline will regard this book as an aid to the continual quest for producing creative design solutions that people will embrace and enjoy, achieving a level of satisfaction that is commensurate with the investment of the stakeholders. If you use Google to perform a search for interior design, the first page that comes up is almost solely devoted to the decoration side of the business. This demonstrates that the major part of the industry is still devoted to furnishing and decoration, and the more architectural side of the discipline is consigned to a smaller share of the business. If you search for 'interior architecture', four of the items that come up refer to educational courses in the subject, and only two practices describe themselves as being interior architects.

Figure 262. Komb House, by Karim Rashid, shown at Le Marche exhibition in Cairo, Egypt, 2010. An eco-friendly house based on Islamic design principles.

Figure 263. Anish Kapoor's *Leviathan*, Grand Palais, Paris, 2011. Photographer: Stefan Tuchila.

Students of art and design will be aware of the close interaction between both of these subjects. Traditionally, art is seen as being portrayed in painting and sculpture, and design is seen as covering commercially driven disciplines, as mentioned in Chapter 2. But in the last fifty years, art has gradually strayed into design, and design has gradually strayed into art.

Figure 263, on the previous page, shows how the scale of an art installation can be comparable with that of a building. Figure 262 shows the effervescent work of the multi-talented all-round designer, Karim Rashid.

The technology and mechanics of production may vary between art and design, but because of this blurring and overlap, the essential result has similarities. It should be clear from this book that I regard interior design as being an art form. The following table is an interesting summary, I think.

ART = DESIGN DESIGN = ART		
	ART	DESIGN
Inspiration	Ideas of form, colour, texture, line, shape, materials and structure	Same
Motivation	Challenge, solving a problem, the expression of something, making a statement	Same
Rationale	Theoretical and philosophical stance	Same
Application	Must work, be fit for purpose, provide user satisfaction	Same

Interior design can be self-promotional in the sense that designers do not have to sit around waiting for a client-driven job to come in. A designer can have an idea for something that may be based on a factory product or a building component. Once he or she has defined the project, ascertained the need for it and conducted market research to confirm acceptance, the next critical stage is to negotiate some kind of financial support to enable the project to have the chance of life.

APPENDIX

PERSONAL JOURNEY

My interest in art began at an early age in school where I first demonstrated my talent for drawing. This was combined with a deep sensitivity to my environment, as post-war Britain was exceedingly grim, especially in Brixton, South London, where I grew up. Bombed out buildings and bomb sites were my playgrounds. Ghastly British Railways green was all too ubiquitous, and the poverty of internal decoration was all around me.

STUDENT EXPERIENCE, 1964

Once hooked on the subject of design I eventually went on to specialise in interior design; first at Hammersmith College of Art and Building[1] (now Chelsea College of Art), and then at the Royal College of Art, London, under Sir Hugh Casson[2]. I always wanted to take an exploratory approach in my design work rather than follow established norms. The illustrations on the right show a pub scheme concept that I did in my second year at the RCA, entitled 'Pub '84', taking my inspiration from George Orwell's book *Nineteen Eighty-Four*. I was inspired by the Lamson pneumatic tube system, which was in use in the big stores in the 1950s, to devise a system of self-service. Customers would insert a credit card (not in public circulation until many years later) into one of three service stations and select their food and drink. Their order would arrive in pre-packed containers down tubes from a central distribution centre above. Once they had finished, they would throw all empty containers under the seating, and these would be sucked back for recycling.

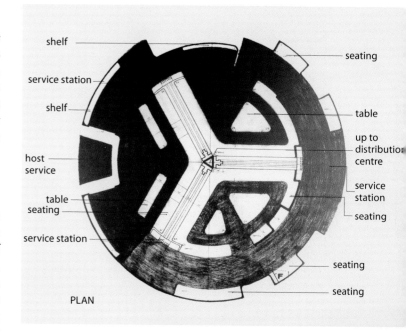

PLAN

Figure 264. *Top*. Plan showing three seating areas, corridor and host contact. Drawing by author.

Figure 265. Plaster model ⅓ full size, 1964. Author's work.

Figure 266. Jones' Jewellery Shop, Knightsbridge, London, 1968. Project team: Anthony Sully for Michael Brown. Client: Annabel Jones, Cob Stenham.

JONES' JEWELLERY SHOP, 1968

The first major project I worked on after graduation allowed me to experiment with efficient use of space on a restricted corner site in Brompton Arcade, Knightsbridge, London. It was Jones' Jewellery Shop, a retail project that I designed for the architect Michael Brown. The site had an existing cast iron column just off-centre, and this inspired me to think of vertical display columns. I then investigated the concept of sliding tubes within tubes, telescopically suspended from the ceiling on a pulley system, with the exception of floor-to-ceiling displays. This enabled the floor space to be free from displays, and meant that customers could pull down tubes containing jewellery, triggering an internal spotlight, to view the jewellery at chest height, as and when desired.

The above image shows tubes suspended from the ceiling as well as floor-to-ceiling tubes. The handles are concealed within the base of the tube, which is locked into the acrylic with a pin tumbler lock. The tubes were made by sub-contractors Rivington Plastics, whose specialism was laying drains made of PVC tubing. When I asked if they would be interested in making these tubular shopfitting items they jumped at the chance, and did a superb job.

IBM SHOWROOM, 1971

The next project that involved re-thinking was examining the way IBM used their showroom in Wigmore Street, London. The image below shows the 'unseen cable concept', with cables under a raised floor rising up through chromium plated steel tubes, directly to the machine on display. All displays could be interchanged to suit product changes.

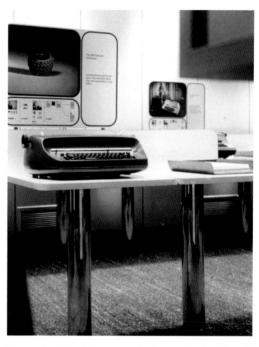

Figure 267. IBM Showroom, Wigmore St, London. Single product display stand – 1971 whilst working for Austin Smith Lord, Architects, London. Project team: Mike Aukett, John Stewart. Shopfitters: Economic Shopfitters. Client: IBM.

INTERCONTINENTAL HOTEL, LONDON, 1977

My next challenge was whilst working on the Intercontinental Hotel, London, for Frederick Gibberd Architects. I designed the internal retail units off the main lobby, but one freestanding newspaper kiosk intrigued me, as the brief from the American HQ was pretty bland – a simple box with shelving, counter and a door.

I allowed the form of stepped magazine racks to be expressed on the exterior. I designed two display units with glass doors either side of double glass doors, which when folded back were the same depth as the showcases, and thus unobtrusive. The whole effect was to increase transparency in a small confined space.

Figure 268. View showing the completed shops with the kiosk in the foreground. Project team: Michael Coombs, Mike Knowles. Client: Intercontinental Hotels.

Figure 270. View of monster in Percy Street from Charlotte Street, London. Photograph by author.

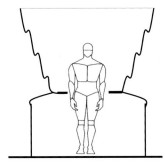

Figure 269. Section showing magazine racks.

COMMUNITY PROJECT, 1975

I designed a static monster on three levels outside the White Tower Restaurant which looked down the whole of Charlotte Street where the Fitzrovia carnival procession took place. I obtained planning permission to erect a temporary scaffolding structure upon which I had designed soft cladding materials to represent a monster. The first level was a stage, on which I hired different acts to perform throughout the day. The second level consisted of concealed colleagues waving the arms up and down, opening the beak, flicking a tongue out, and blinking one eye. I hired a smoke machine from Pinewood Film Studios to belch out smoke at appropriate moments. On the top level I booked a sound engineer from Theatre Projects to make monster sounds with synthesizers, synchronised with the monster's movements. The fact that the *Architects' Journal* published this was perhaps recognition of its environmental value, albeit shortlived.

GLENDOWER HOUSE CHAPEL CONVERSION, 2002

After a long spell of teaching full-time I felt it was time I worked on another interior project. Whilst renting a house in Monmouth, Wales, I found this derelict congregational church in the centre of the town – one of a 'hot dozen' buildings that SAVE[3] had highlighted as desperately needing attention. It consisted of an upper gallery on three sides, supported by seven cast iron columns. The gallery was accessed by two helical stone staircases. I decided to convert it into a home and studio for my family. Sleeping accommodation was on the ground floor, and living spaces were on an open-plan first floor, simply because more natural light entered the building on the upper level. The project qualified for a grant from CADW[4] after listed building consent was obtained.

I introduced a 45° axis as a planning tool on the ground floor to facilitate better use of the space and to enhance the human circulation in the spaces, whilst the upper floor left an opening in the centre so that the full height of the original building could be experienced. This angularity is carried through in section whereby some ground floor rooms have a partial sloping internal roof for which there is no architectural term for the external surface. The columns are given a niche and a defining colour from Dalsouple rubber flooring.

The project appeared on BBC2's *All the Right Moves*, Channel 4's *Britain's Best Home* and ITV's *Our House*. It won a Civic Trust Award from Wales as well as being shortlisted by the RICS for the International Conservation Awards in 2003.

Figure 271. Glendower House 'before'. Photo by author.

Figure 272. Glendower House 'after'. Photo by Ken Price.

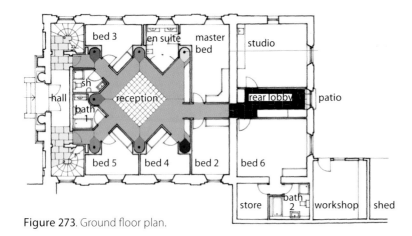

Figure 273. Ground floor plan.

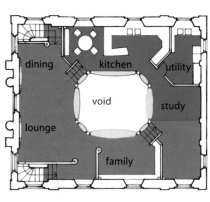

Figure 274. First floor plan.

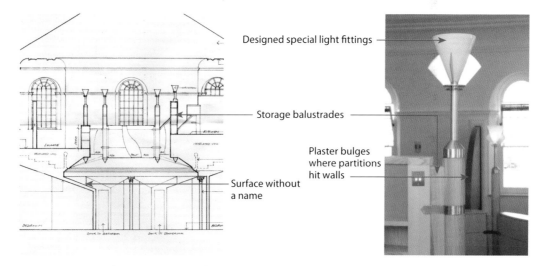

Figure 275. Cross-section showing existing galleried steps.

Figure 276. Interior of house. Photo by author.

DRAWING

Sketching and drawing are important parts of a designer's skill base in that they confirm the ability to record things visually, not only to feed the design process, but also to create artwork in its own right.

Figure 277. *Fitzwilliam Museum, Cambridge, UK. Main Entrance.* Pen and ink on board, 2008. Drawing by author.

Figure 278. *Deceased Artichoke*. Pen and ink, mixed media on A0 card. 2005. Drawing by author.

NOTES

PREFACE

1. Christian Norberg-Schulz, *Intentions in Architecture* (Cambridge, MA: MIT Press, 1965), p.30.

INTRODUCTION

1. Roberto J. Rengel, *Shaping Interior Space*, (New York: Fairchild Publications, 2003), p.5.
2. Building Regulations UK sets standards for design and construction, which apply to most new buildings and many alterations to existing buildings in England and Wales.
3. Frank Lloyd Wright (1867–1959), American architect, interior designer, writer and educator, who promoted organic architecture (exemplified by Fallingwater), and was a leader of the Prairie School movement of architecture in Chicago.
4. Bloomer and Moore, *Body Memory and Architecture* (London: Yale University Press, 1977), p.59.
5. Sigfried Giedion, Space, *Time and Architecture* (Boston, MA: Harvard University Press, 1941), p.xxxviii.

1: THE PRESENT SITUATION

1. The Council for National Academic Awards (CNAA) was a degree-awarding authority in the United Kingdom from 1965 until 1992.
2. The Business and Technology Education Council is the British body that awards vocational qualifications.
3. A listed building in the United Kingdom is a building that has been placed on the Statutory List of Buildings of Special Architectural or Historic Interest. Listing is not a preservation order, preventing change. Listing is an identification stage where buildings are marked and celebrated as having exceptional architectural or historic special interest, before any planning stage which may decide a building's future.
4. John Blake, *Design Magazine* No. 365, May 1979, pp.42–43.
5. Josef Hoffmann (1870–1956) was an Austrian architect and designer of consumer goods.
6. Bruno Zevi, *The Modern Language of Architecture* (New York: Da Capo Press, 1978), p.52.
7. Sven Hesselgren, *The Language of Architecture* (Barking, Essex: Applied Science Publishers, 1969), p.7.
8. Anthony Sully, *Design Courses – Graduates for What Industry?*, conference paper, 'European Academy of Design', Salford, April 1995.

9. The UK Design Commission was established a year ago by the Associate Parliamentary Design and Innovation Group, following its report into design and public procurement.
10. Josef Albers (1888–1976) was a German-born American artist and educator, and student/teacher of the Bauhaus.

2: DEFINITION OF TERMS

1. Richard Buckminster (Bucky) Fuller (1895–1983) was an American architect, author, designer, inventor and futurist, also famous for the geodesic dome.
2. Lawrence Blair, *Rhythms of Vision* (St Albans: Paladin Granada Publishing, 1976), p.46.
3. Bruno Zevi, *The Modern Language of Architecture* (New York: Da Capo Press, 1978) p.61.
4. Lewis Mumford, *The Condition of Man* (London: Martin Secker and Warburg, 1944), p.12.
5. Martin Pawley (1939–2008), English architectural critic and writer.
6. Amos Rapoport, *House Form and Culture* (New Jersey: Prentice-Hall, 1969), p.75.
7. Robert Venturi, *Complexity and Contradiction in Architecture* (New York: Museum of Modern Art, Papers on Architecture, 1966), p.70.
8. Graeme Brooker and Sally Stone, *Basics Interior Architecture, Form and Structure* (Switzerland: AVA Publishing, 2007, p.124).
9. Sigfried Giedion, *Space, Time and Architecture* (Boston, MA: Harvard University Press, 1941), p.xl.
10. J. Malnar and F. Vodvarka, *The Interior Dimension* (New York: Van Nostrand Reinhold, 1992), p.65. Reprinted with permission of John Wiley & Sons, Inc.
11. Edward T. Hall, anthropologist, *The Hidden Dimension* (New York: Anchor Books, 1966).
12. Georgian architectural period in England, 1714–1837.
13. Michael Parker Pearson, *Architecture and Order: Approaches to Social Space* (Material Cultures) (London: Routledge, 1994), p.3.
14. Lewis Mumford, *The Condition of Man* (London: Martin Secker and Warburg, 1944), p.10.
15. Christian Norberg-Schulz, *Intentions in Architecture* (Cambridge, MA: MIT Press, 1965), p.65.
16. From review by Clem Labine of John F. Harbeson, *Lost Secrets of Beaux-Arts Design – The Study of Architecture* (New York: W. W. Norton, 2008). Compared with today's architectural education, the Beaux-Arts method relied less

on bursts of individual inspiration and more on detailed analysis and application of basic principles.

17. Sven Hesselgren, *The Language of Architecture* (Barking, Essex: Applied Science Publishers, 1969), p.250.

18. C. E. Shannon and W. Weaver, *The Mathematical Theory of Communication* (Urbana: University of Illinois Press, 1949).

19. Further reading into semiotics is advised for those interested in exploring more of this subject.

20. Herbert Marshall McLuhan (1911–80) was a Canadian educator, philosopher and scholar – a professor of English literature, a literary critic, a rhetorician and a communication theorist.

21. Edmund Carpenter, *Oh, What a Blow That Phantom Gave Me!* (London: Paladin, 1976), p.50.

22. Tiiu Poldma, *Taking Up Space – Exploring the Design Process* (New York: Fairchild Books, 2009), pp.31, 64.

23. Susan J Slotkis, *Foundations of Interior Design* (London: Laurence King, 2006).

24. Clive Edwards is Professor of Design History at Loughborough University.

25. Victor Papanek (1927–99) was an Austrian designer and educator who became a strong advocate of the socially and ecologically responsible design of products, tools and community infrastructures.

26. John Ruskin, English (1819–1900). Ruskin was one of the greatest figures of the Victorian age; poet, artist, critic, social revolutionary and conservationist. Author of *Seven Lamps of Architecture*, *The Stones of Venice*.

27. David John Watkin (b. 1941) is a British architectural historian and the author of *Morality and Architecture* (University of Chicago Press, 1977), p.9.

3: THE HUMAN BODY

1. J. E. Hochberg, perception psychologist.

2. R. Fletcher, behavioural psychologist.

3. Environmental psychology is an interdisciplinary field focused on the interplay between humans and their surroundings. The field defines the term 'environment' broadly, encompassing natural environments, social settings, built environments, learning environments, and informational environments.

4. Kent C. Bloomer and Charles W. Moore, *Body Memory and Architecture* (Yale University Press, 1977) p.40.

5. Hartley Alexander, *The World's Rim* (Lincoln: University of Nebraska Press, 1953), p.9.

6. Edmund Carpenter, in his book *Oh, What a Blow That Phantom Gave Me!* (London: Paladin, 1976), confesses that as an anthropologist he went to Papua and New Guinea to help civilise the primitives but it transpired that he was destroying, not civilising.

7. The Greek philosopher Aristotle (384–322 BC) developed many theories on the nature of physics. These involved what Aristotle described as the four elements. He spoke intimately of the relationship between these elements, of their dynamics, how they impacted on the Earth, and how they were – in many cases – attracted to each other by unspecified forces.

8. Robert Lawlor, *Sacred Geometry* (London: Thames and Hudson, 1982), p.4.

9. *Small is Beautiful: Economics as if People Mattered* is a collection of essays by the British economist E. F. Schumacher. The phrase 'Small is beautiful' came from a phrase by his teacher, Leopold Kohr. It is often used to champion small, appropriate technologies that are believed to empower people more, in contrast with phrases such as 'Bigger is better'.

10. Philip Steadman, *The Evolution of Designs* (London: Routledge, 1979), p.4.

11. Claude Bernard (1813–78) was a French physiologist and historian of science. Bernard Cohen of Harvard University called Bernard 'one of the greatest of all men of science'. Among many other accomplishments, he was one of the first to suggest the use of blind experiments to ensure the objectivity of scientific observations.

12. From www.darwinproject.ac.uk.

13. René Descartes (1596–1650) was a French philosopher, mathematician and physicist.

14. Georges Cuvier (1769–1832) was a French naturalist and zoologist.

15. Rudolf Wittkower, *Architectural Principles in the Age of Humanism* (Academy Editions, 1949), p.11.

16. Le Corbusier (1887–1965), widely acclaimed as the most influential architect of the 20th century, was also a celebrated thinker, writer and artist – a multi-faceted 'Renaissance man'. His architecture and radical ideas for reinventing modern living, from private villas to large-scale social housing and utopian urban plans, still resonate today.

17. J. S. Atherton (2009), *Learning and Teaching; Piaget's Developmental Theory*. Available at: http://www. learningandteaching.info/learning/piaget.htm.

18. John Dewey, American (1859–1952) has made arguably the most significant contribution to the development of educational thinking in the twentieth century.

19. David Hume (1711–76) was a Scottish philosopher, economist, historian and a key figure in the history of Western philosophy and the Scottish Enlightenment. Hume is often grouped with John Locke, George Berkeley, and a handful of others as a British Empiricist.

20. Child development in behaviour analytic theory has origins in John B. Watson's (American, 1878–1958) behaviourism. B. F. Skinner's (American, 1904–90) radical behaviourism focused the science on private events such as thinking and feeling and how they are shaped by interacting with the environment.

21. Max Wertheimer's (Czech, 1880–1943) unique contribution was to insist that gestalt is perceptually primary, defining the parts of which it was composed, rather than being a secondary quality that emerges from those

parts.

22. Ibid., p.10.

23. Professor Mehrabian's (American, 1971) major theoretical contributions include a three-dimensional mathematical model for the precise and general description and measurement of emotions.

24. Étienne-Jules Marey (1830–1904) was a French scientist and chronophotographer.

25. Eadweard J. Muybridge (1830–1904) was an English photographer, known primarily for his pioneering work with the use of multiple cameras to capture motion, and his zoopraxiscope, a device for projecting motion pictures that predated the flexible perforated film strip that is used today.

26. Robert Sommer, environmental psychologist, wrote *Personal Space: The Behavioral Basis of Design* (New Jersey, Englewood Cliffs, 1969).

27. David Canter, English psychologist, *Psychology for Architects* (London: Applied Science Publishers, 1974).

28. Richard Dawkins, *The Selfish Gene* (Paladin Granada Publishing, 1978), p.21.

29. Juhani Pallasmaa, Finnish architect and theorist, wrote *The Eyes of the Skin* (Chichester: Wiley, 2005), p.72.

4: GEOMETRY AND PROPORTION

1. Steen Eiler Rasmussen, *Experiencing Architecture* (London: Chapman & Hall, 1959), p.135.

2. Dr Keith Critchlow is an artist, designer, author and teacher. He is a leading expert in sacred architecture and Professor Emeritus at The Prince's School of Traditional Arts. Keith Critchlow, *Order in Space* (London: Thames and Hudson, 1969), p.5.

3. Lawrence Blair, *Rhythms of Vision* (St Albans: Paladin, 1976), p.92.

4. Robert Lawlor, *Sacred Geometry* (London: Thames and Hudson, 1982), p.6. Reprinted by kind permission of Thames and Hudson Ltd.

5. Robert Lawlor, *Sacred Geometry* (London: Thames and Hudson, 1982), p.6.

6. Lawrence Blair, *Rhythms of Vision* (St Albans: Paladin, 1976), p.118.

7. Louis Khan, American architect, 1901–74.

8. Le Corbusier (1887–1965).

9. Roger Cook, *The Tree of Life* (London: Thames and Hudson, 1974).

10. Lawrence Blair, *Rhythms of Vision* (St Albans: Paladin, 1976), p.113.

11. Robert Lawlor, *Sacred Geometry* (London: Thames and Hudson, 1982), p.5.

12. Johannes Kepler (1571–1630) was a German mathematician, astronomer and astrologer. This is from his 1596 book, *Mysterium Cosmographicum*.

13. Dan Pedoe, *Geometry and the Liberal Arts* (Harmondsworth: Penguin, 1976) p.72.

14. Leonardo Pisano Bogollo (c.1170–c.1250), also known as Leonardo of Pisa or Fibonacci, was an Italian mathematician.

15. Lawrence Blair, *Rhythms of Vision* (St Albans: Paladin, 1976), p.117.

16. Vitruvius (Marcus Vitruvius Pollio), *Ten Books on Architecture* (80–15 BC), was a Roman writer, architect and engineer. He was author of the first published works on architecture in the world.

17. Arne Emil Jacobsen, usually known as Arne Jacobsen (1902–71), was one of Denmark's most successful architects and a designer of furniture and products. He was inspired by the work of Charles and Rae Eames.

18. Leon Battista Alberti (1404–72) was an author, artist, architect, poet, priest, linguist and philosopher.

19. Sebastiano Serlio (1475–c.1554) was an Italian Mannerist architect who wrote several influential books on architecture.

20. Andrea Palladio (1508–80) was an Italian Renaissance architect and stonemason active in the Republic of Venice. The Palladian style, named after him, adhered to classical Roman principles that he rediscovered, applied and explained in his works. He was famous for his villa designs, and the first architect to graft a temple front on to a house.

21. Callimachus was a Greek architect and sculptor working in the second half of the 5th century BC.

22. J. Malnar and F. Vodvarka, *The Interior Dimension* (New York: Van Nostrand Reinhold, 1992), p.75.

5: PERCEPTION

1. Steen Eiler Rasmussen, *Experiencing Architecture* (London: Chapman & Hall, 1959), p.33.

2. Keith Albarn and Jenny Miall Smith, *Diagram, The Instrument of Thought* (London: Thames and Hudson, 1977), p.36.

3. Sir Jonathan Wolfe Miller is a British theatre and opera director, author, television presenter, humorist and sculptor.

4. Professor M. D. Vernon, natural scientist, *The Psychology of Perception*, (Harmondsworth: Penguin Books, 1962), p.38.

5. Max Wertheimer's (Czech, 1880–1943) unique contribution was to insist that gestalt is perceptually primary, defining the parts of which it was composed, rather than being a secondary quality that emerges from those parts.

6. Sven Hesselgren, Swedish architectural theorist specialising in environmental perception, *The Language of Architecture* (Barking, Essex: Applied Science Publishers, 1969), p.11.

6: EXPRESSION AND MEANING

1. Walter Crane (1845–1915) was an English artist and book illustrator. Influenced by William Morris, he was also a designer of textiles, ceramics and wallpapers.

2. The Great Exhibition of 1851 was held at Crystal Palace and designed by Joseph Paxton, and demonstrated how

Britain was a leading industrial and manufacturing power in the world.

3. The Arts and Crafts Exhibition Society was founded in 1888 in London.

4. William Morris (1834–96) formed the company of Morris, Marshall, Faulkener & Co., which specialised in producing stained glass, carvings, furniture, wallpaper, carpets and tapestries. The company's designs brought about a complete revolution in public taste.

5. Charles Francis Annesley Voysey (1857–1941) was an English architect, furniture designer and textile designer. Voysey's early work was as a designer of wallpapers, fabrics and furnishings.

6. Victor Horta, Belgian (1861–1947). © 2000, Artists' Rights Society (ARS), New York/ SOFAM, Brussels. Photography by C. H. Bastin and J. Evrard, Brussels.

7. Alphonse Maria Mucha, Czech (1860–1939), was an art nouveau painter and decorative artist.

8. Charles Rennie Mackintosh (1868–1928) was a Scottish architect, designer and watercolourist.

9. Emile Gallé (1846–1904), was a French glass designer. He revolutionised the art of glass-making by combining ancient techniques such as enamelling, cameo and inlay with his own influences. He also used heavy, opaque etched glass with Japanese styles.

10. The Bauhaus School was founded by Walter Gropius in Weimar, Germany, and was active from 1919 to 1933.

11. De Stijl, also known as neoplasticism, was a Dutch design movement founded in 1917.

12. Adolf Loos (1870–1933) was a Czech-born Austrian architect famous for his essay *Ornament and Crime*.

13. Louis Sullivan, American architect, 1896.

14. Gillian Naylor, *The Bauhaus* (Studio Vista/ Dutton Pictureback, 1968), p.7.

15. Piet Mondrian (1872–1944), born in Amersfoort in the Netherlands, is one of the brilliant pioneers of abstract art.

16. Theo van Doesburg (1883–1931) was a Dutch artist and architect who founded *De Stijl* magazine in 1917. The magazine gave its name to a group of artists and architects that included Mondrian, Huszar and Vantongerloo, Oud and Rietveld.

17. Second World War, 1938–45.

18. The Design Council is a government agency that was founded in 1944 to promote design excellence.

19. Sir Nikolaus Bernhard Leon Pevsner (1902–83) was a German-born British scholar of the history of art and architecture. Published works: *The Buildings of England* (Harmondsworth: Penguin, 1951–74); *Pioneers of Modern Design* (Harmondsworth: Penguin, 1960).

20. Peter Reyner Banham (1922–88) was a prolific architectural critic and writer. He wrote *Theory and Design in the First Machine Age* (London: Architectural Press, 1960).

21. Frank Lloyd Wright (1867–1959).

22. Ludwig Mies van der Rohe (1886–1969) was a German-American architect. His mature buildings made use of modern materials such as industrial steel and plate glass to define interior spaces.

23. Le Corbusier (1887–1965).

24. In 1919, Walter Gropius founded the Bauhaus School in Weimar, Germany. This academy of architecture and design, although only in existence for fourteen years, established a tremendous reputation amongst the avant-garde for its creative approach to architecture and design, a reputation that lives on to this day.

25. Erich Mendelsohn (1887–1953) was a German Jewish architect, known for his expressionist architecture in the 1920s.

26. Wells Wintemute Coates (1895–1958) was an architect, and a pioneer of industrial design because he demonstrated the importance of understanding the technical processes of prefabrication and industrial methods in order to design competently.

27. Founded in 1933 by a group of architects and critics including Wells Coates, Maxwell Fry and Morton Shand as a 'think tank' for British Modernism, the MARS Group (Modern Architectural Research Group) produced visionary plans and exhibitions before disbanding in 1957.

28. Hugo Alvar Henrik Aalto (1898–1976) was a Finnish architect and designer, sometimes known as the father of modernism in Nordic countries. His work included architecture, furniture, textiles and glassware.

29. Le Corbusier (1887–1965). *Towards a New Architecture* was published in 1923; a later edition in 1986 by Dover Publications.

30. Foster + Partners, architects, London. Foster's earlier designs reflected a sophisticated, machine-influenced, high-tech vision. His style has since evolved into a more sublime, sharp-edged modernity.

31. Herman Hertzberger (b. 1932) was the influence behind the Dutch structuralist movement of the 1960s.

32. Richard George Rogers (b. 1933) is a British architect noted for his modernist and functionalist designs.

33. Their visions for cities of the future inhabited by a mass society were characterised by large-scale, flexible and expandable structures. The architects were Noboru Kawazoe, Kiyonori Kikutake, Fumihiko Maki, Masato Otaka, Kisho Kurokawa and Kiyoshi Awazu.

34. Louis Isadore Kahn (1901/2–1974) was a world-renowned architect of Estonian Jewish origin, based in Philadelphia, USA.

35. The office landscape (*Bürolandschaft* in German) movement was an early (1950s) movement in open-plan office space planning, led by Eberhard and Wolfgang Schnelle.

36. Founded in 1923 in Michigan, USA.

37. Bernard Tschumi (b. 1944, Lausanne, Switzerland) is an architect, writer and educator, commonly associated with

Deconstructivism. He wrote *Architecture and Disjunction* (Cambridge, MA: MIT Press, 1996).

38. Daniel Libeskind (b. 1946 in Łódź, Poland) is an American architect, artist and set designer of Polish-Jewish descent.

39. Peter Eisenman (b. 1932 in Newark, New Jersey) is an American architect.

40. Remment Lucas Koolhaas (b. 1944) is a Dutch architect, architectural theorist and urbanist. He founded the Office of Metropolitan Architecture (OMA) in 1975. Zaha Hadid was one of his students.

41. Frank Owen Gehry (b. 1929) is a Canadian-American Pritzker Prize-winning architect based in Los Angeles, California.

42. Zaha Hadid, CBE (b. 1950) is a notable British-Iraqi architect, having won the Pritzker Prize.

43. Juhani Pallasmaa, *The Eyes of the Skin* (Chichester: Wiley, 2005), p.31.

7: THE THEORETICAL BASIS THAT ALLOWS THE DESIGN PROCESS TO WORK

1. Leonard Bruce Archer CBE (1922–2005), British mechanical engineer and later Professor of Design Research at the Royal College of Art, championed research in design and helped to establish design as an academic discipline.

2. Hans Gugelot (1920–65), Indonesian, born in Ulm, Germany. A renowned architect, industrial designer and furniture designer. Worked for Braun.

3. Morris Asimow (1906–82), Professor Emeritus of Engineering Systems, University of California, USA.

4. John Christopher Jones (b. 1927), Welsh engineering designer. He studied engineering at the University of Cambridge, and went on to work for AEI in Manchester, England. His book *Design Methods* (London: John Wiley, 1970) is considered a major text on design.

5. Geoffrey Broadbent, *Design in Architecture* (London: John Wiley, 1973), pp.25–35.

6. Rosemary Kilmer and W. Otie Kilmer, *Designing Interiors* (Fort Worth: Harcourt Brace Jovanovich, 1992), p.162.

7. Arne Emil Jacobsen, usually known as Arne Jacobsen (1902–71), was one of Denmark's most successful architects and a designer of furniture and products. He was inspired by the work of Charles and Rae Eames.

8. Glendower Congregational Chapel (1854). Conversion to family home, Monmouth, Wales. Designer and owner: Anthony Sully. Architect: Graham Frecknall, 2002.

9. Gaston Bachelard, *The Poetics of Space* (Orion Press, 1964), p.224.

10. George Nelson (1908–86) was one of the founders of American modernism, along with Charles and Ray Eames.

8: SEARCHING FOR CODES

1. Bruno Zevi, *The Modern Language of Architecture*, (New York: Da Capo Press, 1978), p.5.

2. Quinlan Terry (b. 1937) is an English architect who specialises in high-quality traditional buildings of a classical design.

3. Ernst Mach (1838–1916) was an Austrian physicist and philosopher.

4. Robert Adam (1728–92) was a Scottish neoclassical architect, interior designer and furniture designer with influence throughout the Western world. He was the son of William Adam (1689–1748), Scotland's foremost architect of the time, and trained under him.

5. The Roman city of Pompeii was founded in the 6–7th century BC and was destroyed and completely buried during a catastrophic eruption of the volcano Mount Vesuvius, spanning two days in AD 79. Parts of many buildings and artefacts were preserved in the ashes.

6. Sir John Soane RA (1753–1837) was an English architect who specialised in the neoclassical style. In 1792 he bought a house at 12 Lincoln's Inn Fields, London. He expanded to buy numbers 13 and 14 next door. He used the whole property as his home and library, but also entertained potential clients in the drawing room. (Today, this house is a museum.)

7. William Morris (1834–96) was an English textile designer, artist, writer and socialist associated with the Pre-Raphaelite Brotherhood and the English Arts and Crafts Movement.

8. Mario Amaya, *Art Nouveau* (London: Studio Vista/ Dutton, 1966).

9. Charles Rennie Mackintosh (1868–1928).

10. Frank Lloyd Wright (1867–1959).

11. Owen Jones (1809–74) was a London-born architect and designer of Welsh descent. He was one of the most influential design theorists of the 19th century.

12. Eugène Emmanuel Viollet-le-Duc (1814–79) was a French architect and theorist, famous for his 'restorations' of medieval buildings. Born in Paris, he was as central a figure in the Gothic revival in France as he was in the public discourse on honesty in architecture, which eventually transcended all revival styles, to inform the emerging spirit of Modernism.

13. Christopher Dresser (1834–1904) was a Scottish designer and writer on design, now widely known as Britain's first independent industrial designer and as a contributor to the Anglo-Japanese movement and Aesthetic Movement in Britain.

14. Gerrit Thomas Rietveld (1888–1964) was a Dutch furniture designer and architect, and one of the principal members of the Dutch artistic movement called De Stijl.

15. Charles (1907–78) and Rae (1912–88) Eames were American designers who made major contributions to modern architecture and furniture. They also worked in the fields of industrial design, fine art, graphic design and film.

16. Carlo Scarpa (1906–78) was an Italian architect influenced by the materials, landscape, the history of

Venetian culture, and Japan. Scarpa was also a glass and furniture designer of note. During the late 1920s, he began his career as an interior designer and industrial designer.

17. Eva Jiřičná CBE (b. 1939) is a renowned Czech architect and designer, active in London and Prague.

18. High-tech architecture, also known as late Modernism or structural Expressionism, is an architectural style that emerged in the 1970s, incorporating elements of high-tech industry and technology into building design.

19. Tadao Ando (b. 1941) is a Japanese architect.

20. Enric Miralles Moya (1955–2000) was a Spanish architect who died tragically early of a brain tumour, aged 45. In 1993, Enric Miralles formed a new practice with his second wife, the Italian architect Benedetta Tagliabue, under the name of EMBT Architects.

21. Adolf Loos (1870–1933) was a Moravian-born Austrian architect. He was influential in European modern architecture, and in his essay, *Ornament and Crime*, he repudiated the florid style of the Vienna Secession, the Austrian version of art nouveau.

22. For the purpose of teaching geography, John Spilsbury, a teacher in England, created the first jigsaw puzzle in 1767. Adhering his maps to flat hardwood, he used a fine saw to cut along the borders of the European countries, and the jigsaw puzzle was born. Hand-painted and made of wood, the puzzle was a map of England and Wales, with each county making up a separate piece.

23. Founded by Tristan d'Estree Sterk, the Office for Robotic Architectural Media and the Bureau for Responsive Architecture (ORAMBRA) is a small design and technology office interested in rethinking the art of construction alongside the emergence of responsive technologies. Its work focuses upon the use of structural shape change and its role in altering the way that buildings use energy.

APPENDIX

1. Tutors were: Geoffrey Bocking, Keith Critchlow, Robyn Denny, Richard Smith, Robert Heritage, Henry Thornton, Ruskin Spear, Michael Caddy, Bernard Cohen, Frank Height, Roland Whiteside, Harold Bartram, John Prizeman.

2. Tutors were: Tom Kay, Iris Murdoch, John Miller, David Gentleman, Norman Potter, Kit Evans, Chris Cornford, Fred Samson, Elizabeth Henderson, Anthony Froshaug.

3. SAVE – founded in 1975 as a campaign to save Britain's Heritage.

4. CADW – Welsh Historic Monuments ('cadw' is Welsh for 'to keep').

BIBLIOGRAPHY

Abercombie, Stanley, *A Philosophy of Interior Design*, Icon Editions, New York: Harper and Row, 1990

Adler, David, *Metric Handbook*, Oxford: Architectural Press (Reed Elsevier plc Group), 1968

Albarn, Keith & Smith, Jenny Miall, *Diagram, the Instrument of Thought*, London: Thames and Hudson, 1977

Albarn, Keith; Smith, Jenny Miall; Steele, Stanford & Walker, Dinah, *The Language of Pattern*, London: Thames and Hudson, 1974

Alexander, Christopher, *Notes on the Synthesis of Form*, Massachusetts: Harvard University Press, 1964

Alexander, Hartley, *The World's Rim*, Lincoln: University of Nebraska Press, 1953

Amaya, Mario, *Art Nouveau*, London: Studio Vista/Dutton, 1966

Amery, Colin, *Period Houses and their Details*, London: The Architectural Press, 1974

Ashcroft, Roland, *Construction for Interior Designers*, Harlow: Longman, 1985

Bachelard, Gaston, *The Poetics of Space*, Boston: The Beacon Press, 1969

Banham, Peter Reyner, *Theory and Design in the First Machine Age*, London: Architectural Press, 1960

Baudrillard, Jean, *The System of Objects*, London: Verso, 1968

Benton, Tim & Charlotte, *Form and Function*, Crosby, London: Lockwood, Staples with Open University Press, 1975

Blair, Lawrence, *Rhythms of Vision*, St Albans: Paladin Granada Publishing, 1976

Blake, John, 'Don't Forget that bad taste is popular' *Design Magazine*. May 1979, issue no. 365

Bloomer and Moore, *Body Memory and Architecture*, London: Yale University Press, 1977

Broadbent, Geoffrey, *Design in Architecture*, London: John Wiley, 1973

Brooker, Graeme and Stone, Sally, *Basics Interior Architecture, Form and Structure*, Switzerland: AVA Publishing, 2007

Calloway, Stephen & Cromley, Elizabeth, *The Elements of Style*, New York: Simon & Schuster, 1996

Canter, David, *Psychology for Architects*, London: Applied Science, 1974

Carpenter, Edmund, *Oh, What a blow that phantom gave me!* St Albans: Paladin Granada Publishing, 1976

Clay, Robert, *Beautiful Thing, An Introduction to Design*, Oxford: Berg, 2009

Cook, Roger, *The Tree of Life*, London: Thames and Hudson, 1974

Corbusier, Le, *Towards a new Architecture*, London: Architectural Press, 1923
My Work, London: Architectural Press, 1960

Crane, Walter, *The Bases of Design*, London: George Bell & Sons, 1904

Critchlow, Keith, *Order in Space*, London: Thames and Hudson, 1969

Davey, Peter, *Arts and Crafts Architecture*, London: The Architectural Press, 1980

Dawkins, Richard, *The Selfish Gene*, St Albans: Paladin Granada Publishing, 1978

Dodsworth, Simon, *The Fundamentals of Interior Design*, Switzerland: Academia, 2009

Dormer, Peter, *Design since 1945*, London: Thames and Hudson, 1993

Elam, Kimberly, *Geometry of Design*, New York: Princeton Architectural Press, 2001

Edwards, Clive, *Interior Design, a Critical Introduction*, Oxford: Berg, 2011

Fletcher, Banister, *A History of Architecture*, London: B. T. Batsford, 1905

Gelernter, Mark, *Sources of Architectural Form*, Manchester: Manchester University Press, 1995

Ghyka, Matila, *The Geometry of Art and Life*, New York: Dover Publications Inc, 1977 (first published 1946)

Giedion, Sigfried, *Space, Time and Architecture*, Massachusetts: Harvard University Press, 1941

Glazier, Richard, *A Manual of Historic Ornament*, London: Batsford, 1899

Hall, Edward T., *The Hidden Dimension*, Garden City, New York: Doubleday, 1966

Hanks, David A., *The Decorative Designs of Frank Lloyd Wright*, London: Studio Vista, 1979

Hesselgren, Sven, *The Language of Architecture*, Barking: Applied Science Publishers, 1969

Jones, John Christopher, *Design Methods: Seeds of Human Futures*, London: John Wiley & Sons Ltd. 1970

Jung, Varl G., *Man and his Symbols*, London: Aldus Books and Jupiter Books, 1964

Kilmer, Rosemary and Otie, W., *Designing Interiors*, Fort Worth: Harcourt Brace Jovanovich, 1992

Kruft, Hanno-Walter, *A History of Architectural Theory*, New York: Princeton Architectural Press, 1994

Lawlor, Robert, *Sacred Geometry*, London: Thames and Hudson, 1982

Malnar, Joy and Vodvarka, Frank, *The Interior Dimension*, New York: Van Nostrand Reinhold, 1992

Mann, A.T., *The Round Art*, Cheltenham: Dragon's World, 1979

Massey, Anne, *Interior Design of the 20th Century*, London: Thames and Hudson, 1990

Mumford, Lewis, *The Condition of Man*, London: Martin Secker and Warburg Ltd, 1944

Muybridge, Eadweard, *The Human Figure in Motion*, New York: Dover Publications Inc, 1955

Naylor, Gillian, *The Bauhaus*, London: Studio Vista/Dutton Pictureback, 1968

Nesbitt, Kate, *Theorizing a new Agenda for Architecture*, New York: Princeton Architectural Press, 1996

Norberg-Schulz, Christian, *Intentions in Architecture*, Cambridge, MA: MIT Press, 1965

Pallasmaa, Juhani, *The Eyes of the Skin*, Chichester: Wiley, 2005

Panero, Julius & Zelnik, Martin, *Human Dimension and Interior Space*, New York: Whitney Library of Design, 1979

Papanek, Victor, *Design for the Real World: Human Ecology and Social Change*, New York: Pantheon Books, 1971

Pawley, Martin, *The Private Future*, London: Thames and Hudson, 1974

Pearson, Michael Parker, *Architecture and Order: Approaches to Social Space* (Material Cultures), London: Routledge, 1994

Pedoe, Dan, *Geometry and the Liberal Arts*, Harmondsworth: Penguin Books, 1976

Pennick, Nigel, *Sacred Geometry*, Wellingborough: Turnstone Press Ltd, 1980

Pevsner, Nikolaus, *Pioneers of Modern Design*, Harmondsworth: Penguin Books, 1960

Pevsner, Nikolaus, *An Outline of European Architecture*, Harmondsworth: Penguin Books, 1943

Pile, John, *A History of Interior Design*, London: Laurence King, 2000

Pile, John, *Interior Design*, New York: Prentice Hall and Harry N. Abrams, 1988

Pirsig, Robert, *Zen and the Art of Motorcycle Maintenance: An Inquiry into Values*, New York: William Morrow & Co. 1974

Poldma, Tiiu, *Taking up Space – Exploring the Design Process*, New York: Fairchild Books, 2009

Rapoport, Amos, *House Form and Culture*, New Jersey: Prentice Hall, 1969

Rasmussen, Steen Eiler, *Experiencing Architecture*, London: Chapman & Hall, 1959

Read, Herbert Edward, *Art and Industry*, London: Faber & Faber, 1934

Rengel, Roberto J., *Shaping Interior Space*, New York: Fairchild Publications, 2003

Ruskin, John, *The Seven Lamps of Architecture*, London: J. M. Dent & Sons,1907

Salingaros, Nikos A., *Fractals in the New Architecture,* first published in *Archimagazine* (2001)

Sausmarez, Maurice de, *Basic Design, The Dynamics of Visual Form*, London: The Herbert Press, 1964

Scott, Geoffrey, *The Architecture of Humanism*, London: Methuen & Co. 1914

Shannon, C.E. & Weaver, W., *The Mathematical Theory of Communication*, University of Illinois Press, Urbana, 1949

Slotkis, Susan J., *Foundations of Interior Design*, Laurence King, 2006

Sommer, Robert, *Personal Space: The Behavioral Basis of Design*, New Jersey: Prentice Hall, 1969

Sparke, Penny, *An Introduction to Design and Culture in the Twentieth Century*, London: Routledge, 1986

Sparke, Penny, *Design in Context: History, Application and Development of Design*, London: Bloomsbury, 1987

Steadman, Philip, *The Evolution of Designs*, London: Routledge 1979

Stewart, Richard, *Design and British Industry*, London: John Murray, 1987

Stoppard, Tom, *Travesties*, London: Faber & Faber, 1975

Sully, Anthony, Conference Paper *Design Courses – Graduates for What Industry?* European Academy of Design, Salford, April 1995

Summerson, John, *The Classical Language of Architecture*, London: Thames and Hudson, 1980

Tangaz, Tomris, *The Interior Design Course: Principles, Practices and Techniques for the Aspiring Designer*, London: Thames and Hudson, 2004

Thompson, D'Arcy, *On Growth and Form*, Cambridge: Cambridge University Press, 1961

Tschumi, Bernard, *Architecture and Disjunction*, Cambridge, MA: MIT Press, 1996

Venturi, Robert, *Complexity and Contradiction in Architecture*, New York: The Museum of Modern Art, 1966

Vernon, M.D., *The Psychology of Perception*, Harmondsworth: Penguin Books Ltd, 1962

Watkin, David, *Morality and Architecture*, London: University of Chicago Press, 1977

White, Antony and Robertson, Bruce, *Architecture and Ornament*, London: Studio Vista, 1990

Wigley, Mark, *The Architecture of Deconstruction*, London: MIT Press, 1996

Wittkower, Rudolf, *Architectural Principles in the Age of Humanism*, London: Academy Editions, 1949

Zeisel, John, *Inquiry by Design*, Cambridge: Cambridge University Press, 1981

Zelanski, Paul and Fisher, Mary Pat, *Shaping Space*, Fort Worth: Harcourt Brace College Publishers, 1987

Zevi, Bruno, *The Modern Language of Architecture*, Da Capo Press, New York, 1978

GLOSSARY

Analysis – The ability to break down, organise and categorise information to assist with problem solving.

Anthropometrics – Recording the measurement of the human form in a variety of postures, including all possible movements that the figure can do.

Bubble diagram – Groups of circles delineating an activity to determine their relationship to each other, in order to help the planning process.

Building form – The three-dimensional shape and form of a building in its simplest terms.

Building regulations – these set standards for design and construction and apply to most new buildings and many alterations to existing buildings in England and Wales.

Chiffonier – An ornamental cabinet.

Computer Aided Design (CAD) – A means of producing digitised architectural layouts, constructions and presentation drawings. CAD can also organise and co-ordinate information in relation to these drawings.

Contract – A legally binding agreement between all parties concerned with a building.

Credenza – A buffet consisting of drawers and doors and resting on a carved base.

Design concept – a mental construct that is given shape and form through the drawing skills of the designer.

Duality – Two parts of a design problem whose combined union has a major impact on the final design proposal.

Element – Constituent part of the interior design field of work.

Enclosure – This defines any structure that surrounds an internal space.

Ergonomics – The study of designing equipment and devices that fit the human body, its movements, and its cognitive abilities in relation to a particular activity.

Expression – The embodiment and spirit of a design which reflects on the culture of the time.

Fitted kitchen – This term is used to describe a kitchen all of whose functions are provided for by built-in units fixed to the structure of the building.

Green issues – Ecological sustainability aims to use natural solutions where possible guided by adaptable re-use and environmentally friendly products and manufacturing processes.

Ideology – Ideas or a way of thinking that formulates a particular philosophy of approach to design.

International style – An architectural movement that emphasises space instead of mass. Led by early Modernists, it became a global phenomenon.

LED – A light-emitting diode. It is a semiconductor light source with low energy and a high efficiency rating.

Lux – A unit for measuring illumination. One lux is one lumen per square metre.

Mosaic – Small pieces of coloured glass, marble or wood cemented together to create a pattern, usually on floors or walls, but can also be laid onto ceilings and other surfaces.

Motif – A dominant decorative theme used to embellish furniture or interior structure.

Newbuild – A newly designed building. Both the design of the building and the interior could be executed at the same time.

Plenum – This is the space between a suspended ceiling and the structural slab above. Usually used for fitting building services such as wiring and ductwork.

Services – The services within a building such as power, water supply and drainage.

Symmetry – A balance of shapes either side of a central axis.

Tambour – A flexible sliding door composed of narrow strips of wood joined together and fitted to a cabinet or bureau.

User – Someone who uses the interior of a building: both occupiers and visitors.

Vernacular – In the style that matches or conforms to an existing style of design and building.

Whatnot or étagère – A cabinet of open shelves, sometimes pyramidal in shape, usually placed in the corner of a room.

INDEX